Issues in Ghana's Electoral Politics

Issues in Ghana's Electoral Politics

Edited by

Kwame A. Ninsin

CODESRIA

Council for the Development of Social Science Research in Africa
DAKAR

© CODESRIA 2016
Council for the Development of Social Science Research in Africa
Avenue Cheikh Anta Diop, Angle Canal IV
BP 3304 Dakar, 18524, Senegal
Website : www.codesria.org
ISBN : 978-2-86978-694-3

Typesetting: Alpha Ousmane Dia
Cover Design: Ibrahima Fofana

Distributed in Africa by CODESRIA
Distributed elsewhere by African Books Collective, Oxford, UK
Website: www.africanbookscollective.com

The Council for the Development of Social Science Research in Africa (CODESRIA) is an independent organisation whose principal objectives are to facilitate research, promote research-based publishing and create multiple forums for the exchange of views and information among African researchers. All these are aimed at reducing the fragmentation of research in the continent through the creation of thematic research networks that cut across linguistic and regional boundaries.

CODESRIA publishes *Africa Development,* the longest standing Africa based social science journal; *Afrika Zamani,* a journal of history; the *African Sociological Review*; the *African Journal of International Affairs*; *Africa Review of Books* and the *Journal of Higher Education in Africa.* The Council also co-publishes the *Africa Media Review*; *Identity, Culture and Politics: An Afro-Asian Dialogue*; *The African Anthropologist, Journal of African Tranformation, Méthod(e)s: African Review of Social Sciences Methodology, and the Afro-Arab Selections for Social Sciences.* The results of its research and other activities are also disseminated through its Working Paper Series, Green Book Series, Monograph Series, Book Series, Policy Briefs and the *CODESRIA Bulletin.* Select CODESRIA publications are also accessible online at www.codesria.org

CODESRIA would like to express its gratitude to the Swedish International Development Cooperation Agency (SIDA), the International Development Research Centre (IDRC), the Ford Foundation, the Carnegie Corporation of New York (CCNY), the Norwegian Agency for Development Cooperation (NORAD), the Danish Agency for International Development (DANIDA), the French Ministry of Cooperation, the United Nations Development Programme (UNDP), the Netherlands Ministry of Foreign Affairs, the Rockefeller Foundation, the Open Society Foundations (OSFs), Trust Africa, UNESCO, UN Women, the African Capacity Building Foundation (ACBF) and the Government of Senegal for supporting its research, training and publication programmes.

Table of Contents

List of Tables, Figures and Boxes

Tables

Figures

Boxes

Contributors

Cyril K. Daddieh, Professor and Director of Graduate Studies, Department of Political Science, Miami University, USA.

George M. Bob-Milliar, Lecturer, Department of History and Political Studies, Kwame Nkrumah University of Science and Technology, Kumasi.

Joseph R. A. Ayee, Professor and Independent Consultant, and First Emeka Anyaoku Visiting Professor of Commonwealth Studies, University of London.

Kofi Quashigah, Associate Professor and Dean, Faculty of Law, University of Ghana.

Kwabena A. Anaman, Professor of Economics, Institute of Statistical Social and Economic Research, University of Ghana.

Kwame A. Ninsin, Emeritus Professor of Political Science, University of Ghana.

Maame Adwoa A. Gyekye-Jandoh, Lecturer, Department of Political Science, University of Ghana.

Maxwell Owusu, Professor of Anthropology, University of Michigan, Ann Arbor, USA.

Ziblim Iddi, Lecturer, Department of Political Science, University of Ghana.

Preface and Acknowledgements

The essays in this volume are essentially about elections in Ghana. In a wider sense they are about elections as an academic discourse. In the narrower sense they are about the fact that elections give practical expression to the sovereignty of the citizens of Ghana. Both of these perspectives converge where the democratic rights of citizens become central to governance. Our interest lies in both, because underlying both perspectives is the centrality of elections to democracy and the role of citizens as key participants in governance, particularly in the policy-making process where alternative policy choices regarding what is good for society are made.

Existing discourse on elections tends to focus on formal institutional structures by which the electorate choose their representatives, and thereby participate indirectly in the decision-making process. Explanations of why people vote have been based on responses to questionnaires as well as trends in voting behaviour leading to formal explanations of the highly complex relationships between voters and their representatives, and the attribution of rationality to voters. Yet electoral politics is mediated by a number of social, political and economic factors as well as developments within and outside the immediate environment of the voter and which affect the processes leading to electoral outcomes and the meaning of representation. A study of elections that takes into consideration the environmental factors that affect the choices made by the voter promises to further give an insight into the nature of the contribution of the electorate, if any, to the policy process. A contrary approach to the study of elections is bound to raise questions about whether the electorate are able to make a sound and reasonable judgement via their vote?

The nine chapters in this volume seek to give a better understanding of the relationship between the electorate and their representatives. In a large measure they depart from the study of formal structures by which the electorate choose their representatives and instead apply a methodology that does 'a more abstract and normative evaluation of the institutional forms' that representation may take. This makes it possible for the authors to study elections outside the specific institutional form that democratic theory presumes as mandatory to arrive at the actual nature of the relationships that are formed between the voters and their representatives, and 'to judge them in terms of their contributions to democracy' (Castiglione and Warren 2006:3).

This anthology was conceived in 2008 when the Department of Political Science could not raise funds to undertake a study of the elections of that year. It then dawned on me that the situation offered an opportunity to study Ghanaian elections from a different methodological perspective. I take this opportunity to commend the contributors to this volume for accepting the challenge of this methodology, which is premised on abstract and normative interpretation of elections, and working diligently to complete their respective chapters. We missed several opportunities to meet at a seminar as a collective to dialogue on this methodology, and also to seize the moment to tap into the wisdom of colleagues within the political studies fraternity. Nonetheless, all of us approached the subjects that we had individually chosen and analysed the relevant issues with perspicacity. I am sure that the essays in this anthology will further enrich existing knowledge about Ghanaian elections in particular and Ghanaian politics in general.

It is difficult to single out colleagues at home and abroad – within and outside academia – who have indirectly contributed to the success of this work. Surely several scholars and non-scholars have – through direct and indirect conversations and through their publications which have been cited extensively in this volume. I wish to acknowledge the contributions of all such unknown partners in this scholarly enterprise, as well as share the joy of successfully completing this anthology.

Kwame A. Ninsin
Department of Political Science
University of Ghana

Introduction

Understanding Ghana's Electoral Politics

Kwame A. Ninsin

Ghana attained independence from Great Britain in 1957. Between that date and 1992 when a new constitution came into force, she went through what may be described as an endless political transition. An *endless* political *transition* is a process of political change, from one regime to another, that is circuitous and endless. The politics of the Federal Republic of Nigeria from the 1980s to the early 1990s was characterized by such an interminable succession of regimes described by Diamond, Kirk-Green and Oyederan (1997) in *Transition Without End: Nigerian Politics and Civil Society Under Babangida.*[1] In Ghana, during the period 1966 to 1993, democratic constitutions by which civilian regimes were established were abrogated with reckless abandon through a quick succession of military coups d'état. Before then the independence Constitution of 1957 had been replaced in 1964 with a single party socialist constitution that lasted until January 1966 when the military abrogated it. Following widespread social unrest and political agitations the military regime supervised the writing of a new constitution in 1969 that ushered in a democratically elected government in that year. In barely two and a half years of constitutional civilian government the military intervened in Ghana's politics again and ruled the country from 1972 till 1979, and again from 31 December 1981 to January 1993.

All the civil constitutions since 1957 contained elaborate institutional arrangements for separation of powers and checks and balances which usually entrenched executive, legislative and judicial powers, and also provided that each arm of government would work more or less in an independent but coordinated manner. The only exception was the Republican Constitution of 1960 under which the executive was vested with superordinate powers. By the 1979 constitution human rights and media independence would become enshrined constitutional provisions. The purpose of these constitutional provisions was to guarantee the rights and freedoms of the citizens through democratic governance.

At each juncture of the transition from an authoritarian regime to constitutional rule these institutional arrangements for democratic governance were restored. The various restorations notwithstanding, the institutional foundations for democratic governance were not necessarily strengthened. The rampant military coups aborted the process of strengthening the institutions of state.

Political parties have been an integral part of the country's transition to democratic politics. However, the political party system also went through a similar cycle of rebirth and suppression. Between 1954 and 1957 when the people were struggling for independence from British colonial rule, as many as eight political parties emerged to participate in the independence struggle. Between 1969 and 1972 when the country freed itself from the first military regime, between five and 12 political parties were formed to join hands in the agitation to restore democratic rule in the country. In 1979 when Ghanaians again embarked on agitations to reclaim their government from the military and place it on the path to democratic rule there was an explosion of political parties: 11 political parties mushroomed. By 1981 the scramble to form political parties had simmered down reducing the number to six which existed at various levels of engagement in the political process until the last and longest military regime truncated the budding democratic process in December 1981 and thereby ended the growth of various governance institutions, and ruled the country until December 1992. Throughout the transitions to democratic rule, the emergence of political parties was linked to elections through which the core values of democracy were affirmed: namely, political and civil rights as well as social and economic rights.

The 1992 Constitution under which democratic rule was restored guarantees various rights, including political and civil rights such as freedom of political association, speech and self determination. Like their predecessors, the political parties that emerged within the framework of the 1992 Constitution have been driven by the core values of democracy. The country's history of military dictatorship and abuse of human rights were compelling reasons for insisting especially on the basic political and civil rights that are guaranteed by the Constitution. Between May 1992, when the ban on political parties was lifted, and November of the same year, 13 political parties were registered in response to the democratic opening, namely,

Democratic People's Party

New Generation Party

Ghana Democratic Republican Party

National Independence Party

Peoples Heritage Party
Every Ghanaian Living Everywhere Party
National Convention Party
National Democratic Congress
New Patriotic Party
People's National Convention
People's Party for Democracy and Development
National Justice Party, and
National Salvation Party

Some of the political parties, for example, the New Patriotic Party (NPP), had emerged from an old political tradition dating back to the 1950s and subscribed to conservative liberalism (Jonah 1998:72-94).[2] Others such as the National Salvation Party were entirely new political entities; they had no roots in Ghanaian politics and did not expatiate on any specific political ideology. A number of these political parties did not survive the competitive as well as organizational and financial demands of electoral politics. Three of the political parties went into alliance with the National Democratic Congress that won both the presidential and parliamentary elections held in November-December 1992. Six others joined the New Patriotic Party to form an alliance of opposition parties to challenge the emergence of the NDC and its allies as hegemons in Ghanaian politics. Four years into constitutional rule, eight of the political parties had survived to contest the 1996 elections. By 2004 the political arena had stabilized enough to allow only the better-organized political parties to sustain their participation in Ghana's democratic politics, especially electoral politics. In the 2000 parliamentary elections the number of contesting political parties had dropped to seven, but rose to eight in the 2004 parliamentary elections.

While the number of political parties contesting the parliamentary elections remained more or less stable between, for example, 1996 and 2004, those contesting the presidential elections varied from time to time: three (3) in 1996, seven (7) in 2000 and four (4) in 2004. Clearly the better-organized political parties, which were also the best endowed with funds and other material resources, were the ones that could field candidates in both the parliamentary and presidential elections. Apart from the NPP and NDC the other political parties could not field candidates in all the constituencies even for the parliamentary elections. This pattern of rise and fall of the political parties has continued into post-2000 electoral politics that further indicates the contrasting financial and organizational capacity of the array of political parties that populates Ghana's political arena.

In the light of this unstable political history, governance institutions could not develop appropriate rules and procedures (Huntington 1968[3]) that would be rooted in society and in the consciousness of the rank and file of citizens, and ensure general compliance as well as guarantee their longevity and stability. Again, the prevailing institutions could not gain the necessary maturity and embedded principles and norms that would dictate that governance would be in consonance with the general interest and demands for social security and wellbeing. Ghanaian politics in general and electoral politics in particular should be understood within this environment of institutional fragility that above all was underpinned by a weak commitment to an overriding national purpose.

I postulate that the 1992 Constitution ended the circus of political transitions from authoritarian regimes to constitutional/civilian regimes without resolving the problem of fragile institutions. Rather it introduced another cycle of political transitions that would further subvert the newly established governance institutions. This new development is the transition from one democratically elected government to another. Central to all such transitions is election, which embodies the sovereign right of the people to chose and change their government through free and fair ballot, as well as produce a governing regime that enhances the enjoyment of their human rights. There is a presumption, backed by a strong current of opinion that equates free and fair elections to democracy and democratic consolidation, especially in the newly democratizing countries of Africa. Bratton (1999:19) has argued that 'while elections and democracy are not synonymous, elections remain fundamental, not only for installing democratic governments, but as a necessary requisite for broader democratic consolidation. The regularity, openness, and acceptability of elections signal whether basic constitutional, behavioural, and attitudinal foundations are being laid for sustainable democratic rules.'[4] This school of thought recognizes certain requisites such as respect for civil and political rights, inclusiveness in the choice of leaders and policies. They nonetheless assert that once citizens are able to regularly exercise their franchise in a free and fair manner as well as enjoy their human rights, the outcome of an election is a democratic regime. This is why Ghana is celebrated as a beacon of democracy in Africa having successfully organized six presidential and parliamentary elections – in 1992, 1996, 2000, 2004, 2008, and 2012.

In all these instances, the exception being the 1992 elections, both foreign and local observers underscored the democratic nature of the elections on the basis of formal attributes such as transparency in electoral management, the extent of external interference in the citizens' exercise of their franchise – for example, the incidence of voter intimidation and obstruction during voting; the enjoyment of civic and political rights, and vote rigging among others. Elite consensus is an equally important ingredient in democratic politics. Since the 1996 elections the Ghanaian political class has been commended for the disposition of its losing faction to concede defeat despite a litany of grievances that the losers might have compiled concerning the conduct and outcome of the election.[5] Furthermore, compared to the tendency toward post-election violence, the Ghanaian political class has been disposed to settling election disputes amicably, usually by resorting to the judiciary for adjudication. The current election petition, which is before the Ghanaian Supreme Court challenging the 2012 presidential election results as declared by the Electoral Commission, may soon be cited as a classic illustration of the disposition of the Ghanaian political class to comply with prevailing institutional norms and practices governing elections.[6]

Such euphoria about Ghana's democratic politics notwithstanding, there is mounting evidence that governance institutions are not working according to global standards. For example, parliament is unable to exercise its oversight functions due to extreme partisanship and gaps in the existing enforcement regime (Ninsin 2008), and political parties cannot perform their integrative and policy articulation functions effectively. They have become instruments for sectarian, ethnic and money politics. The media do not perform their civic duty by acting as the conscience of the nation and holding government accountable, ensuring transparency, building consensus on national issues through dispassionate and educative journalism, and generally promoting common national values and national unity. They tend to function as instruments for peddling ethnic and partisan division and acrimonious politics in the country. In general they have become complicit in bad governance for purely partisan ends, especially during an election year (Karikari 2013).

The essays in this volume draw attention to a number of flaws in Ghana's electoral politics. They delve beyond the veil of formal attributes of democratic elections in the country, and interrogate a wide range of substantive issues that have become standard assumptions about the centrality of elections in actualizing democratic politics, especially in the developing countries of Africa. The essays point to one underlying weakness of Ghana's democracy – the fragility of governance institutions that derogate from the standard practice of liberal democratic politics.

In their chapter on parliamentary primaries Daddieh and Bob-Milliar recall the claim by theorists of democracy that where the individual party member is able to play a greater role in the internal affairs of the party the party is more democratic, and the more decentralized its procedure the greater the possibilities that its members would be able to play a role in its internal governance (quoting Billie 2001). This claim about citizen participation in the internal processes of political parties is made mandatory by Article 55(5) of the 1992 Constitution which requires that 'the internal organization of a political party shall conform to democratic principles'. It may justifiably be argued therefore that the conduct of party primaries that occurs through the decentralized structures of the political parties is in conformity with these principles of participation.

However, as the authors point out, party primaries are only formally democratic. Despite the mass base of the political parties, voting in the primaries is restrictive: only certain categories of party members are allowed to vote. Voters in the primaries are also subjected to a number of extraneous influences, including the exercise of undue influence, imposition of candidates and manipulation of procedures by party officials at the local and national levels despite the existence of 'explicit formal rules'. There is also the use of money to get candidates to vote in a particular way or for particular candidates. Regarding the latter problem, the authors assert categorically that unregulated use of money in Ghanaian elections could determine the outcome of crucial primaries, and that such palpable trends are the result of growing competitiveness in the race for parliament.

Since 1992 Ghanaian elections have grown in the intensity of competition for parliamentary seats and for executive office, especially as the multiparty system resolved itself into a virtual two-party competition between the National Democratic Congress (NDC) and the New Patriotic Party (NPP), and also as the margin of victory between the presidential candidates in elections since 2008 became smaller. In 2008, for example, the victorious presidential candidate of the NDC won by just 50.3 per cent of the votes against the NPP candidate's 49.7 per cent – a difference of just over 41,000 votes. Furthermore, as Ninsin argues in his chapter on '*Elections and Representation in Ghana's Democracy*', 'the rising level of elite competition for parliamentary seats is due to the prevailing view of elections as a means to control the state for private accumulation ...'. The engagement of political parties in electoral politics is therefore driven by the imperative to win power at all cost. Hence candidates as well as their political parties are wont to employ unorthodox strategies to win, especially the presidential election.

As a winning strategy in an election, the two leading political parties do not hesitate to provoke serious controversy about various aspects of election management, including voter registration, the voters' register, whether it is credible, the creation of new constituencies and several other issues that could otherwise be settled consensually. Such contestations have had the tendency to undermine the legitimacy of elections as well as the credibility of election results, leading to post-election disputes – for example, in 1992, 2000, 2008 and 2012. Admittedly, those disputes were resolved without undermining the peace and stability of the nation; they nonetheless left a mark of profound anxiety over the prospect for consolidating the country's democracy.

Maame Gyekye-Jandoh argues in her chapter titled '*Civic Election Observation and General Elections in Ghana under the Fourth Republic: Enhancing Government Legitimacy and the Democratization Process*' that such threats to Ghana's democracy have been averted largely through the intervention of civil society organizations which continue to function as election monitors and observers in support of the country's democratic politics. She employs the case of the Coalition of Domestic Election Observation (CODEO), which started on a modest scale as a domestic election observer group in 1996. About 18 years later CODEO has grown into a giant and dynamic domestic election observation group capable of conducting election observation without the intervention of foreign observers and monitors. Hence she argues:

the Ghanaian experience shows clearly that democracy can be consolidated and democratic reversals pre-empted, when civil society organizations take the initiative to enhance domestic/societal ownership of the electoral process through active observation and monitoring of elections. Success in performing these roles instils credibility and transparency in the electoral process, so that election results would be accepted by all (to a large extent) and post-election violence and conflict prevented.

Above all, she concludes:

> If political legitimacy, the authority to rule in accordance with law or with the established legal forms, is necessary for a peaceful and well-functioning democracy, then election observation and monitoring of Ghana's general elections (by civic bodies) since 1996 have been a critical factor in furthering the democratic process. They have given considerable credence to elections and election outcomes and legitimatized newly elected governments.

There is no doubt that robust monitoring and observation by civil society organizations have been crucial in ensuring successful elections and legitimizing election outcomes. The explosion of CSOs engaged in election monitoring and observation, civic education and citizens' empowerment actions, examples of which are the Institute for Democratic Governance (IDEG), Centre for Democratic Governance (CDD–Ghana), Institute for Economic Affairs (IEA) and other citizens' networks and faith-based organizations underscores the dynamic relationship between democratic elections in Ghana, political stability and civil society. All said and done, the Ghanaian experience provides grounds for reflecting on the role of civil society in consolidating democracy in Africa. It underscores the need for autonomous and impartial civil society. CODEO embodies these attributes, and warns political actors in Africa's democratic politics of the absolute need for impartial civil society actors if the political order is to remain legitimate, stable and democratic. Where the actions of civil society are marked by impartiality and autonomy there is a strong likelihood that their intervention in domestic politics will produce outcomes that inspire popular confidence and acceptance. Anything short of this is likely to encourage dissent and violence leading to the breakdown of the political order.

The literature on elections in Africa have also focused on the quality of the vote – whether the electorate vote for candidate A or candidate B on presumably *rational* bases such as public policy, ideology or class, or they are influenced by factors such as ethnicity, religion and personality of candidates to vote. The chapters by Ziblim Iddi and Joseph Ayee address this issue from different angles. Iddi uses the choice of a presidential running mate in the 2008 elections to test the claim that the electorate are more likely to vote for a party that has a member of their ethnic group on the presidential ticket or that the electorate vote on the basis of clientelism. Did ethnicity or clientelism affect the choices made by the voters in the home region (the Northern Region) of the running mates for the NPP and NDC, respectively? Iddi concludes that ethnicity was a major factor in Gonjaland working in favour of the NDC and its Gonja running mate. However, in the Mamprugu traditional area clientelism and party loyalty were more significant factors than ethnicity, which adversely affected the electoral fortunes of the NPP and its Mampruga running mate.

Several of the contributions to this volume allude, however obliquely, to the determinate role played in the electoral choices made by Ghanaian voters. Ayee, for example, postulates that such factors as ethnicity, clientelism and personality of candidates are bound to influence the electorate despite the fact that there is a long tradition in Ghanaian politics whereby political parties publish manifestos on the eve of an election. However, the fact still remains that Ghanaian political parties have not developed the capacity to set the public policy agenda to shape the choices of the electorate at the polls. According to him, the lack of a public policy agenda exposes the electorate to 'irrational' factors in the choices they make at the polls. Ayee concludes: 'Voters are not always the rational or well informed actors that the doctrine of mandate suggests. Voters are influenced by a range of "irrational" factors such as the personality of the leaders, the public image of the parties, habitual allegiance and social conditioning.'

As stated earlier, the literature on the transition to liberal democratic politics in Africa postulates that free and fair elections, despite the widespread ambiguities and contradictions which characterise them, are central to the process.[7] In this regard, I should recall my earlier argument: 'The freedom that democracy embodies become manifest during an election: the freedoms of association, choice, speech, movement; the right to participate and differ, the right to peaceful assembly and other latent fundamental human rights are brought alive and exercised by the citizens, including the franchise itself which expresses the fundamental equality of the citizen' (see *Africa Development* Vol. XXXI No. 3, 2006:9). The quality of the vote or how people perceive their vote is therefore of paramount importance if democratic governance is not to be debased. The value of the right to vote in a democracy lies in its empowerment of citizens to demand the embedded purpose of citizenship that includes the enjoyment of rights and entitlements such as access to quality education and health, employment and a living wage, among others. Where a democratically chosen government fails to deliver on these citizenship entitlements citizens have the right to replace it with one that promises to provide them with the opportunities for improved livelihood. In the chapter titled '*Elections and Representation in Ghana's Democracy*', Ninsin queries whether the enthusiasm of the Ghanaian electorate to vote in their numbers at each general election is an expression of their sovereign power to choose a government and affect the course of public policy. He argues that on the contrary the embedded power of accountability in the vote that the Ghanaian electorate are expected to exercise over those they vote for is circumscribed by the logic of patron-client relations and poverty and by the lack of a learning process that enables them to exercise 'enlightened' political judgment. Therefore the electorate ultimately vote for their representatives merely because of the trust that the latter would facilitate the allocation of collective goods in the form of local development in exchange for their vote, and in so doing give the political elite a *de facto* mandate to use state power to enrich themselves and enhance their status in Ghanaian society. Notwithstanding the patron-clientelist nature of Ghanaian politics, citizens are able use elections to demand some form of development in their communities. Electoral politics, which has been showing a strong tendency towards permanent electoral mobilization, is somehow affected by the imperative to meet the developmental needs of the electorate.

Since the 1992 elections, there have been two *transition elections* – in 2000 and 2008, during which there was a change of governing parties. In the chapter titled 'Political transitions, electoral mobilization, and the problem of state capacity', Ninsin argues that the prevailing weak governance institutions provide just the conducive environment for acrimony and instability during the process of change from one elected government to another. In the process, the transition process is privatized by the incoming political elite who fashion new rules and procedures to regulate the transition in a manner that will secure their monopoly of power and enable them to effectively marginalize the outgoing faction of the political class. The contending elite factions in the transition process take advantage of the weakness of governance institutions to drag out the process almost indefinitely, and thereby create uncertainty about the future of the political contest. They assume adversarial positions on almost every issue arising from the transition process. Between the two contending political elites there is no trust, no dialogue and no consensus about the transition process. In the absence of regulatory governance institutions there is a strong tendency to abuse power through various actions and inactions. The weakness of governance institutions benefits the political elite as a whole; therefore no faction of the political class has the incentive to strengthen the institutions of the democratic state. Where the political environment is volatile, as happens during democratic political transitions, and state institutions are weak the governing political elite is able to engage in wanton corruption and inefficient economic management that adversely affect social development.

Anaman draws a direct link between democratic political transitions and the general state of the economy. He argues that incumbent governments control substantial wealth of the nation to either manage or mismanage the economy.

> [In the absence of strong governance institutions] they tend to spend excessively and with impunity, especially during an election year leading to inflation in the immediate post election years. Inflation has adverse effect on corporate, group and personal income; it weakens the domestic currency and ultimately slows down the development of the nation.

Concluding, he states:

> Overall, in terms of human development, it is observed that election years produce poorer macroeconomic management which is characterized by higher inflation, higher budget deficits, negative balance of payments figures and lower levels of gross international reserves. The poorer macroeconomic management translates into poorer economic conditions of the people and lower quality of human development.

In '*Democracy without Development: The Perils of Plutocracy in Ghana*' Maxwell Owusu affirms the point made in the preceding paragraphs about the implications of weak governance institutions, which includes the reckless choices public officeholders do make, and the adverse effect these have on democratic politics and on social development. The pathos of public life is that anti-corruption laws are not enforced, and anti-corruption and accountability institutions do not carry out their legal mandate to the hilt. Hence Owusu argues that in the absence of strong institutions the governing elite indulge with impunity in political and administrative dishonesty and corruption.

The pursuit of self-interest does not encourage economic progress which is a necessary requirement for sustainable democratic governance. A sprinkling of elections, however free and fair, on a sea of corruption, economic mismanagement and plutocracy, cannot cure the problem of social and economic backwardness. According to Owusu, if the political elite would strengthen the governance institutions and replace the politics of self-interest that predominates in public life with the pursuit of the public good there will be prosperity, sustainable growth and development, and democracy will flourish.

Quashigah, in '*Ghana's 2008 Elections, The Constitution and the Unexpected: Lessons for the Future*', sums up the thrust of the analyses in the preceding chapters; namely, that institutions do matter, but where institutions are weak operating rules and procedures are easily and wilfully flouted and abused for personal advantage regardless of the consequences for society. The problem of Ghana's politics is that its institutions are weak; the 1992 Constitutions did not provide the framework for the functioning of established institutions. This omission is compounded by the political attitude and behaviour of the plutocrats for whom power is a means to the acquisition of wealth and status, and they have shown that they have ample disposition to employ any means to achieve and monopolize it. Hence,

> The two main political parties, the New Patriotic Party (NPP) and the National Democratic Party (NDC) deliberately manipulated the electoral process and the legislative system to hopefully achieve desired ends. [...] In general so much money is spent on Ghana's electioneering campaign and related activities that the stakes become extremely high and loss becomes devastating. Consequently everything possible is done to win an election, [...] without regard to its repercussions for the whole democratic process or for the integrity and stability of the nation as a whole.

However, unlike Gyekye-Jandoh who postulates that the efficacy of civil society intervention has redeemed the situation from the machinations of the contending political elites, Quashigah argues that the institutional weaknesses and their perverted outcomes are due to human agency: they are 'more a reflection principally of the determination of political attitude [...]'. Nonetheless he believes that a change in political attitude and behaviour will correct the institutional lapses and nurture the governance institutions into maturity. This is what Owusu (ibid) also has to say about the responsibility of the political class in perverting Ghana's electoral politics: if the political class would strengthen the governance institutions and replace the politics of self-interest that predominates in public life with the pursuit of the public good there will be prosperity, sustainable growth and development, and democracy will flourish.

In addition to the imperative for attitudinal and behavioural change among the political class, Quashigah believes that social engineering would compliment this human effort. In apparent approval of the current constitutional review processes initiated by the previous NDC government, he states:

> Nevertheless ... (new) constitutional provisions could complement political attitude in ensuring a smoother operation of the electoral and transition processes. The experience in Ghana confirms the belief in the need for a complement between the political attitude and the constitutional and statutory aspects. The electoral process in Ghana could benefit from some conscious re-engineering of the timetable for elections as well as a statutorily regulated transitional process [...].

Notes

1. The introduction by the editors ('The Politics of Transition Without End') provides a concise understanding of this kind of political change in especially the new democracies of Africa.
2. In general, the politics of the rise and fall of political parties during the 1992-1996 period is discussed by this author – Jonah 1998:72-94.
3. See Huntington (1968) on institutionalization of organization.
4. See also Diamond et al. (1988:xvi) and Ambrose (1995:33) reported in Joseph Takouganag (2003:265-266)
5. See Ninsin (1998:185-202) for a description of the delicate political negotiations that followed the 1992 elections and the boycott staged by the alliance of opposition political parties, and what finally produced elite consensus as an essential ingredient of democratic politics.
6. On 29 September 2013, the Supreme Court of Ghana gave its verdict in favour of John Mahama, by majority decision, as the duly elected president of Ghana. The petitioners, led by Nana Addo-Dankwa Akufo-Addo, immediately accepted the court verdict. He further declared to the nation that consistent with his belief in the rule of law and to affirm his commitment to the principles of democracy, he would not seek a review despite a swell of pressure from factions in his party, the New Patriotic Party.

7. For a wide ranging discourse on the role of elections in Africa's transition to democracy and the inherent ambiguities see Bratton (1999), Gyimah-Boadi (1999) and Diamond and Platter (1999), chapters 11 – 16; also Berhanu (in Salih 2003:115-147).

References

Ambrose, B.P., 1995, *Democratization and the Protection of Human Rights in Africa: Problems and Prospects,* Westport, CT: Praeger Publishers.

Berhanu, K., 2003, 'Party Politics and Political Culture in Ethiopia' in M.A. Mohamed Salih (ed.) *African Political Parties: Evolution, Institutionalization and Governance,* London: Pluto Press.

Bratton, M., 1999, 'Second Elections in Africa' in L. Diamond and M.F. Platter (eds.) *Democratization in Africa,* Baltimore and London: Johns Hopkins University Press.

Diamond, L. *et al.,* 1988, *Democracy in Developing Countries:* Africa, Boulder, CO: Lynne Rienne Publishers.

Diamond, L., A. Kirk-Green and O. Oyederan (eds.), 1997, *Transition Without End: Nigerian Politics and Civil Society Under,* Ibadan: Vantage Publishers.

Diamond, L. and Platter, M.F. (eds.), 1999, *Democratization in Africa,* Baltimore and London: Johns Hopkins University Press, Chapters 11-16.

Gyimah-Boadi, E., 1999, 'The Rebirth of African Democracy' in L. Diamond and M.F. Platter (eds.) *Democratization in Africa,* Baltimore and London: Johns Hopkins University Press, Chapters 11-16.

Huntington, S.P., 1968, *Political Order in Changing Societies,* Yale University Press).

Jonah, K 1998, 'Political Parties and the Transition to Multi-Party Politics in Ghana' in K.A. Ninsin (ed.) *Ghana: Transition to Democracy,* Accra: Freedom Publications.

Karikari, K., 2013, *The Ghanaian Media: National Peace and Cohesion* Ghana Speaks Lecture Series No. 2 2001, Accra: Institute for Democratic Governance.

Ninsin, K.A., 1998, 'Postscript: Elections, Democracy and Elite Consensus' in K.A. Ninsin (ed.) *Ghana: Transition to Democracy,* Accra: Freedom Publications.

Takouganag, J., 2003, *Democracy, Human Rights, and Democratization in Africa"* in J.M. Mbaku and J.O. Iihonvbere (eds.) *The Transition to Democratic Governance in Africa: The Continuing Struggle,* Westport, CT: Praeger Publishers.

1

In Search of 'Honorable' Membership: Parliamentary Primaries and Candidate Selection in Ghana*

Cyril K. Daddieh and George M. Bob-Milliar

Introduction

Ghana's democratic achievements have become a cause for celebration in Africa. Perhaps the country's most notable achievement has been the progressive improvement of election management and the increasing acceptance of election results as 'free and fair' by the contestants, their supporters, and by domestic and international observers alike. Ghana is now endowed with a more open political system and a number of stable democratic institutions. Five successive general elections have been held: the National Democratic Congress (NDC) won the 1992 and 1996 elections, but lost power in the 2000 elections to the New Patriotic Party (NPP), which secured another victory in the 2004 elections (see Daddieh, 2009; 2011; Gyimah-Boadi 2009a; Whitfield 2009). The 2008 elections ushered in a second alternation of a ruling party, with the NDC regaining the reins of power. The country has witnessed five successive multi-party elections since the return to constitutional rule in 1992. This constitutes the longest timeframe in Ghana's history over which we can observe parliamentary primary elections within a single civilian regime.

A crucial function of political parties concerns their gate-keeping role in nominating candidates for office. This key function of political parties has potential implications for levels of intra-party conflict and the composition of parliaments as well as emerging governments (Norris, 2006). The major political parties in Ghana have been democratizing their candidate selection process, allowing candidates to be freely selected through primary elections.[1] Nevertheless, the procedures employed by the parties to fill internal party positions or how they select candidates for parliamentary and presidential elections have not attracted the level of scholarly attention they deserve. Indeed, in a preface to one of the few extant studies of candidate selection in sub-Saharan Africa and other new democracies, Gyimah-Boadi (2002) lamented the dearth of empirical research in this area. This article makes a modest attempt to bridge this knowledge gap.

In the early years of Ghana's Fourth Republic, competition for nomination to represent parties in the legislature was hardly keen. In fact, some of the pioneer Members of Parliament (MPs) had to be cajoled by their local communities and other power brokers to run for the office.[2] The major political parties conducted primary elections irregularly and the nomination process was generally undemocratic. The NDC imposed candidates on constituencies and then claimed the nominees were the 'consensus' candidates. The NPP, for its part, organized constituency primaries to select candidates for parliament but the process was not without controversies or its detractors. Since then, parliamentary primaries have assumed greater importance and have become the scenes of bloody contestations, partly because of the growing recognition that the office of MP carries with it not only status and prestige but also certain privileges, including financial perks and even power, especially for the fortunate few who get tapped for ministerial positions.[3] Not surprisingly, as District and Municipal Chief Executives (DCEs and MCEs) and other government functionaries have become interested in the office, it has created intense rivalries and even animosity between them and incumbent MPs. Incumbent MPs feel a sense of entitlement. As such, they view the challenge posed by these other officeholders in primary contests not as a sign of a more vibrant democracy but as tantamount to usurpation of their rights as 'honorable' MPs. Nevertheless, parliamentary primary elections are becoming so keenly contested and so expensive that these days both aspiring MPs and incumbents raise their campaign funds overseas (Lindberg 2010). Some candidates have allegedly gone to such great lengths as resorting to the use of black magic (or juju) to eliminate potential rivals.[4] There have been numerous reports of decidedly undemocratic practices being employed during primary elections for selection of candidates for parliament. Party leaders have been accused of preventing primaries from taking place in some constituencies and, in others, poorly-run or flawed primaries created conflicts that proved electorally costly to both major parties in general elections.[5]

This chapter focuses on the conduct of parliamentary primaries by the two leading parties in Ghana, the NDC and NPP. It interrogates the nature of parliamentary primaries, how they are conducted in Ghana by the political parties, the factors that determine their conduct, and the degree to which they enhance or undermine democratic norms. The article also tries to confront the increasingly acrimonious nature of these parliamentary primaries and how they may be influencing general election outcomes. It provides a tentative assessment of the degree to which such primaries are promotive of Ghana's democratic experiment or act as a drag on it. The balance of this article is divided into six sections. The opening section provides a theoretical overview of the subject of candidate selection. Next, we examine Ghana's emergent two-party system followed by the dynamics of primary elections. We then problematize primary elections in Ghana, interrogating whether, as currently practiced, they enhance or weaken our democracy. Finally, we shine the spotlight on the office of MP itself, the object of desire of primary contestants. We then draw some general conclusions from the study of primary elections in Ghana.

Primary Elections and Candidate Selection: An Overview

Political parties in both presidential and parliamentary systems the world over rely increasingly on primary elections to select candidates for public offices. Where they are adopted, primaries are generally touted as ensuring 'openness and internal party democracy.' Nonetheless, United States (US) scholars have suggested that primaries select candidates who are weaker in general election competition than other selection methods (Carey and Polga-Hecimovich 2006). They contend that primary voters are more myopic in their choice of nominees than the seasoned party leaders who controlled nominations in the good old days before the advent of primaries. This 'primary penalty' argument is predicated on the nature of the primary process. It maintains that primaries that are fiercely contested leave even their winners 'scarred from political battle, exhausted (financially, at least), and therefore weaker in the general election' (Carey and Polga-Hecimovich 2006:530). And yet the authors posit that the electorate values openness, transparency, and internal party democracy in the selection of candidates. Primary elections deliver these qualities in larger measure than other candidate selection procedures. In this context, primaries will provide a 'stamp of legitimacy that is an asset to candidates relative to rivals selected by other procedures' (Carey and Polga-Hecimovich 2006:534).

In their study of parliamentary nominations of the NDC and NPP for the 2004 and 2008 elections, Ichino and Nathan (2010) found evidence to support an 'aspirant demand' explanation for primaries. The underlying assumption is that party leaders are not interested in the policy positions of potential nominees. They demonstrated that, contrary to claims in the literature, primaries are not more likely in competitive constituencies or weaker parties. Instead, the probability of primaries increases with the predicted success of the nominee in the general election. Elsewhere, empirical research has shown that candidate selection has wide-ranging and significant implications for political parties, party members, leaders, and democratic governance (Hazan and Rahat 2006). Indeed, Gallagher (1988:2) identifies candidate selection as the 'key stage' in the recruitment process of political parties.

If we accept the argument that candidate selection takes place almost entirely within political parties, then we must be more concerned about the machinations of the candidate selection process. In emerging democracies in sub-Saharan Africa, this most crucial of links between democratic selection and democratic governance has not always been fully appreciated. While candidate selection has not attracted enough scholarly attention in sub-Saharan Africa, the subject has been extensively studied in Western democracies (see Gallagher 1980; Gallagher and Marsh 1988; Hazan and Rahat 2006; Rahat 2008; Rahat and Hazan 2001; Ranney 1965). Sartori (1976:64) has observed that the selection of candidates is the core activity that globally distinguishes parties from other organizations.

Further, as Schattschneider (1942:101) observed in *Party Government*, 'the nominating process has become the crucial process of the party. He who can make the nominations is the owner of the party.' Ranney (1981:103) affirms this observation by suggesting that what is at stake in candidate nominations 'is nothing less than control of the core of what the party stands for and does.' Candidate selection has also become an important test of the internal democratic strength of party organizations. According to Gallagher (1988: 1) 'the way in which political parties select their candidates may be used as an acid test of how democratically they conduct their internal affairs.' Bille (2001:363–364) advanced two reasons why it is important to study how parties select candidates for election to the representative assemblies of a political system and whether the selection process has become more democratic. On the one hand, the candidate selection process is very crucial to any party, whatever the type. The way parties are organized is an important indicator when trying to characterize and understand the functioning of a democratic regime. On the other hand, a democratization of the candidate selection process might promote an increased sense of involvement of either members or voters. Furthermore, the importance of candidate nomination goes beyond the borders of the political party. Crotty observed that:

> The party in recruiting candidates determines the personnel and, more symbolically, the groups to be represented among the decision-making elite. Through recruitment, the party indirectly influences the types of policy decisions to be enacted and the interests most likely to be heard. Candidate recruitment then represents one of the key linkages between the electorate and the policy-making process (1968:260).

In Ghana, Ichino and Nathan (2010) report that party leaders do not value the policy positions of their legislative candidates. The Ghanaian political system is weighted heavily in favor of the executive branch of government. As a result of this presidential or executive dominance, the policy views of parliamentary candidates are less important, especially given the lack of opportunity for ordinary MPs to initiate private members bills. In that case, all bills submitted to parliament emanate from the executive. To sum up this brief overview, first, Gallagher insists that political parties serve as vehicles for popular participation. Second, Schattschneider (1942) and Ranney (1981) have argued that candidate selection is one of the core functions of political parties. We argue that these observations provide a powerful universal justification for the significance of parliamentary and presidential nomination contests in Ghana as elsewhere.

We hasten to confess, however, that as the dominant mode of candidate selection, primary elections fall squarely within the liberal representative democratic tradition. We concede that this is certainly a far cry from direct participatory democracy; neither does it resemble an African community-centered democratic project which traditionally took place under the baobab tree or village square and which involved broader participation and consensual decision making. Besides its participatory and consensual limitations, the process may produce outcomes that favor elites and harm or ignore the interests of peasant majorities and the working poor in Africa. It must be recalled that Flt. Lt. Jerry John Rawlings, the military strongman who had come to power for the second time via another successful coup d'Etat, had to be pushed by a combination of sustained domestic pressure and at least an international nudge before he reluctantly accepted this liberal democratic arrangement. In that regard, parliamentary candidate selection via primaries is compatible with the interests of elites and international democracy promoters alike.

Ghana's Emergent Two-Party System

Following extensive constitutional deliberations between 1988 and 1992, a plurality electoral system in single-member constituencies was adopted in Ghana. In the contested and highly flawed first multi-party elections in 1992, the main opposition parties led by the NPP boycotted the parliamentary elections, rendering the first parliament of the Fourth Republic an essentially 'rubber-stamp' institution (see Jeffries and Thomas 1993; New Patriotic Party, 1993; Nugent 1996). The second multi-party elections, held in 1996, were essentially free and fair, and with only minor irregularities. The third consecutive round of elections in 2000 continued the positive trend and was judged free and fair with all parties and a number of independent candidates participating (see Ayee, 2002). The 2000 elections produced an alternation of power, with John Agyekum Kufuor and the NPP emerging victorious in the run-off presidential election. In 1992, 463 candidates ran for office of MP. The overall turnout was 29 per cent in the parliamentary poll. In 1996 and 2000, 780 and 1,078 candidates respectively competed for the 200 parliamentary seats on offer. The overall number of candidates running for office has since increased. In 2004, the electoral commission (EC) used its redistricting powers to create 30 new constituencies bringing the total number of parliamentary seats to 230. However, only a total of 953 candidates ran in the 2004 election. The general election of 2008 witnessed a significant increase in the number of candidates. A total of 1,062 candidates competed. Moreover, even though the Ghanaian political system features multiple parties, the NDC and the NPP have appropriated and monopolized the entire electoral space. By sucking the political oxygen from the other parties, they have managed to create a *de facto* two-party system. Only roughly 5 per cent of the votes is divided among several smaller parties including the Nkrumahist-inspired Convention People's Party (CPP) and the People's National Convention (PNC) and independent candidates.

Last but not least, it is worth reflecting on the gender mix of parliamentary candidates, albeit only briefly. Even though females constitute roughly 52 per cent of Ghana's population, the vast majority of the candidates were male. This gender reality flies in the face of the solemn pledges made by all the political parties to promote gender equality as well as increased female representation in the legislature. For example, the number of women who contested the parliamentary elections in 1992 was a mere 23 and 16 won, while in 1996, 18 out of the 57 female candidates were elected to the 200-member legislature (see Electoral Commission 2009). In 2000, 95 women contested out of which only 19 won, while 25 out of the 104 women who competed in the 2004 parliamentary elections emerged victorious (Ibid 2009). Clearly, Ghana's electoral landscape is dominated by the NDC and the NPP as well as by male candidates, making the Ghanaian state highly gendered.

The Dynamics of Primary Elections

To begin with, political parties are enjoined to practice and promote internal democracy. To this end, article 55 (5) of the 1992 constitution states that 'the internal organization of a political party shall conform to democratic principles and its actions and purposes shall not contravene or be inconsistent with this Constitution or any other law.' The general assumption among democratic theorists is that the greater the role of the individual party members, the more democratically the party conducts its internal affairs and, additionally, the more decentralized the procedure, the greater the possibilities for individual party members to play a role (Bille 2001:363).

Unlike the president, who is restricted by the 1992 constitution to two consecutive terms of office, parliamentary incumbents are only limited by the favorable or unfavorable verdicts of the voters. However, in constituencies in which a party already held the seat, potential aspirants had to wait and ascertain the intentions of the incumbent MP before they were able to weigh their options to run or to sit out an election. As suggested earlier, increasingly there is mutual suspicion between MPs and the government-appointed DCEs and MCEs. The former view the functions of the latter in the constituency as creating an enabling environment for a run for their seats. Theoretically, District and Municipal Assemblies and the office of DCEs and MCEs provide fertile breeding grounds, if properly cultivated, to enable many a DCE/MCE to unseat incumbent MPs. The decentralized nature of the Ghanaian political system is such that it imposes collaboration on local officeholders and MPs. The development of the constituency is supposed to be fostered through collaboration between local governments and MPs. Funds are allocated to District and Metropolitan/ Municipal Assemblies to be used for development at the local or constituency level.

In this arrangement, development is the joint responsibility of MPs, assembly members, and DCEs or MCEs. However, DCEs and MCEs who harbor ambitions of becoming future MPs themselves have been known to act in ways that deliberately undermine and frustrate the incumbent MP. To illustrate our point, MPs have access to a modest 'common fund' to be used to initiate development projects in their constituencies. In instances where there is rivalry between the two parties, projects designed by an incumbent MP for the assembly's approval are either ignored or rejected. While this is calculated to make the MP look incompetent and ineffective in the eyes of the constituents, it is ultimately the people of the constituency who suffer. They are deprived of potentially beneficial development projects that are shelved or their constituency funds may be misappropriated or inefficiently utilized to promote politically-expedient or misguided projects. This situation is worst if the MP is from an opposition party. The convention is that unsuccessful parliamentary aspirants of the ruling party are the ones the president usually appoints as DCEs and MCEs. In such situations, the DCEs and MCEs who are hungry for election to parliament would take credit for any development projects that are executed by the assembly in their constituencies. Notwithstanding this, it is also important to note that there are plenty of instances where incumbent DCEs and MCEs have lost their bids to become MPs even after securing their parties' nominations, a testament to the growing sophistication of the Ghanaian electorate.

Meanwhile the number of candidates running for the two major parties increased in the 2000 and 2008 elections. These were transitional elections in the sense that they coincided with the end of presidential terms. While in 2000 1,078 nominations were certified by the EC to run for the 200 parliamentary seats, the 2004 elections registered a total of 953 candidates; the NDC presented the highest number of candidates for the parliamentary elections. Ashanti region, which has 39 constituencies, recorded the highest number of contestants. Generally there were no unopposed candidates (Electoral Commission 2005). These figures underscore the competitive nature of the parliamentary contest during this period. The highest number of candidates for a constituency was seven in Upper West

Akim constituency in the Eastern region and the lowest number of candidates was two in Akrofrom and Ahafo Ano South constituencies, both in the Ashanti region (Electoral Commission 2005). The NPP and the NDC had serious problems in some constituencies during the selection of parliamentary candidates. Some of the aspiring MPs who failed in their bid but who assumed that they had a large enough following, ran as independent candidates. There were also instances of violent demonstrations staged by disgruntled activists that destroyed party property. We recall here the furor over the defeat of Clement Eledi, the popular choice of the party activists, by Adama Keglah, the Chairman's preference, in the Wa Central constituency during the 2004 NPP primary. The defeat of Eledi provoked a backlash: party activists[6] adopted the strategy of 'shirt and blouse.'[7] They deserted their own party and voted for president JA Kufuor in the presidential elections and for Bernard Mornah, the parliamentary candidate of the PNC.

Parliamentary Primary Election System

Candidate selection is, according to Ranney (1981:75), the 'process by which a political party decides which of the persons legally eligible to hold an elective office will be designated on the ballot and in election communications as its recommended and supported candidate or list ofcandidates.' Under the 1992 constitution, general elections are held in Ghana every four years, starting from 1992. The electoral law permits both party-sponsored and independent candidates. To be elected, a parliamentary candidate requires only a plurality of the valid votes cast (first-past- the-post); a presidential candidate requires a clear majority (any figure above 50%). Who are eligible to seek the nomination for parliament in Ghana's two major parties, the NDC and NPP? Candidates seeking nomination on the ticket of the NDC and NPP formally go through four stages: nominations, certification, campaign, and elections. The certification process, defining who is eligible to pursue the nomination for MP, is influenced by a number of factors. In the last two general elections, the NDC and NPP parliamentary nominations generally adhered to the following prescriptions contained in their constitutions.

Article 42 of the Constitution of the National Democratic Congress (2002: 38–39) regulates the nomination of candidates for parliament and the conduct of parliamentary primaries. The National Executive Committee (NEC) is mandated to notify all Constituency Executive Committees (CECs) as to the timing of the opening of nominations for the conduct of primaries for the parliamentary seat in each constituency. When the information reaches the CEC of each of the 230 constituencies, the CEC is expected to send a circular within seven days to all polling divisions inviting nominations from prospective candidates. The CEC then fixes a date which shall not conflict with the overall national party calendar of political activities. A meeting is convened by the CEC and all prospective candidates who meet the eligibility criteria of the party are invited for the selection of the candidates. At the regional level, the Regional Executive Committee (REC) is mandated to supervise the selection process for parliamentary candidates at the constituency level.

After the selection of prospective candidates who meet the eligibility criteria, the REC and CEC are required to forward the details of such candidates to the party headquarters for consideration by the NEC. The NEC is required to do proper due diligence on all lists of candidates submitted by the REC and CEC. This is to ensure that such candidates are qualified to contest the constituency primaries. The NDC constitution further stipulates that a member shall not be qualified to contest primaries for any parliamentary seat if he/she is disqualified under national electoral laws from contesting a parliamentary seat; is not an active member of the party at the constituency level for the two years immediately preceding the date of filing nomination; and is for any reason disqualified from being a party member as spelt out under article 8 of the NDC constitution. Only after certification by the NEC can parliamentary primaries be conducted in a constituency. However, if a candidate fails to meet the eligibility criteria, the NEC shall communicate this to the CEC. In addition, NEC issues guidelines regarding the selection of parliamentary candidates. When the primary election is held, any candidate who wins by a simple majority of votes cast is duly elected as the party's parliamentary candidate.

The NPP, for its part, bases the selection of parliamentary candidates on article 11 of its constitution (New Patriotic Party 2009:52–54). On the issue of eligibility, the party's constitution states that no member shall be nominated or endorsed as the official candidate in any parliamentary election unless the member has been selected in accordance with the provisions of article 11. The selection of parliamentary candidates is advertised for 18 months prior to the date of the national election and parliamentary candidates are to be elected at least 12 months before the national general election. The NEC is mandated to determine separate dates for elections in constituencies with incumbent MPs.

Any NPP member may, prior to the expiration date of the period set out in article 11 (2), submit an application for nomination as the party's parliamentary candidate. No member is entitled to apply for nomination as the party's parliamentary candidate for any constituency unless he or she is a known and active member of at least two years; is a registered member and a voter in the constituency which he or she seeks to represent, although in appropriate cases the CEC may suspend the requirement; is of good character; is otherwise of good standing; has paid the pre- scribed fees for a parliamentary candidate by the deadline set by the NEC; qualifies under the electoral laws to be a parliamentary candidate for the constituency; and has signed the 'undertaking for parliamentary candidates.' It is incumbent upon the member seeking nomination as the party's parliamentary candidate to satisfy all three tiers (CEC, REC and NEC) of the organizational structure of the party that the conditions stipulated in article 11 (4) have been fulfilled. An application that did not comply with these conditions was to be rejected.

The rules guiding the selection of parliamentary candidates in both parties are fairly standard and uncontroversial. An interesting difference between the official positions of the two parties is that the NDC leaves the determination of the timing of parliamentary primaries entirely in the hands of its CEC; it has no set dates for the holding of primaries. By contrast, the NPP runs an advertisement 18 months prior to the national elections and primaries must be held at least one month to the national elections. Another instance in which the parties differed is that there is a higher burden of proof in the NPP than the NDC. As noted earlier, an NPP aspirant must first satisfy the CEC, then the REC and finally the NEC. Nevertheless, there is a convergence around the duration of membership in both political parties insofar as to be considered for nomination in the NDC and NPP a candidate must have been a registered member for at least two years.

The primary election system used by the parties has evolved over time. Initially, the NDC and NPP adopted different procedures for selecting parliamentary candidates. The NDC operated like an electoral machine resurrected every four years to win elections and then went into hibernation.[8]

NDC parliamentarians in the first parliament of the Fourth Republic never faced any real challenges as the party held few primary elections. The NDC's procedure for selecting candidates for parliament as well as for the presidency remained 'informal' until after the 2000 election. The party's revolutionary ideology and populist rhetoric predisposed it to a preference for bottom–up processes and for consensus building in its operations. In this context, article 48 of the NDC constitution (2002: 43) states that '[e]xcept as otherwise provided in this constitution, at any party meeting decisions shall be reached by consensus and in case of failure to reach a consensus, by a majority of the votes cast.' In addition, the party claimed that the old procedure it had adopted was based on a time-tested African tradition – selection based on consensus of the key actors in a constituency. Accordingly, nominees were endorsed when there was overwhelming support from all politically-relevant people in the constituency.

Nevertheless, in 1996, a selection system based on constituency congresses was attempted by the NDC. This minimalist attempt at democratizing the candidate selection process backfired as evidenced by the high level of dissatisfaction within party circles. Two main issues of contention emerged. First, the open system of parliamentary selection introduced the use of money in the process, thus indirectly disqualifying candidates without deep pockets. The excessive use of money in parliamentary primaries, many NDC activists argued, threatened the very foundations of the party's status as the party of ordinary Ghanaians. Second, too few of the old MPs were retained and the new candidates selected lacked parliamentary experience. A former MP succinctly described the situation in the following terms:

> We entered a one-sided parliament in 1992, many of us with no experience of parliamentary proceedings. Majority of us [sic] came from working class backgrounds, e.g. pupil teachers, clerks and farmers but we were fortunate because the NPP and the other Nkrumahist parties boycotted parliament. In the run-up to the 1996 elections, the NPP big lawyers and PhD titleholders dominated the print and electronic media and they almost won the debate on the economic front. We were told parliament would be a battleground and that the party needed to run primaries and also get some titleholders to match the NPP. (Interview with a former MP, Accra, 18 May 2009)

The views of the MP lend credence to Nugent's (1998: 14) observation that the NDC wanted more 'big men in parliament who could hold their own against the heavyweights of the NPP. The fact that the party appeared content to let loyal foot soldiers go to the wall in the process did not reflect well on the leadership.' Some nominees for parliament were elected at poorly-organized constituency congresses while others were chosen directly by the Regional Executive Committee for the endorsement of the National Executive Committee. The National Executive Committee of the NDC decided which constituencies would be allowed to hold primaries and which would have nominees selected by the national leadership. This decision appears to have been motivated by two considerations. On the formal level, incumbent MPs were evaluated before a decision was taken about whether they should be allowed to seek reelection. This decision was clearly based on the NDC's perceived need to have more qualified individuals represent it in parliament. Unofficially, the national and regional executives wanted loyalists to stand unopposed in safe seats (Interview with a former Lawra-Nandom MP, 17 September 2009).

In contrast to the rather lax rules used by the NDC, the NPP constitution laid out a more explicit procedure for parliamentary candidates to be elected in constituency primaries by local party activists. The NPP held primary elections in many constituencies fairly consistently from 1996 to the present. Nonetheless, there was still some amount of 'imposition' from the National Executive Committee, with the result that some constituencies did not hold competitive primaries. Overall, however, primaries have become increasingly common and more keenly contested in recent years. The NDC, whose parliamentary and presidential candidates were initially not selected through primary elections, was put under the microscope and it began to receive criticism for the way it handled its selection process which was considered undemocratic. The NDC began to take internal party democracy seriously after it lost to the NPP in 2000, partly because a post-mortem revealed that the centralized approach to candidate selection had undermined the party by creating internal discontent (Interview, Accra, 18 May 2009). Subsequent constitutional amendments in 2002 saw the party move to a system that more closely resembled that of the NPP.

Both parties went into the 2004 and 2008 elections having conducted parliamentary primaries based on similar formal procedures. In the majority of cases, the nominees were selected by a constituency-level electoral college made up of polling station executives. In essence, Ghanaian parliamentary and presidential primaries remain restrictive and closed rather than open. Only certain categories of voters or individuals within the party are allowed to participate in the process.[9] Meanwhile, a new trend that augurs well for political party development is that, notwith- standing the sometimes acrimonious and polarized nature of Ghanaian politics, party executives from the different political traditions are invited to witness primaries at the presidential level; at such functions they are given an opportunity to deliver solidarity messages.[10] In 2004, some civil society organizations (CSOs) became involved in the organizing and supervision of parliamentary primaries.[11] However, as already indicated, the existence of explicit formal procedures did not prevent manipulation by party executives and other interested agencies. Some nominees con- tinued to be selected without competitive elections. The size of constituency electoral college – eligible voters are the chairpersons of each polling station executive committee and the constituency executive – has attracted criticism because it is fairly easy for aspirants to manipulate the results by paying off individual voters (Lindberg 2010).

Campaign financing also heavily influences primary election outcomes. The call for 'clean politics' has resulted in many democracies adopting regulatory mechanisms to police the behavior of politicians and the parties they represent. Elsewhere, laws have been enacted to limit the amount of cash donations individuals and/or special interest groups can make to political parties. More stringent disclosure, reporting and auditing requirements have also been instituted for both the political parties and the donors (see Ferdinand 2003; Nassmacher 2003). In Ghana, the constitution mandates the EC to regulate the behavior of political parties. However, the EC's monitoring and the regulation of the behavior of political parties and of their financing has not been robust (see Bob-Milliar 2011). Indeed, the conclusion reached by the 2004 *Global Integrity* report is that the lack of transparency regarding the financing of Ghana's political parties has given rise to abuse and corruption. Broadly, Saffu (2003) has observed that political financing is relatively under-regulated in Africa. He concluded that 'the raising of funds by parties and candidates is a matter of unregulated self-help' (Saffu 2003:21).

In the specific case of Ghana, the legal framework of party financing includes constitutional provisions, laws governing political parties and their financing as well as those governing election campaigns as enshrined in Act 55 (14) of the

1992 constitution and the Political Parties Act (Act 547) of 2000. These two acts leave political party financing completely unregulated, with the sole exception of banning non-citizens and foreign corporate entities from making donations, in cash or in kind, to parties. Neither the constitution nor the acts impose limits on donations from citizens, including corporate citizens; there are not disclosure laws that allow us to follow the flow of monies. There are also no limits on the amount of money individual candidates or the parties can spend on elections. As a result, the NPP made elections 2004 and 2008 Ghana's most expensive elections on record. The party shelled out a whopping (by Ghanaian standards) US$30 million and US$100 million[12] of its 'own' money on advertising and entertaining supporters (*Africa Confidential* 2004:5). It is not just political parties that can engage in this feeding or spending frenzy. Political candidates are also free to raise unlimited amounts of money without questions being asked. As money is the holy grail of politics, it is not hard to imagine how unregulated financing of campaigns can determine the outcome of crucial primaries or general elections. It is also significant to note in the Ghanaian case, especially if the experience of Alan Kyerematen is any guide, that there is a limit to how many votes money can buy. As an NPP presidential candidate for the December 2007 primary, Alan 'cash,' as he became famously known, raised GH¢15 million (or US$13 million) in a single night (see Bob-Milliar and Bob-Milliar 2010; Bebli 2007:1, 15). More importantly, he failed to win the nomination. He lost to his nemesis, Nana Addo Dankwa Akufo-Addo who, in turn, lost the December 2008 general election to the current president, Professor John Evans Ata Mills.

Problematizing Primary Elections in Ghana: Democracy Promotion and Deficits

Given the evidence presented thus far about primary elections in Ghana, how sanguine can we be about this aspect of the Ghanaian democratic experiment? In other words, is the parliamentary primary selection process employed by the two leading political parties in Ghana contributing to further democracy promotion in the country or acting as a drag on it? As a general proposition, political parties the world over employ primaries presumably to make the selection process more open, transparent, and democratic. To the extent that this is true, primaries may be general election assets rather than liabilities. However, in the case of Ghana, the two main parties ran primaries in which only the local party executives were enfranchised, giving them enormous leverage to extract personalized goods from candidates. According to Ichino and Nathan (2010:23), parliamentary primaries in Ghana are 'demand-driven.' In this context, the demand for a primary election in a safe seat is usually high and party leaders are more likely to allow a primary to proceed in such situations.

Party executives continue to intervene selectively, deliberately forcing out aspirants in order to pave the way for their favorite candidates to sail through unopposed.[13] Party leaders become involved in a primary election when there are only two aspirants seeking the nomination. It is much easier to construct attractive incentives for one aspirant to drop out of a race than to do so for multiple aspirants. However, democracy suffers when political contestation is short-circuited in this way. Imposing candidates is not without inherent political risks since it has the potential to alienate local activists and other power brokers; it may also produce angry supporters who may take out their anger on the party at the polls or fail to turn up to vote for the party in the general election. Similarly, contested primaries run the same risk, particularly if the election is poorly organized or is perceived to privilege a particular candidate. Furthermore, primaries can drive disgruntled losers to stand as independent candidates and take their supporters with them as was the case in many poorly-run NPP primaries. Much of this reflects the fact that the competition for parliamentary seats had never been keener.

Party executives play a very important role in this process. Vetting is one of two ways in which party leaders could prevent contested primaries from taking place without suspending the formal procedures for these elections. For instance, many constituencies, especially in rural areas, face resource constraints. As a result, during the parties' primary season there are usually several failed attempts and postponements. Such situations place the national party (headquarters) at the center of organizing primary elections. Where the national party cannot provide support for a constituency to organize primary elections, local party patrons usually step in to perform this role. This process is operationalized on two levels: an aspirant who can financially support a constituency for the primaries is viewed more favorably and generally has an advantage over rivals. The second dimension involves the parliamentary candidates themselves trying to influence the decision of the electorate by 'hosting' them, providing 'transportation' and 'refreshment' money and sometimes resorting to outright bribery on election day. While some local executives benefit from and encourage the process, some have always defended their prerogative from direct interference from Accra. Meanwhile, the central and local levels have sometimes collaborated in the nomination of 'good aspirants,' not least because of an obvious mutual interest in ensuring that a candidate who emerges victorious at a party's primary election is also electable in the constituency (Interview, Accra, Kokomlemle, 14 January, 2008).

The vetting process gives party executives (national and constituency) room to exercise veto power over the slate of candidates who may contest the primaries. Disqualified aspirants and their supporters frequently complained that the vetting committees had invented phantom or 'non-existent' clauses to push them out of the race or applied the rules unfairly to benefit preferred aspirants. A case in point is the 2008 NPP parliamentary primary election in the Tema West constituency in which the aspirant, Irene Naa Torshie Addo, was threatened with disqualification. The constituency chairman appealed to the national executives to have the aspirant disqualified on the grounds that there was not sufficient evidence that the candidate was in good standing with the party. In her defense, Ms Addo claimed that her dues had been paid upfront covering four years (2005–8) even though entries in her membership card indicated payments were made at different times. The chairman countered that the card entries showing dues paid were not entered in the record books of the constituency. The chairman also revealed that the signatories in Ms Addo's card endorsing payment of dues were not authorized by the constituency executives to do so. In effect, there was no record of payment of dues in the books of Tema West constituency.[14]

What is indisputable is that Ms Addo was running against a very powerful incumbent, Abraham Ossei-Aidoo, Minister of Parliamentary Affairs and also the majority leader with 12 years standing in parliament.[15] The evidence pointed to party leaders conniving to prevent the primary from taking place; however, they did it in such a way as not to tip their hand that they were protecting a politically-important MP. This kind of 'back room' manipulation of the primary outcome seems more common than overt intervention in the process.

The case of Ms Vicky Bright, a Deputy Minister at the Office of the President, is equally revealing. She filed her nomination papers to contest the NPP parliamentary primary in the Okaikoi-South constituency but was disqualified by the vetting committee on the grounds that she had not 'nurtured the constituency.' In political party parlance, a prospective MP must 'nurture the constituency' for which he or she intends to seek the nomination. 'Nurturing a constituency' simply means providing all kinds of social amenities and related services such as community toilets, roofing sheets, street lights, paving of streets, paying school and medical bills of constituents, attending festivals, funerals and other social gatherings, and making substantial financial donations. In some cases, the prospective candidate provides funds for the running of party activities in the constituency. In short, 'constituency nurturing' implies a commitment to the party and its programs and taking good care of constituents like any good nurturer. Laying claim to constituency nurturing, Nana Akomea, the incumbent MP, had his nomination confirmed by popular acclamation. However, the Greater Accra Regional Chairman of the NPP, Sammy Crabbe, invalidated the acclamation of Nana Akomea as Okaikoi-South parliamentary candidate. According to the chairman, the process of acclamation violated the party's constitution. 'I know that we have procedures in this party, we have a constitution which governs the way we conduct ourselves including the selection of parliamentary candidates' (Bebli and Kamal, 2008:1). He went on to reiterate that the meeting that acclaimed Nana Akomea's candidature was not properly constituted. 'I believe that what happened was illegal and that any decision coming out of what happened is null and void' (Bebli and Kamal, 2008:1).

The National Chairman of the NPP, Peter Mac Manu, upheld the acclamation procedure. The disqualification of Ms Bright, argues Mac Manu, was right since quite a number of the executives of the party claimed they 'did not know her.' In other instances, all aspirants but one dropped out after passing through vetting, allowing the nominee to emerge unopposed. It is quite likely that some of these cases involved behind-the-scenes manipulation to ensure a particular outcome, including payments to aspirants to drop out of the contest. In another celebrated case, an aspirant was disqualified to maintain party unity. Barely two months to the 2008 general election, the popular MP and Minister of Finance, Kwadwo Baah Wiredu, suddenly passed away in South Africa where he was receiving medical treatment. Six aspirants were vetted for the Asante-Akim North constituency. Kwame Appiah Kubi, a contestant in the previous primary, had his nomination rejected because he was alleged to have used juju (or black magic) to kill the popular minister. Party activists staged demonstrations in the constituency and later at the party headquarters in Accra with placards, some of which read, 'Andy the murderer' (see *Chronicle* 2 October 2008:1, 15). Party leaders asked the aspirant to withdraw his nomination for security reasons. The constituency executives argued that it would be difficult for the aspirant to campaign at Agogo, a town where Baah-Wiredu hailed from, because he 'failed to attend the one-week observation of the death of Baah-Wiredu at Agogo' (see Boadu 2008:1, 3).[16]

The Office of Member of Parliament in Ghana: A Coveted Trophy

We turn finally to the object of such intense interest and desire among the Ghanaian political class. Successful party nomination is only the first but crucial step in the search for 'honorable' membership in the august body called the Ghanaian Parliament. There is a popular Ghanaian saying that 'once an honorable member always an honorable member.' This saying best captures the perceived importance of the office of 'MP.' When the occupants of the office exit parliament either voluntarily or from suffering defeat at the polls, they still expect to be addressed by the title 'honorable.' Indeed, Lindberg (2010:117) asserts that the institution of the office of MP in Ghana is strongly influenced by 'informal norms in ways that favor the provision of private goods in clientelistic networks.'

The office of MP has its powers embedded in two constitutional provisions. First, the constitution stipulates that the president must appoint at least half of the ministers of state from the legislature (parliament), thus undermining the separation of powers and providing the executive with a powerful instrument of co-optation and subordination of MPs (see Lindberg 2009a). This provision has so far served both government and party well. Even though the risk of a hung parliament has been averted since the new constitution came into effect in 1992, the convention of appointing ministers from the parliament compromises the independence of the legislature. For instance, NPP MPs were under severe and constant pressure from the executive to toe the national party line. The sanctions for errant MPs included the denial of constituency development projects as well as denial of seats on lucrative tender boards. Lindberg (2009b) reports that, during the administration of the NPP, President Kufuor created 147 lucrative seats on procurement and tender boards that he could distribute to MPs on the basis of loyalty to him. In this context, the office of MP becomes very attractive and coveted. For instance, a teacher whose annual salary is equivalent to the sitting allowance of an MP would view the office very favourably.[17] But in order to be considered, one had to demonstrate party loyalty by supporting and defending the government's legislative agenda, and not engage in any real executive oversight activities (Lindberg 2010:131).

Second, as indicated earlier, legislators in Ghana are entrusted with some form of local development funds for constituency development. The national Government sets aside 7.5 per cent of revenues into the District Assembly Common Fund (DACF) to be spent on local development by the District Chief Executive (DCE) and the district assembly in each of 170 districts. The MP for each constitu- ency has spending authority over a 5 per cent share of that local fund. Each MP had at his or her disposal the equivalent of about US$34,000 annually from this source (Lindberg 2010:121). In addition, when Ghana subscribed to the Heavily Indebted Poor Country (HIPC) initiative towards the end of 2001, development funds accrued from this initiative. The same decentralized sharing formula was applied to the HIPC funds, generating an additional US$9,000 per year. The annual salary including allowances for MPs is currently about US$24,000 (Lindberg 2010:121). As we suggested earlier, although these figures are modest, by current Ghanaian standards they are alluring enough. Added to the other perks and the psychic satisfaction of the status symbol of 'honorable' MP and one has the makings of a coveted position, which aspirant politicians and political parties have every incentive to struggle to conquer in competitive primary elections.

Conclusion

The objective of this chapter has been to examine the conduct of parliamentary primaries by the two leading parties, the NDC and NPP. Candidate nomination is widely recognized as one of the most consequential functions political parties perform in representative democracies. It is also considered an essential element of any definition of a political party. Furthermore, the methods by which candidates are nominated have a powerful effect on the types of people who are elected as well as influence how these people behave once in office. Finally, a party's candidate selection process can provide invaluable insights into how the party functions internally and more generally on where political power is located in a country.

As a mode of parliamentary and presidential candidate selection, primaries have grown in importance in Ghana. Initially, the NDC's method of selecting candidates for the office of MP lacked transparency and a democratic veneer. Nevertheless, it served the party's leadership interest and so the process was generally condoned. However, as the country deepened its democracy and institutionalized selection processes, the NDC abandoned the consensus method of nominating candidates for parliament. The NPP, on the other hand, instituted a more formal procedure for parliamentary candidates' selection but it was not unproblematic. Parliamentary seats are keenly contested. All parties now have well-defined formal procedures regulating the conduct of parliamentary primaries. However, the existence of formal rules does not prevent executive manipulation of the election system.

The constituency and national executives continue to influence the conduct and outcome of primaries. The relative size of the primary electorates or caucuses makes it possible for formal rules to be narrowly interpreted to give some contestants undue advantage. Again, the ill-defined roles of the MP and the MCE/DCEs at the grassroots continue to affect the conduct of primaries for better or for worse. Indeed, the Asantehene acknowledged as much when he said: 'Politics has become the shortest route to riches and people will do whatever is necessary to get there... the practice of occultism is rife in our politics... Ritual murders, burying of cows alive and various nefarious activities, I am told, have become part of the repertoire. It is to win and lord over the people but not to change the destiny of the people' (see *Daily Guide*, 8 December, 2010.) While significant progress has been made in the selection process by both major parties, there is plenty of room for improvement to make it more empowering of voters in the constituencies and therefore truly democratic. There is a need for a continued push toward the opening up of the primary process to involve more registered voters, as well as greater institutionalization and decentralization of the process to permit greater local control. Finally, although the Ghanaian public had previously revealed itself to be either ambivalent or hostile to state funding of political parties (see Gyimah-Boadi 2009b; Center for Democratic Development [CDD]-Ghana 2005a, 2005b), the time may have come to reengage the public on this issue along with the enactment of more robust legislative and legal instruments to regulate campaign financing and spending. Left unaddressed, campaign financing and expenditures may have a more corrosive effect on candidate selection and democratic governance down the road.

Notes

* First published by SAGE in the Journal of Asian and African Studies 47(2) 2012. We are grateful for permission to reprint it as part of this anthology.
1. The media hype surrounding presidential primaries makes them more prominent in Ghana; however, it is only the NPP that had selected all its presidential candidates through competitive party primaries. The NDC adopted competitive primary election for its presidential candidate fairly late in 2002.
2. Interview with a former Lawra-Nandom MP, 17 September 2009.
3. See Akwefey, 2008: 1, 15.
4. See 'Allegation of using Juju to kill Minister,' Chronicle, 2 October, 2008.
5. For example the poorly-run NPP primaries in Bekwai and Suhum caused the party to lose the safe seats to independents.
6. Over 500 foot soldiers from the Sokpayiri section of the Wa Central Constituency defected from the NPP to the People's National Convention (PNC). They attributed their defection to the 'undemocratic manner in which Mr Clement Eledi was kicked out of the parliamentary race for Wa Central,' GNA, 26 October 2004.
7. It means voting for a party's presidential candidate and voting for the opposing parliamentary candidate or vice versa.
8. Vincent Asiseh, former NDC secretary, speaking on a Joy FM programme, 16 July 2001. The story appeared as 'NDC is not a political party- Vincent Asiseh declares' in Chronicle, 17 July 2001:1 and 8.
9. In 2009, the NPP's National Delegates' Conference approved the expansion of the electoral college for the selection of the party's parliamentary and presidential candidates as well as other party officers from 2,340 delegates to about 115,000 delegates.
10. Authors' observation of the National Congresses of the NDC and NPP.
11. See report on CDD-Ghana's 'Candidates' debate forum for aspiring parliamentary candidates – 2004 General Elections.'Available at: http://www.cddghana.org/documents/ Report%20on%20Candidates%20 debate%20forum_elect_2004.pdf (accessed 22 January 2008).
12. The total election expenditure could exceed US$100 million, according to a senior party executive interviewed in Accra on 16 July 2010.
13. For example, in the recently-held (30 April 2011) NPP parliamentary primary to select candidates for the 2012 general elections, filing fees paid depended on incumbency and gender. A male aspirant paid GH¢10,000 for contesting against an incumbent MP and a female aspirant who competed against an incumbent MP paid GH¢5,000. In addition, all male aspirants paid a filing fee of GH¢6,000 compared to female aspirants who paid GH¢3,000 each. In total, a male aspirant who competed against an incumbent MP paid a total of GH¢16,000 and a female aspirant who competed against an incumbent MP paid a total of GH¢8,000. A male aspirant running in an orphan constituency (i.e. a constituency whose current MP is not from the NPP) paid a total of GH¢6,000 and a female aspirant paid a total of GH¢3,000.

14. See Atteukah, 2008: 14.
15. See GNA, 2008.
16. Appiah Kubi refused the directive from the Constituency Executive Committee (CEC). The CEC recommended to the National Executive Committee (NEC) that his nomination should be rejected and the NEC complied. He threatened his accusers with a lawsuit.
17. For a powerful satirical account of the allure of a parliamentary and cabinet salary for a poor pupil teacher, see Achebe (1967).

References

Achebe, C., (1967). *A Man of the People*. New York: Anchor Books.

Africa, Confidential., (2004), Ghana, now for the hard work. 17 December. *Africa Confidential* 45(25) 3–5. Akwefey I (2008) Suhun NPP primary turns bloody. *Chronicle* 9 July: 1, 15.

Atteukah, RK., (2008), Tema NPP primary takes new twist – Irene Addo not in good standing, chairman calls for her disqualification. *Chronicle* 17 July: 14.

Ayee, J., (2002), The 2000 general election and presidential run-off in Ghana: An overview. *Democratization* 9(2): 148–174.

Bebli, B., (2007), NPP presidential race Alan bags ¢13b. *Chronicle* 9 October: 1, 15.

Bebli, B and Kamal B. (2008), Efforts to go unopposed? ... Crabbe pulls stopper on Akomea. *Chronicle* 3 June: 1, 15.

Bille, L., (2001), Democratizing a democratic procedure: Myth or reality? *Party Politics* 7: 363–380.

Boadu, KA., (2008), Search for Baah-Wiredu's successor Appiah-Kubi disqualified. *Daily Graphic* 9 October: 1, 3.

Bob-Milliar, GM., (2011), Political party activism in Ghana: Factors influencing the decision of the politically active to join a political party. *Democratization*. Epub ahead of print.

Bob-Milliar, GM., and Bob-Milliar, GK., (2010), The economy and intra-party competition: Presidential primaries in the new patriotic party of Ghana. *African Review of Economics & Finance* 1(2): 51–71.

Carey, J., and Polga-Hecimovich, J., (2006), ,Primary elections and candidate strength in Latin America. *The Journal of Politics* 68(3): 530–543.

Center for Democratic Development, (CDD)-Ghana (2005a), A report of a survey on political party financing in Ghana conducted in May 2004. *Research Paper* 13, February. Accra: Ghana Center for Democratic Development.

Center for Democratic Development, (CDD)-Ghana, (2005b), *Financing Political Parties in Ghana: Policy Guidelines*. March. Accra: Ghana Center for Democratic Development. Constitution of the National Democratic Congress (NDC) (2002) Accra: NDC.

Crotty, W., (1968), The party organization and its activities. In: Crotty W (ed.) *Approaches to the Study of Party Organization*. Boston, MA: Allyn & Bacon, 247–306.

Daddieh, C., (2009), The presidential and parliamentary elections in Ghana, December 2008. *Electoral Studies* 28: 642–647.

Daddieh, C., (2011), Democratic consolidation without a second turnover: Ghana's remarkable 2004 Elections. In: Saine A, N'Diaye B, Houngnikpo M (eds) *Elections and Democratization in West Africa 1990– 2009*. Trenton, NJ: African World Press, 43–74.

Electoral Commission, (EC) of Ghana, (2005), *Ghana's Parliamentary and Presidential Elections 2004*. November. Accra: EC, with support of the Friedrich Ebert Stiftung.

Electoral Commission (EC) of Ghana (2009) Available at : http://www.ec.gov.gh/ (accessed 2 October 2009).

Ferdinand, P., (2003), Party funding and political corruption in East Asia: The cases of Japan, South Korea and Taiwan. In: Reginald A, Tjernström M (eds) *Funding of Political Parties and Election Campaigns Hand Book Series*. Sweden: International Institute for Democracy and Electoral Assistance (IDEA), 55–66.

Gallagher, M., (1980), Candidate selection in Ireland: The impact of localism and the electoral system. *British Journal of Political Science* 10: 489–503.

Gallagher, M., (1988), Conclusions. In: Gallagher M, Marsh M (eds) *Candidate Selection in Comparative Perspective: The Secret Garden of Politics*. London: Sage Publications, 236–283.

Gallagher, M., and Marsh, M, (eds) (1988), *Candidate Selection in Comparative Perspective: The Secret Garden of Politics*. London: Sage Publications.

Global Integrity (2004) *An Investigation Report Tracking Corruption, Openness And Accountability In 25 Countries*. Available at: http://www.globalintegrity.org/reports/2004/default24ff.html?act=8 (accessed 12 April 2008).

GNA, (2008), Lawyer/diplomat Irene Naa Torshie Addo unseats NPP majority leader. *GNA* 2 August.

Gyimah-Boadi, E., (2002), Preface. In: Öhman M (ed.) Determining the Contestants: Candidate Selection in

Ghana's 2000 Elections. *Critical Perspectives* 8. Accra: Ghana Center for Democratic Development. Gyimah-Boadi E (2009a) Another step forward for Ghana. *Journal of Democracy* 20(2): 138–152.

Gyimah-Boadi, E., (2009b), State funding of political parties in Ghana. *Critical Perspectives* 24 (October). Accra: Ghana Center for Democratic Development, CDD-Ghana.

Hazan, R, and Rahat, G., (2006) Candidate selection: Methods and consequences. In: Katz R and Crotty W (eds) *Handbook of Party Politics*. London: Sage Publications, 109–121.

Ichino, N., and Nathan, N., (2010) *Primaries on Demand? Nominations to Parliament in Ghana*. Available at: http://www.gov.harvard.edu/files/uploads/IchinoNathan_primaries_20100916.pdf (accessed 26 October 2010).

Jeffries, R., and Thomas, C., (1993) The Ghanaian elections of 1992. *African Affairs* 92(368): 331–366.

Lindberg, S., (2009a), Parliament in Ghana: Cooptation despite democratization. In: Barkan J (ed.) *Emerging Legislatures in Emerging Democracies*. Boulder, CO: Lynne Rienner, 147–176.

Lindberg, S., (2009b), Byzantine complexity: Making sense of accountability. *Working Paper* 28, *Political Concepts Series*. Gainsville, FL: International Political Science Association: Committee on Concepts and Methods.

Lindberg, S, (2010), What accountability pressures do MPs in Africa face and how do they respond? Evidence from Ghana. *Journal of Modern African Studies* 48(1): 117–142.

Nassmacher, KH., (2003), The funding of political parties in the Anglo-Saxon Orbit. In: Reginald A, Tjernström M (eds) *Funding of Political Parties and Election Campaigns Hand Book Series*. Sweden: International Institute for Democracy and Electoral Assistance (IDEA), 33–51.

Norris, P., (2006), Recruitment. In: Katz R and Crotty W (eds) *Handbook of Party Politics*. London: Sage Publications, 89–109.

New Patriotic Party, (NPP), (1993), *The Stolen Verdict: Ghana November 1992 Presidential Elections*. Accra: New Patriotic Party.

New Patriotic Party, (NPP), (2009), *Constitution of the New Patriotic Party*. Accra: NPP

Nugent, P., (1996) *Big Men, Small Boys and Politics in Ghana: Power, Ideology and the Burden of History, 1982–1994*. Accra: Asempa Publishers.

Nugent, P., (1998), *The Flight-Lieutenant Rides (To Power) Again: National Delusions, Local Fixations and the 1996 Ghanaian Elections*. Occasional Paper No. 76. Edinburgh: Centre of African Studies, University of Edinburgh.

Öhman, M., (2002) Determining the contestants: Candidate selection in Ghana's 2000 elections. *Critical Perspectives* 8.Accra: Ghana Center for Democratic Development.

Rahat, G, (2008), *Which Candidate Selection Method Is More Democratic?* Paper posted on the eScholar- ship Repository, University of California. Available at: http://repositories.cdlib.org/cgi/viewcontent.cgi? article=1152&context=csd (accessed 13 March 2009), 1–18.

Rahat, G., and Hazan, R, (2001), Candidate selection methods: An analytical framework. *Party Politics* 7(3): 297–322.

Ranney, A., (1965), *Pathways to Parliament: Candidate Selection in Britain*. London: Macmillan.

Ranney, A., (1981), Candidate selection In: Butler D, Penniman H, Ranney A (eds) *Democracy at the Polls*. Washington, DC: American Enterprise Institute, 75–106.

Saffu, Y., (2003), The funding of political parties and election campaigns in Africa. In: Reginald A, Tjernström M (eds) *Funding of Political Parties and Election Campaigns Hand Book Series*. Sweden: International Institute for Democracy and Electoral Assistance (IDEA), 21–29.

Sartori, G., (1976), *Parties and Party Systems: A Framework for Analysis*. Cambridge and New York: Cambridge University Press.

Schattschneider E (1942) *Party Government*. New York: Rinehart.

Whitfield, L., (2009), Change for a better Ghana: Party Competition, Institutionalization and Alternation in Ghana's 2008 elections. *African Affairs* 108(433): 621–641.

2

Civic Election Observation and General Elections in Ghana under the Fourth Republic: Enhancing Government Legitimacy and the Democratization Process

Maame Adwoa A. Gyekye-Jandoh

Introduction

This chapter argues that civil society groups actually propelled the Ghanaian democratic process forward in the post-transition period (1993-present), through domestic observation practices that frustrated electoral fraud and enhanced the credibility and transparency of electoral outcomes. This is very important for the fact that disputed and flawed elections have derailed several democratic processes in Africa and in some cases led to instability and violent conflict (e.g. Liberia in 1985, Angola in 1992, Sierra Leone in 1998, and Ivory Coast in 2000 (Agyeman-Duah 2005); among others.

Regular, free and fair elections are an integral part of democracy and of any democratization process, and this must be ensured as far as is possible. It is important that domestic election observation should take place during the electoral period (pre-election, particularly election-day, and post-election) to confer an aura of neutrality, fairness, transparency, and ultimately, legitimacy on the process. This chapter therefore contends that particularly in elections where the stakes are extremely high (as in Ghana's 1992, 2000, 2008 and 2012 elections), professional domestic observation is a highly important tool for securing acceptance of election outcomes by citizens and all stakeholders and for imbuing new governments with legitimacy. When election outcomes are rejected as illegitimate, it is usually because the election processes themselves are regarded as unfair and not transparent. Ineffective and partial observation practices can just as easily contribute to a rejection of election outcomes or disputed elections.

Elections do not make a democracy, and one can have elections without democracy, but one cannot have democracy without elections (Bratton 1999), because elections afford participation, choice, competition, and accountability to the electorate. Free and fair elections that have widespread acceptance and confer legitimacy on a nation's leaders constitute the prima facie condition for democratic practice, and increases the chances of further deepening it. What this research adds to the literature is the saliency of election observation practices in the acceptance of election outcomes, and thereby their potential contribution to the consolidation of democracy in Africa.

Methodology

A qualitative and comparative analysis was employed to investigate the impact of election observation in Ghanaian elections since 1996. The study used a combination of secondary and primary research methods, supplemented published works with relevant newspaper articles, and archival documents from the Electoral Commission of Ghana, the Center for Democratic Development and other civil society organizations (CSOs). Extensive interviews were also conducted with some of the domestic election observers and representatives of CODEO that took part in the various elections.

This chapter contributes to both the empirical and theoretical meanings of democracy. At the empirical level, we are able to gain in-depth knowledge of Ghana's electoral system and the way it actually works on the ground during election periods via the practices and experiences of domestic election observers, as well as the extent to which the observers' reports enhance the legitimacy of the elections or raise doubts and questions about them. A closer look is taken at domestic election observers as their numbers and involvement in election observation have gradually eclipsed that of international observers since 1992. Their involvement inspires greater confidence in the electorate about the legitimacy or otherwise of the elections because they, domestic election observers, are seen as having a local touch and more intimate knowledge of the terrain and the people. Our findings can be used as building blocks in the accumulated lessons for other countries in Africa.

The study contributes to democratic theorizing, particularly with respect to civil society and its role in democratization. It offers another angle from which to look at civil society and its involvement in pressurizing governments to further democratize other than through public demonstrations, for example, and shows that for Africa, as well as other regions of the world, civil society can work towards the furtherance of democracy, but not just in the conventionally known and theorized ways; namely, education, holding governments accountable, fostering communal and national identity, challenging government policy, among others.

The Concepts of Civil Society, Government Legitimacy, Democratisation, Democracy and Election Observation

The importance of civil society (out of which domestic election observers emerge) and the associational life of citizens in bridging the political participation gap outside elections, in holding officials accountable, in promoting human rights, in helping legitimate governments/states, in short, in promoting and consolidating a stable democracy, has been recognized and emphasized by several scholars (including De Tocqueville 1835/1840; Lipset 1960; Almond and Verba 1963; Diamond, Linz, and Lipset 1995). In fact, some have argued that for democracy to become sustainable, it has to grow roots in society (Meyns 1993:597). This paper examines civil society's role in helping to consolidate democratic government, and argues that this is an extremely important role that has been underemphasized in the literature.

The existence of different dimensions of civil society has also been highlighted in the literature, particularly three dimensions of it which, according to Bratton (1994), constitute the observable aspects of the theoretical concept of civil society. While the three dimensions are the material (Hegel 1821; Marx and Engels 1932), the organizational (De Tocqueville 1835/1840), and the ideological (Havel 1985), the focus in this chapter is on civil society's organizational dimension here. Following Bratton (1994) we distinguish between civil society and the state or political society. Civil society is 'public'; it is not confined to the domestic or household arena, and entails collective action whereby individuals join to pursue shared goals (Bratton 1994:56). Civil society is also distinct from the institutions of political society, such as political parties, legislatures, and elections (Stepan 1988).

This study appropriated Drah's (1993) definition of civil society, as denoting 'the presence of a cluster of intermediary organizations/associations that operate between the primary units of society (like individuals, nuclear and extended families, clans, ethnic groups, and village units) and the state. These intermediary groupings include labour unions and associations of professionals, farmers, fishermen, women, youth and students; religious and business organizations, cultural and recreational clubs, as well as political parties' (Drah 1993:73). The study, however, excludes political parties from the definition of civil society, as political parties can contest elections and suddenly become the ruling party. Ultimately, civil society is both a repository of consent and dissent, depending on whether or not it accepts the right of a particular elite to exercise state power. So far, through the role of domestic election observers, civil society in Ghana has, since 1996, acted as a repository of consent, although its potential to dissent is never in doubt. The concept of government legitimacy in this study simply denotes the rightness of the exercise of political power by a particular party that is duly elected to form a national government. In other words, government legitimacy exists when the citizens, particularly the electorate, perceive and accept that it is right and proper for a particular government to be in power.

The concept of democratization is used here to refer to a 'movement of a country along a continuum of change from a condition of 'authoritarian government' to one of consolidated democratic government' (Armijo 1993:20). It involves a 'movement over time from less accountable to more accountable government, from less competitive (or non-existent) elections to freer and fairer competitive elections, from severely restricted to better protected civil and political rights, from weak (or non-existent) autonomous associations in civil society to more autonomous and more numerous associations' (Potter, Goldblatt, Kiloh, and Lewis 1997:6). This definition subsumes all the attributes of Dahl's rendition of democracy or polyarchy. In his view democracy is a form of government characterized by three conditions: meaningful and extensive competition (excluding the use of force) among individuals and political parties for all effective positions of government power at regular intervals, a highly inclusive level of political participation in the selection of leaders and policies at least through regular and fair elections, such that no major (adult) group is excluded; and a level of political liberties – freedom of expression, freedom of the press, freedom to form and join organizations – sufficient to ensure the integrity of political competition and participation (see also Diamond et al. 1990; Lipset 1981; Linz and Stepan 1978; Dahl 1971; Schumpeter 1950). This definition summarizes both the procedural (regular competitive elections) qualities of democracy and its substantive norms (freedoms, equality, and universal suffrage). Most important, democracy gives leaders legitimacy and stability (c.f. Gyekye-Jandoh 2006). However, it must be noted that the pursuit of the substantive goal of democracy is a process and their attainment is a matter of degree. I examine Ghana's democratization on the basis of this procedural and minimalist definition of democracy.

Finally, election observation is usually done by one or more independent parties, typically from another country or a non-governmental organizations (NGOs), primarily to assess the conduct of an election process on the basis of national legislation and international standards. The groups or individuals rate elections to check whether they meet free and fair standards. There are domestic and international election observers. Observers do not directly prevent electoral fraud; they rather record and report any fraudulent acts. Domestic observer groups are constituted by individuals and organizations from the country hosting the election. They may be representatives of political parties or of civil society organizations that are committed to issues of democracy and human rights (Carothers 1999:26). Domestic observer groups can also be constituted by individuals from professional associations, social service organizations, or of university student organizations (Bjornlund 2004:39). Domestic observers are able to contribute to the quality of monitoring missions because they not only understand the language and culture of the host nation; they are also well aware of the political situation in which the election is taking place (Squire 2012). The term 'election observation' is used interchangeably in this study with 'election monitoring'.

Election observation plays a vital role in assessing whether and under what circumstances elections permit the free expression of the will of the people in a variety of contexts and settings. One of the basic functions of election observation is deterring election fraud (Carothers 1997a). Accordingly, election observers have in many cases pointed out election fraud at various elections. Both domestic and international audiences make use of the information provided by election observer groups. Outside Africa, two very prominent cases are the Philippines in 1986, where US observers raised the alarm when President Ferdinand Marcos tried to steal the 1986 elections, and Panama in 1989, when the incumbent General Manuel Antonio Noriega tried to steal the elections for his handpicked presidential candidate (Carothers 1997a).

While the work of international observers is commendable, Carothers argues that it does not cure all the ills associated with elections. International observers cannot force deeply polarized political factions to cooperate with one another; they cannot offset the anti-democratic sentiments of an autocrat bent on maintaining power at all costs, or guarantee that any findings of electoral fraud will be followed by sanctions from the international community or individual nations. Most of these problems exist because election observation has attracted too many groups, many of which are amateurish in their work (Carothers 1997a; c.f. Squire 2012). The focus, however, of this chapter, is not on international observers, but on how domestic election observers can make a difference by ensuring the acceptance of electoral outcomes.

A Historical Sketch of Civil Society in Ghana

At independence in March 1957, the Convention People's Party government, led by the late Osagyefo Dr. Kwame Nkrumah under the First Republic, used its hold on power and national resources to co-opt most of the vibrant and active civil society organizations. Among them was the United Ghana Farmer's Co-operative Council (UGFCC) and the Ghana Co-operative Council. Some vocal anti-government organisations (e. g. cocoa co-operatives) were dissolved and their assets given to their competitor, the UGFCC. Similarly, worker unions that were vehemently against the co-optation by government were also silenced with the promulgation of the Industrial Relations Act which made it compulsory for all labour unions to come under the Trades Union Congress (TUC) and made it very difficult for them to embark on industrial action without the approval of the co-opted TUC. This made it difficult for churches and businesses that were not affiliated to the CPP and the government to be heard (Drah 1993).

The Nkrumah-CPP government was removed in a military coup on 24 February 1966. The National Liberation Council (NLC) did not do much to promote a free atmosphere for civil society to thrive. It eventually handed over power to the Progress Party (PP) administration in 1969 with K.A. Busia as Prime Minister under a new republican constitution. The obvious expectation was that the PP would be very liberal with civil society. Contrary to expectations, the PP government got embroiled in disputes with civil society groups, notably the TUC and the National Union of Ghana Students (NUGS) (Darkwah et al. 2006).

The PP government was removed in a military coup on 13 January 1972 by Col. Acheampong who initially formed the National Redemption Council (NRC), later the Supreme Military Council (SMC). This period perhaps saw civil society activism reaching its peak since independence even though many also got co-opted. Some politically active civil society groups emerged to challenge the UNIGOV proposal of the SMC. Notable groups include the People's Movement for Freedom and Justice, Prevention of Dictatorship, and the Third Force. The SMC was eventually removed from power in a Junior Officers uprising on 4 June 1979 and replaced by the Armed Forces Revolutionary Council (AFRC), which enjoyed considerable support from a number of anti-SMC elements. In addition, a number of civil society groups emerged supporting and defending the revolution. This includes the June Fourth Movement, New Democratic Movement and the Kwame Nkrumah Revolutionary Guard. Most of these organizations maintained their support for the AFRC until the 'second coming' of Rawlings in 1981. The military-style government of the Provisional National Defense Council (PNDC) forced a 'culture of silence' on the Ghanaian people and even on civil society. The oppressive atmosphere gave little or no room for civil society to organize and act independently.

Significantly, opposition to Rawlings' regime grew, eventually becoming a 'pro-democracy movement' that was a fusion of several distinct groups and political agendas. In August 1990, an alliance of politicians and groups that had existed in the previous three republics re-emerged, forming the Movement for Freedom and Justice (MFJ). This group received support from some professional groups such as the Ghana Bar Association (GBA), the National Union of Ghana Students (NUGS), Catholic Bishops Conference, and the Trades Union Congress (TUC). The PNDC, however, still controlled several civil society organizations. The NDC's electoral victory in 1992 and 1996 is attributed to the crucial support of these groups (Ayee 1998: 321).

The 1992 elections that brought Jerry John Rawlings to power as a civilian president marked the beginning of the 4th Republic under which Ghana has had six consecutive multi-party elections – in 1992 when the Rawlings-NDC won; in 1996 when the NDC government won re-election with Rawlings as president; in 2000 when there was the first peaceful transfer of power from one elected government to another, in this case from the NDC to the John Agyekum Kufuor-New Patriotic Party (NPP) government; in 2004 when the Kufuor-led government won re-election; and in 2008 when a second regime handover occurred from the NPP government to an NDC government, led by Prof. John E.A. Mills, who died in office in July 2012. His Vice-President, John Dramani Mahama, who was sworn in as president via constitutional mandate, won his own mandate as president of Ghana in the controversial 2012 general elections whose results were challenged at the Supreme Court by the main opposition NPP party. The verdict of the Supreme Court on 29 August 2013 confirmed Mahama as the duly elected president of Ghana.

Of these six general elections, the stakes were particularly high in four because of the closeness of the elections, especially the contests between presidential candidates of the two major political parties in Ghana – the NDC and the NPP. Ghanaian elections have always been high stakes due to the zero-sum and winner-take-all nature. Each political party, particularly its presidential candidate, tends to believe that it must win power at all costs or lose the perks and other privileges they have enjoyed in the past or that they seek to enjoy. The contest is keenest when an incumbent president comes to the end of the constitutionally-mandated two terms of office as it creates the impression that without the advantage of incumbency the electoral competition would be fairly open for the presidential candidate of the opposition party to strive to win political power.

These extremely high stake elections tended to intensify political tension around election issues, especially regarding the possibility of a contested election outcome, and to put citizens on the edge. The 1992 elections were crucial because they marked a transition from decades of military rule to democratic-civilian rule; the 2000 elections marked the end of Rawlings' two terms in office as the first president of the 4th Republic and ushered in a period of uncertainty about whether he would willingly cede power and if so, who would accede to power. The 2008 elections also marked the end of the two-term presidency of John Kufuor of the NPP. This period also led to intense political rivalry during the succeeding elections. Finally, though the 2012 elections were to mark the second term of the Mills' (NDC) presidency, the sudden death of President Mills gave the NPP presidential candidate Nana Addo Dankwa Akufo Addo the conviction that he and his party could defeat John Mahama at the polls and terminate the NDC control of the presidency after the first term. Hence the 2012 elections were fraught with intense political acrimony, leading to a contested presidential election results followed by an election petition filed at the Supreme Court to nullify the election results announced by the Electoral Commission. Civil Society, acting as domestic election observers, contributed immensely to the peaceful outcome of those elections, including the most contested 2012 presidential election results.

Civil Society Impact on General Elections and Democracy in Ghana since 1992

The best evidence of civil society impact and the importance of observers was the sheer scale of the domestic observation effort since 1996, and Rawlings' complicated relationship with domestic observers, especially in 1996. The impact of civil society can be measured first through the dramatic growth in domestic election observation capacity of civil society over time (1992-2008). From the 1992 to the 2004 elections, the number of domestic election observers and polling stations covered by domestic observers increased, while the number of international observers decreased with each election during the same period. For example, over 4,100 domestic election monitors were trained at the national, regional and district levels, in addition to another 100 monitors, and these were deployed to about 3,100 polling stations all across Ghana, in all 200 constituencies for the 1996 general elections. This contrasted with just 200 individual domestic observers in 1992 (Gyimah-Boadi, Oquaye and Drah 2000:21).

Furthermore, although in 1996 when there were six international organizations comprising several monitors, in the 2000 elections there was just one umbrella international observer group, the Donors Working Group (DWG), comprising High Commissions and Embassies of donor countries in Ghana. These country representatives coordinated the conduct of the elections and helped to provide the necessary financial and material support for the successful conduct of the elections (Boafo-Arthur 2001:99,103). Notably absent were the OAU, Carter Center, the Commonwealth, and the National Democratic Institute (NDI) (Boafo-Arthur ibid). By the 2000 elections, there were even more domestic election observers. In fact, CSO coalitions recruited, trained, and deployed more than 15,000 observers to cover about 50 per cent of the over 20,000 polling stations during the first round of the elections. This represented a substantial increase in – in fact a tripling of – the number of monitors in the 1996 elections.

Second, the domestic observers had their presence felt in both rural and urban areas, especially in trouble spots in some constituencies during the 2000 elections. Third, during the 1996 election the Rawlings-NDC government had frowned upon the election observation activities, particularly of the Network of Domestic Election Observers (NEDEO). Although it did not ban the group or place legal restrictions on it the government remained suspicious and uncooperative.

Fourth, in 1996 and 2000 donor funding went directly to the CSOs rather than to the NDC government. In 1992, the PNDC government received almost all donor democracy-support funds. In the 1996 election year, most of those funds went to local NGOs and civic organizations rather than to the government (Gyimah-Boadi 1999). Ghana Alert received a total of $73,000 of donor funding, of which $38,000 came from the Danish Embassy, $20,000 from the American

Embassy, and $15,000 from the Canadian High Commission (NEDEO Report 1997:99). The Institute of Economic Affairs (IEA) received about $200,000 from the United States Agency for International Development (USAID) and the National Democratic Institute (NDI), and $50,000 from the National Endowment for Democracy (Gyimah-Boadi, Oquaye and Drah 2000:21). This massive support for CSOs shows that the donor community had recognized CSOs as making significant contributions to ensuring free and fair elections and the legitimacy of election results.

Table 1 below suggests strongly that civil society groups had gained more autonomy from government and made an impact on domestic political development especially in the latter half of the 1990s and since 2000. In the table civil society is divided into three types: private media, traditional CSOs, and newer CSOs. Private media refers to radio, television, print, with radio being the most ubiquitous throughout the country, especially in the rural areas due to the low level of literacy of many rural folk. Television and print media are important sources of information in the urban areas where many residents are literate in the English language. Traditional CSOs include long-standing professional groups such as the Ghana Bar Association (GBA), the Christian Council, and the Trades Union Congress (TUC). More recent CSOs comprise GONGOs, QUANGOs, and 'political' NGOs. GONGOs refers to government-sponsored NGOs, which abounded in Ghana in the Nkrumah era (1957-1966) and proliferated under the Rawlings PNDC/NDC regimes. These GONGOs were attempts by Rawlings to encroach upon civil society space and co-opt as many civil society groups as possible. Examples include the 31st December Women's Movement (DWM) and Mobisquads of the National Mobilization Programme, instituted in the 1980s immediately after the PNDC came to power. QUANGOs are quasi NGOs; an example is the Ghana Private Road Transport Union (GPRTU). 'Political' NGOs, according to Gyimah-Boadi et al. (2000:9), are independent policy research and advocacy institutions that aim at promoting respect for human rights and protection of democratic freedoms in particular, and in general, aim at the facilitation of democratic consolidation in Ghana. Examples include the Institute of Economic Affairs (IEA), the Ghana Center for Democratic Development (CDD-Ghana), and Ghana Alert.

Table 2.1: Indicators of Relative Civil Society Autonomy in Ghana

Civil society	Resource base (Weak, Moderate, Strong)	Level of funding in-dependence of do-nors (Low, Moderate, High)	Government co-option (in terms of funding and agenda(s) pursued; Yes, No)	Mobilizational capa-city (Weak, Moderate, Strong)	Regional representation and organizational strength (Weak, Moderate, Strong)
Private media (radio, television, print) (post-transition/1992-2004)	Moderate; survive on advertising and private funding (1992-2004)	High; not much fun-ding from internatio-nal donors yet (1992-2004)	No; not much dependence on government funding (1992-2004)	N/A	Strong; presence in the urban areas and regional capitals (1992-2004)
Traditional CSOs (professional groups, religious bodies, and unions) (pre- and post-transition/1980s -2004)	Moderate resource and asset base (mid- and upper-income brac-ket membership base) (1980s-2004)	Moderate; many have benefited greatly from donor support, but have substantial sup-port from membership and other local sources (1980s-2004)	No; have achieved conside-rable degree of autonomy from the state, and have relatively high degree of financial independence (1980s-2004)	Moderate; most have large membership base, but many lack strong links with farmers' groups and rural wor-kers (1980s-2004)	Moderate to Strong; have offices and representatives in all ten regions of Gha-na, and reasonably well-organized and generally strong on internal demo-cracy (1980s-2004)
Newer CSOs (GON-GOs, QUANGOs, and especially 'poli-tical' NGOs) (post-transition/1992-2004)	Moderate; relatively improved material and technocratic resources; but generous donor fun-ding for pro-democracy activities (1992-2004)	Low; especially the 'political' NGOs (due to the relatively weak private sector); most of the newer CSOs do not want to depend on go-vernment (1992-2004)	No (except for GONGOs such as the DWM); howe-ver, the NDC government has tried to regulate NGOs (1992-2004)	Strong (for many GONGOs and QUANGOs); modera-te for many of the 'poli-tical' NGOs which lack a wide membership base and links to rural workers and farmers (1992-2004)	Strong; large organizatio-nal structure of GON-GOs and QUANGOs due to government spon-sorship; moderate for 'po-litical' NGOs which are typically based in Accra (1992-2004)

Source: Gyekye-Jandoh, M.A.A. 2006, *Explaining Democratization in Africa: The Case of Ghana*, Doctoral dissertation: Temple University

NEDEO and the 1996 General Elections

The NEDEO and its junior partner, Ghana Alert, played a crucial role in increasing public confidence in the 1996 presidential and parliamentary elections and the outcome, and in the perception of the process as free and fair. NEDEO consisted of 23 national CSOs, and was led by a retired appeals court judge and former electoral commissioner (1979-1983), Joseph Kingsley-Nyinah, while Ghana Alert was led by a renowned journalist Ben Ephson. NEDEO's CSOs included the Christian Council of Ghana, Catholic Secretariat, the Ghana Civic Coalition (GHACICO arising from the Committee on Human and People's Rights which comprised the Ghana Bar Association (GBA), Civil Servants Association (CSA), Ghana Registered Midwives' Association (GRMA), Ghana Registered Nurses' Association (GRNA), Ghana Journalists Association (GJA), Ghana National Association of Teachers (GNAT), and others. These two groups helped to mobilize much of the domestic human and material resources available for non-governmental election observation (Gyimah-Boadi 1999:413; Gyimah-Boadi, Oquaye and Drah 2000:21).

NEDEO and Ghana Alert began early preparations in July 1996, five months before the election. The advantage they had over international observers was that they were better placed to observe pre-election, election, and post-election developments (Gyimah-Boadi 1999:413). NEDEO trained more than 4,100 domestic election observers at the national, regional, and district levels, while Ghana Alert trained 100 observers, and all of them were deployed to about 3,100 polling stations – 21 per cent of the 200 constituencies – on election day, 7 December 1996 (Boafo-Arthur 2001:96; Gyimah-Boadi, Oquaye and Drah 2000:21). The observers were selected from the various civic organizations comprising the coalition, and each observer watched his or her own polling station and at least three other nearby polling stations (this was improved upon in subsequent elections).

From the Election Observers' Reports, it was clear that most polling stations opened on time; security was adequate in most places; party agents were present at most of the stations visited; and electoral officers performed their duties with diligence (NEDEO Report 1997:98). A few problems reported by observers were the inadequate election materials, poor visibility during vote counting, and a few election malpractices at trouble spots. These problems convinced the electoral observers (NEDEO and Ghana Alert) of the need to intensify voter and civic education for the future. For example, at the Gumbare polling station in the Bawku West Constituency in the Upper East region, there were 300 presidential ballot papers for 354 registered voters. In the Cape Coast constituency, an NPP counting agent was allegedly beaten up by the bodyguards of the Central Regional Minister, Mr. Valis Akyianu, at the DC Junior Secondary School at Esuekyir. The most serious problem that was reported is the incidence of child voters who had identity cards and names on the register in Tamale, Salaga, Bimbilla, Kpandai, and Wulensi. They were actually teenagers but claimed to be 38 years old or above (NEDEO Report 1997:102). These reports show the value of having domestic election observers who understand the context, the terrain, and the people better. According to Ghana's leading daily newspaper (Daily Graphic 30 December 2000), local observers' reports served to improve subsequent elections.

In selecting observers, Ghana Alert and NEDEO went into the communities in which potential observers lived and cross-checked their political neutrality from both ruling party and opposition circles. Ghana Alert focused on 24 constituencies with various political flash points (between the parliamentary candidates) as well as a history of ethnic tension (in four of the main conflict areas, Bimbilla, Wulensi, Kpandu, and Salaga). These were chosen for observation at the request of the Canadian High Commission. Observers who did not know each other were paired as a further assurance of neutrality in observation and reporting. In collaboration with the EC, a checklist was designed which observers filled in at each polling station. Ghana Alert had a Command Center in Accra, which was responsible for coordinating the activities of observers, analysing completed observation forms, and analysing and publishing hourly updates based on provisional results (NEDEO Report 1997:101).

The EC cooperated fully with NEDEO and Ghana Alert, giving them access to its facilities and offices, and participating in all the training sessions for observers (Gyimah Boadi, Oquaye and Drah 2000:21). Such full and unhindered collaboration in the electoral process between the domestic observers and the EC served to deter fraud and other irregularities in the elections, while simultaneously enhancing the EC's credibility (Gyimah-Boadi 1999:414). The participation of 80,000 party and candidate agents as observers in the voter registration exercise and in the elections also bolstered NEDEO's efforts (Ninsin 2006:65).

The huge involvement of CSOs in the 1996 elections was in sharp contrast to what pertained in 1992, when just about 200 local observers were involved, a number which was woefully inadequate to deter fraud. In 1992, the electoral observation environment was dominated by the PNDC and its agencies, while international observers, including the Carter Center, African American Institute, the Commonwealth Secretariat, the OAU, and International Foundation of Electoral Systems (IFES), played a limited watchdog role (Gyimah-Boadi 1999). In 1996, international observers included the Commonwealth, European Union, the National Democratic Institute, the OAU, the UN, and the UNDP, all of which played a supplementary role in election observation (Boafo-Arthur 2001:95). NEDEO and Ghana Alert were the dominant actors in election observation, and in fact presented their own independent analyses of the political situation to the international observers before the elections.

The active roles played by NEDEO and its constituent CSOs underscored civil society's increasing ability to support Ghana's democratization process. As Ninsin (2006) has rightly argued, this was 'an invaluable contribution [which] was made by the network of domestic and foreign election monitors and observers' to the process of institution-building, particularly elections (Ninsin 2006:65). It is remarkable that in 1996, there were no significant election disputes when Rawlings won the presidential elections. A majority of the electorate accepted the outcome of the elections, and Rawlings' opponents openly congratulated him.

CODEO and the 2000 General Elections

By the 2000 national elections, the role of domestic election observers had become indispensable (Boafo-Arthur 2001:96). The uniqueness of the 2000 elections was that there were very few international observers; domestic civil society groups led the election observation process (Gyimah-Boadi 2001:73); and election observation was basically a domestic affair, undertaken by CSOs committed to sustaining democratic principles (Boafo-Arthur 2001:99).

The 2000 elections marked the first time that CODEO (Coalition of Domestic Election Observers) observed general elections in Ghana. About 24 national civil society organizations (CSOs), large membership organizations made up of nurses, journalists, teachers, religious groups, and women's and professional groups came together to form CODEO (Larvie 2009, interview). These groups embraced a wide section of Ghanaian society.[1]

In contrast, there was just one umbrella international observer group, the Donors Working Group (DWG), comprising High Commissions and Embassies of foreign donor countries. They coordinated the conduct of the elections and provided the necessary financial and material support for the successful conduct of the elections (Boafo-Arthur 2001:99,103). The notable absence of the OAU, Carter Center, the Commonwealth, and the National Democratic Institute (NDI) confirmed the growing recognition, by both external organizations and domestic bodies, that Ghana had developed local capacity to ensure the credibility of the electoral process and confidence in the electoral system as a whole (Agyeman-Duah 2005:26; Boafo-Arthur 2001). Surely, domestic CSO observation was helping to enhance the legitimacy of the elected government, and this was manifested in the growing strength of civil society over time. For instance, in 1996, the NDI had opened an office with technical staff to assist the NEDEO, while the International Federation of Electoral Systems (IFES) provided extensive technical support to the EC. In 2000, CODEO was initiated and managed solely by local experts, and IFES' role was limited to a 'token expert assistance' to the EC (Agyeman-Duah 2005:26). Previous experience had shown that the involvement of international election observers was not adequate in inspiring the necessary confidence in the electoral system. Domestic election observers filled this gap;

they instilled confidence in the system (CODEO/CDD-Ghana 2001). Election observation in the 2000 general elections depicted this growing importance of CODEO. The outcome of the elections was largely accepted by the public.

The training of observers and their neutrality and objectivity in 2000 was very important in this regard. At the end of each training session, observers were asked to sign an 'Oath of Objectivity and Neutrality' to indicate their willingness to be impartial and neutral in the observation process (CODEO/CDD-Ghana 2001:7). A significant aspect of election observation is the final observers' report. In 2000, the final observers' report showed that domestic observers were important in being able to ascertain for the Ghanaian public the generally calm and peaceful manner in which the elections were conducted, the non-partisan and professional conduct of electoral officials, the diligence and vigilance of party agents, and the transparent and free nature of the process.

In Election 2000, CODEO engaged not only in election-day observation but also in observing the pre-election environment and monitoring media coverage of political party activities from May to December 2000. For the pre-election exercise, CODEO selected from the ten regions of Ghana twelve constituencies deemed to be potential trouble-spots, and sent specially trained observers to monitor the political environment there, especially to note the activities of the EC, the conduct of party primaries, the incident of violence, and signs of abuse of incumbency by the ruling NDC party. The twelve constituencies were Bolgatanga, Jirapa, Gulkpega/Sabongida, Choggu/Tishigu, Sunyani West, Bantama, Akropong Central, South Dayi, Tema East, Agona East, Agona West, and Efia Kwesimintim. The aim was to publicize the monitors' report, drawing attention to infractions and irregularities that could undermine the integrity of the elections (Agyeman-Duah 2005:25). Thus, monitoring of the pre-election environment itself was an important contribution by CODEO, as it served to alert EC officials and the political parties to the potential problems and irregularities in the election environment. Through those monitoring activities CODEO further contributed to the assurance of a level playing field for all political parties and candidates. Significantly also, the elections in most of the potential trouble-spots mentioned above were peaceful, free, and fair. This outcome is partly due to increased public awareness and intensive voter and civic education which resulted from the efforts and keen reporting of CODEO observers in the pre-election period (CDD-Ghana/CODEO 2001). All CODEO activities undertaken in pursuit of its mission were highly publicized. Press conferences were held on the eve of the 7 December general elections and the and 28 December presidential election run-off. At the press conferences, CODEO announced its programmes and readiness for the elections and sought public support for its activities. On the day after each election, two press statements were also released as preliminary statements on the conduct of the elections.

CODEO's final observers' report underscores the importance of its role in the elections. For instance, for the 7 December general elections, 5,155 (93.7%) of the 5,500 checklists were returned by CODEO observers. CODEO observers were interested in two critical issues, among others, namely: 'was the balloting free and fair overall?' and 'did the process work satisfactorily?' Overall, 99.6 per cent of the observers reported that the balloting was free and fair, while 99.8 per cent found the process had worked satisfactorily (CDD-Ghana/CODEO 2001). For the 28 December presidential election run-off, CODEO modified its operations in addition to the deployment of 5,500 observers: two CODEO observers were deployed in each of the 200 constituency collation centres to observe the process of tallying the results from polling stations and 5,062 observers' checklists were analyzed. Over 99 per cent of the observers saw the elections as free and fair and also thought that the process worked satisfactorily (CDD-Ghana/CODEO 2001). Reports from 191 of the 200 constituency collating centres were also analyzed: 97.4 per cent of observers described the collation process as satisfactory. The observers noted that almost all the ballot boxes brought to the centre were sealed. Significantly, an overwhelming percentage of observers (95.8%) reported no recount of ballots at collating centres (CDD-Ghana/CODEO 2001).

Problems which were encountered, despite the peaceful nature of the elections, included the incidence of under-age voters at polling stations, the inability of the EC to supply adequate voting materials to a number of polling stations on time, a few reported cases of impersonation, as well as the occurrence of multiple voting at a few polling stations (CDD-Ghana/CODEO 2001:13). However, in CODEO's view these problems were not widespread enough to dent the credibility of the election results. John Kufuor of the New Patriotic Party (NPP) won the presidential election with 57 per cent of the vote, wresting power from the incumbent National Democratic Congress (NDC), whose former vice-president, Prof. John Atta Mills, polled only 43.1 per cent of the vote.

Thus, in addition to inspiring confidence in the process by helping to minimize the incidence of fraud and other irregularities, CODEO observers were also at a vantage point to see and report problems for the attention of the EC, which enabled the latter to rectify them before the next elections. The training, experience, and presence at polling stations of non-partisan observers enhanced transparency and contributed to public confidence as well as the strengthening of the electoral process (Daily Graphic 30 December 2000). That is, despite the presence of political party agents at most of the polling stations, it took the presence of local observers to give the electorate as well as political parties and their candidates the confidence that no election fraud would take place on a large scale.

CODEO and the 2004 General Elections

By the 2004 general elections, CODEO had expanded its operations to include pre-election observation that began about six months prior to the election. Pre-election observation covered political party activities, registration of voters, nomination of candidates, political party primaries, and exhibition of the voter's register. Also the number of CODEO election-day observers had increased from 5,500 in 2000 to 7,360 making it possible for CODEO to undertake several election observation and democracy-supporting activities which were beneficial to both the candidates and the electorate. For example, it embarked on a snap study of political party financing and organized a Parliamentary Candidates' Forum in 25 selected constituencies, where it trained the moderators of the forums and provided a profile of important national issues to the different candidates. CODEO also held workshops for the parliamentary candidates prior to the forums to help them build capacity, including what they were to do when they met their constituents. These forums were heavily patronized by the candidates, with the exception of those candidates who thought that the constituencies concerned were their strongholds and therefore did not appear.[2]

The forums were successful in the sense that both the electorate and candidates appreciated the opportunity they had to meet and dialogue on practical issues of development that were important to the electorate, such as women empowerment, welfare of the disabled, and sanitation. These forums were beneficial also because they were found to be more beneficial than political rallies that gave little or no room at all for the electorate to dialogue with competing candidates.[3]

There were also international observers in the 2004 elections, but they were not as many as in 1992 and 1996. The international observers were not grounded in Ghana, and their best resource first and foremost was the domestic observers. For example, the international observers interacted significantly with CODEO through the Programs Coordinator, discussing with CODEO their programme specifics and the ways in which they could embark upon it. Through its monthly reports, CODEO shared information about its pre-election activities with the international observers and the Ghanaian public at large; it shared information about good as well as bad developments observed during the pre-election observation and offered recommendations.

Despite problems encountered during the 2004 elections – disagreements, quarrels, fights, irregularities, use of abusive language – the credibility of the elections was unquestioned to a large extent, because the problems were not of such magnitude as to create any doubt in the minds of the principal stakeholders about the results (Ninsin 2006:67). CODEO affirmed this overall assessment of the presidential and parliamentary elections: 'based on the reports from our observers deployed throughout the country, the elections were generally free, fair, and transparent and the election process was satisfactory' (CODEO 2005:50).

CODEO's success in election observation was due to several factors. First, it endeavoured to be as objective and non-partisan as possible through the quality of observation by its agents in the field; the credibility enjoyed by the CSOs forming the Coalition (many of which have a long and tested image as CSOs); and from the calibre of its leadership - Justice V.R.A.C. Crabbe and Professor Miranda Greenstreet who are its joint chairpersons. Next was CODEO's strict adherence to a set of principles that guided recruitment, training, screening, and deployment of observers. First was its policy to recruit local observers from their own communities and districts/regions ensured that its volunteers were known by the people who might work as poll workers or as supervisors. For example, CODEO prefers that a person who is going to observe in the Ashanti region should come from that region. This principle won the confidence and trust of the electorate. The second principle CODEO strictly adheres to is the one that requires that the civic body sending the volunteers should know and be able to vouch for their knowledge of the environment, of the electoral system, of their own districts or regions, and their familiarity with candidates of political parties. This principle was not difficult to enforce because most of the volunteer observers were either head teachers, executive members of the Ghana Trades Union Congress or other member CSO, doctors, lawyers, and others who were at the management or supervisory level of their respective careers. One key criterion by which an observer is chosen is that he or she must be influential and respected by his or her community.[4] Where the volunteers are recommended to be trained as observers CODEO conducts a serious check on whether they are actively partisan (e.g. whether they are seen with candidates or party officials) or non-partisan.

The third principle is that once observers are sent by the civic organizations that recommended them, CODEO conducts thorough interviews at the Secretariat in Accra before finally recruiting them. It must be noted that CODEO is more interested in observing how the elections process runs, not who wins, in order to safeguard the democratic process.

While the first three CODEO principles involve the recruitment, training and screening of observers, the fourth principle is concerned with the actual observation by the observers it has deployed. Compared with the 2008 elections when CODEO embarked upon both strategic and random deployment, in the 2004 elections, it undertook strategic deployment only. Strategic deployment means that CODEO did not go to all polling stations; rather, in its bid to deter fraud and raise the confidence level of voters, it identified historically-proven hot spots (from previous elections) mainly polling stations, in certain constituencies and regions.

CODEO's sources of funding in 2004 were again primarily from the donor community. While these sources were varied, the main source of funding was the United States Agency for International Development (USAID). The Fredriech

Naumann Foundation, as well as the UNDP (United Nations' Development Program) and CIDA (Canadian Development Agency), also helped with some funds. The funding process works this way: the Ghana Center for Democratic Development (CDD-Ghana), which is CODEO's parent organization, writes a proposal for funding and discusses it with CODEO. If funding is approved by a donor, it is given in the name of both CDD-Ghana and CODEO. CDD-Ghana manages the funds, disburses and accounts for the use of the money to the donor. Most of CDD-Ghana's fieldwork is done through CODEO.[5]

Significantly, there was an increase in funding for CODEO between 2000 and 2004, due primarily to the increase in the number of CODEO observers in 2004 (by almost 2,000). CODEO received more funding for the 2004 elections observation than it did in 2000. This increase in funding helped make a difference in the scope and effectiveness of CODEO's election observation practices, as it was able to observe more polling stations than in 2000.

CODEO and the 2008 General Elections

The 2008 general elections, held on 7 December 2008, constituted a major test of Ghana's burgeoning democracy. This is because for the first time in Ghana's political history, the two major political parties, the ruling New Patriotic Party (NPP) and the opposition National Democratic Congress (NDC), having each exercised presidential office and parliamentary dominance for two terms (of eight years), vied seriously for another stint in the Executive Office and a majority in Parliament. While both parties worked hard to win the elections, in reality, only one party could win the general elections. It was therefore crucial that the outcome of the elections be regarded as legitimate.

Electoral outcomes usually depend on the actual election processes, which must therefore be seen as free, fair, and transparent, in order to confer any semblance of legitimacy on the winner of the presidential election as well as winners of parliamentary majority. In 2008, the three main purposes of election observation were well served because the observers trained by the EC and the Ghana Center for Democratic Development (CDD-Ghana) Election Monitoring Mission complied with all the expectations of duty as well as the instructions embedded in the Code of Conduct for Election Monitors. This Code stipulates that 'monitors will maintain strict impartiality in the conduct of their duties and will, at no time, publicly express or exhibit any bias or preference in relation to national authorities, parties, candidates, or … any issues in contention in the election process… monitors will not interfere in the electoral process, and may raise questions with election officials and bring irregularities to their attention, but they must not give instructions or countermand their decisions' (CDD Election Monitoring Mission Document 2008:15-16). In addition, monitors are to 'remain on duty throughout election day, including observation of the vote count, and if instructed, the next stage of tabulation .... monitors will comply with all national laws and regulations, and will exhibit the highest levels of personal discretion and professional behaviour at all times' (CDD Election Monitoring Mission Document 2008:16). The effectiveness of domestic election observers helped to confer legitimacy on the election process, by preventing widespread fraud and cheating.

Equally important was the recognition, by political parties, the Electoral Commission (EC), civil society organizations (CSOs), and the donor community, of the importance of the 2008 elections. This recognition was underscored particularly by the EC's publication in December 2007 of a Framework for Domestic Election Observation. The purpose of the Framework was to 'ensure that the way domestic election observers go about their work is consistent with internationally acceptable standards of election observation' and to strengthen the democratization process by, among other things, calming particularly the nerves of the public and opposition politicians who were distrustful of the government (EC Framework 2007:7). The Framework was used to educate domestic election observers and the public on what election observation entails, what to observe, how observers are to comport themselves and also gather facts, and interpret facts. They were further taught the skill of report writing. These constitute important election observation practices that if carried out well, can enhance the credibility of any elections. Most important, the EC put premium on accreditation of all election observers and monitors. This ensured that no dubious or extremely partisan persons (including political party activists) engaged in election observation (EC Framework 2007:15-16).

In the 2008 pre-election period, observers were to look out for the flaws in election-related legislation; for example, cases where the law was vague and subject to varying interpretations, and lacked sufficient guarantees for civil and political rights; the nature of judicial implementation, such as the lack of due process in court proceedings; the behaviour of the electoral management body (the EC) – for example, whether it was under political pressure or lacked independence from the executive; election logistics and operational management; the conduct of the registration of candidates and political parties, as well as voter registration; flaws in the ballot, such as ballots circulating outside of polling stations on or before election day; the adequacy of voter information and education; the degree of freedom as well as level of violence in the political campaign; and problems associated with campaign resources and the media – such as unequal use of public resources by the incumbent and the other actors in the electoral process – for example, political parties and candidates by the public media.

On election day, observers looked out for: election-related violence or disturbances, intimidation of voters, confusion or disorganization at polling stations, and the presence of unauthorized persons at polling stations. They also monitored the vote count, whether it was done by polling-station officials or other persons etc., and the tabulation of ballots, including any incidence of ballot-box stuffing or switching and disorderly counting procedures. Finally, post-election monitoring involved: monitoring the declaration of results including an unreasonably delayed announcement; the denial of access to observers to this process; discrepancies between the election-day record of results and the final results at any level of the election administration; post-election day complaints and appeals process; and implementation of election results, including disqualification of winning candidates (CDD Election Monitoring Mission Document 2008:16-22).

These guidelines for election observers during the pre-election, election-day, and post-election periods were comprehensive and democracy-enhancing rules geared towards the achievement of free, fair, and transparent elections. The responsibility for securing the integrity of the electoral process lay primarily with the election observers themselves – their conduct and diligent discharge of their duties, as well as the political parties and their polling agents, election officials, security agents, and voters.

The 2008 general elections turned out to be a tough fight for the presidency and parliamentary majority, with extremely close results. The NDC's John Evans Atta Mills won the presidency, after a second round of voting, with 50.3 per cent of the vote, while his very close rival, Nana Addo Dankwa Akufo-Addo of the NPP, won 49.7 per cent. Furthermore, the incumbent NPP lost several seats in parliament – from 128 seats (out of 230) to 109, making it the largest opposition party in parliament. The NDC's parliamentary fortunes were better: the number of parliamentary seats it won increased to 116. This included the seat won by the NDC member in the Chereponi parliamentary bye-election held on September 29, 2009 following the death of the NPP MP, Ms. Seidu, in July 2009.

In contrast to previous general elections in the Fourth Republic (1996, 2000, and 2004), half of the electorate was not so ready to accept the results peacefully, and there was talk of a recount in some constituencies. By July 2009, Ghana was still in the post-election mood pending the re-run of elections in six polling stations of the Akwatia Constituency. On 18 August 2009, the NPP won the Akwatia parliamentary election giving it 109 seats in parliament. There was also a re-run of the presidential election in Tain constituency in the Brong-Ahafo region on 2 January 2009. This very closely fought election and the ensuing allegations of rigging, violence, and disenfranchisement of some voters, begs the question of whether the domestic and international election observers performed their duties diligently, and what their experiences actually were on the ground.

To answer this question, we must recall a few key facts about CODEO's operations in 2008. The number of civic groups involved in CODEO had increased to about 34 from 25 civic groups in 2004. The civic groups included the Trades Union Congress (TUC), associations of journalists, nurses, students, and teachers, among others. In the 2008 pre-election period, CODEO repeated the Parliamentary Candidates' Forums that it had held for candidates in selected constituencies in 2004. For the first time, and because of the high competitiveness of the 2008 elections, CODEO deployed teams of Rapid Response Observers and Ordinary Observers, after recruiting and training them. CODEO deployed observers both strategically and by random sampling. In addition, it employed the Parallel Vote Tabulation (PVT) system. PVT is a method that independently verifies the accuracy of the official vote count at the end of the election day. Observers watch as the votes are counted at the randomly selected polling stations before the ballots are collated or transported away. This enables observers to get as close as possible to an actual count. Observers then immediately transmit the vote tabulation for each candidate and party by text messaging to the CODEO Observation Center for comparison with the official results. In the 2008 elections PVT observers were sent to all 230 constituencies, while strategic deployment of observers took place at sensitive polling locations.

CODEO trained about 4,000 local observers, down from the 8,000 local observers who were trained in 2004. CODEO had planned to train 8,000 observers, but received funding that could support the training and remuneration of only 4,000 local observers. The number was cut back in order to ensure sound technical training for the observers[6]. Nevertheless, CODEO's 4,000 observers constituted by far the largest deployment of election observers in the 2008 general elections.

Supported by the National Democratic Institute (NDI) with technical assistance and funds, the PVT was very successful; it drew a sample out of the 10 regions of the country and a total of 21,008 polling stations. Using a stratified sampling method, CODEO produced a representative sample of 1,007 polling stations, each of which was given a personal identity number. By this method, CODEO was able to reach each of the 230 constituencies, either at polling stations or at its data collection points. An average of 15 CODEO observers was sent to each constituency. Out of this number, some were regular observers deployed to strategic locations, while the rest of them were part of the 1,007 PVT polling station observers. The PVT observers were screened to find out whether they would be able to withstand the stress of the PVT and dispatched to the selected polling stations. The names of the PVT polling stations were not disclosed to the public or political party agents prior to the elections to ensure total anonymity in the observation of party agents and other people at the polling stations (Larvie 2009, interview).

Due to the need for accuracy in managing the PVT, CODEO had to train observers to understand the tools that they would use at the polling station level only. PVT observers were trained to text anything that they observed throughout election day (at five scheduled times during the day) to the Command Center at the Kofi Annan International Peacekeeping Training Center in Accra. These text reports were put into a database by data entry clerks and telephone operators at the CODEO Observation Center (or Command Center), enabling CODEO to release press reports by midday and at regular intervals after that. This scientific process was very thoroughly managed (Larvie 2009, interview).

The important contribution of mobile information technology (incoming text or SMS messages) in relaying both qualitative data on the conduct of the election, and quantitative data that helped verify the official results issued by the EC was unprecedented. As one international observer of the 2008 elections put it, 'mobile phones were ringing constantly with calls from the observers in the field' (Verclas 2008). In fact, 'systematic SMS reporting by trained local citizen observers about how well an election is conducted can prevent rumours, and is an independent and reliable indicator of the quality of the election process' (Verclas 2008).

CODEO used the same polling stations again on 28 December 2008 in the run-off elections. Its PVT was very accurate, and it was even able to predict the approximate number of spoilt ballots at those polling stations. In the Tain elections on 2 January 2009, for example, CODEO observed all the 144 polling stations in the constituency and predicted the results (NDC won 20,000 more votes in Tain) quite accurately. It is clear therefore that the PVT provided a very reliable indicator of the veracity of the EC's official vote count for the initial round of elections, the run-off and the Tain elections. In the words of Katrin Verclas, an international observer: 'an observer from the EU noted that the system CODEO and NDI developed was by far 'the most impressive' election observation system using mobile technology that he had seen. And the news so far from the Rapid Response Observers has been encouraging: there have been few incidents and voting is going largely smoothly' (Verclas 2008). The successful use of PVT in the 2008 elections therefore underscored the fact that CODEO election observers contributed significantly to the acceptance and legitimacy of the new Mills government.

CODEO's contribution to the legitimation of the elections as largely free and fair is evident from the following CODEO actions. CODEO has engaged in extended election observation since 2004. The pre-election observation of the 2008 elections took almost two years having begun its operations almost two years before election day; that is, immediately the NDC party opened its primary season and elected its presidential candidate, Prof. John. E. A. Mills, both of which occurred in 2006 .

From March 2008 when the EC began its final preparations towards the elections, CODEO recruited 60 observers and deployed them to 56 strategically selected constituencies across Ghana to follow and observe procedures for the replacement of voter identity cards, voter registration, and also political parties' meetings, campaigns and rallies. CODEO observers prepared weekly reports that were put together in monthly reports and released to the public. In 2008, CODEO released eight monthly reports on the pre-election environment. Furthermore, it released press statements on the conduct of the elections throughout election day. This enhanced the credibility of the election outcome. CODEO first released a press statement on the eve of the elections to tell the world what it was expecting a keenly contested election, with close election results. CODEO's second report was the crucial one it made at noon of election day regarding the opening of polls, the sufficiency of ballots, etc. The third report came out between 4.00 and 5.00 pm on 7 December 2008, in which it reported on progress and reported incidents; for example, that some people could not find their names in the register, some voting materials were missing, late arrival of voting materials, and shortage of voting materials in some places. For each of the reports, CODEO made some recommendations on how to meet the challenges on the ground.

Reported incidents were highest in the Ashanti region, especially during the run-off, followed by the Eastern region. It is noteworthy that CODEO observers reported what they saw, not what they heard (Larvie 2009, interview). On the morning of the following day, CODEO gave a report on the close of the polls and counting of ballots. CODEO's coded checklist for observers covered all of such issues.

CODEO complied with the law that stipulates that the EC should be the first to declare election results by announcing its tally of results from the PVT soon after the EC had made the official declaration of the results. CODEO's estimated election results had a margin of error of $+/\_$ 1.6, with a confidence level of accuracy of 95 per cent. During the first round of the elections on 7 December 2008, for example, when officially the EC recorded 49.1 per cent for NPP's Nana Akufo-Addo, CODEO had 49.8 per cent, with a margin of error of $+/\_1.6$. When official EC results for Prof. Mills in the first round was 47.9 per cent of the vote, CODEO gave him 47.4 per cent. In the presidential run-off elections held on 28 December 2008, official EC results for Nana Akufo-Addo of the NPP stood at 49.87 per cent of the vote, while CODEO's PVT gave him 49.81 per cent. For the NDC's Atta Mills, the EC put the figure at 50.13 per cent, while the PVT tally was 50.19 per cent . Finally, for the Tain presidential election re-run, NPP's Nana Akufo-Addo officially obtained 49.77 per cent of the vote, while NDC's Atta Mills received 50.2 per cent. CODEO's PVT tally recorded 50.23 per cent for Prof. Mills of the NDC (Larvie 2009, interview). This high level of accuracy shown by CODEO's PVT system increased confidence in the electoral process. It further underscored the transparency of the system in the sense that the results were verifiable (Larvie 2009, interview).

In the post-election period, beginning immediately after election day, CODEO had to quickly act to help contain tensions arising from the alleged inconclusive election results. Indeed, the attitude and posture of the two major political parties regarding the veracity of the results, especially between the run-off and the Tain election, and the behaviour of some FM radio stations in declaring the results prematurely heightened political tensions in the country. Under the auspices of the CDD-Ghana, a press release was issued in which CODEO implored the NPP presidential candidate, Nana Akufo-Addo to accept the results.

While the number of domestic election observers has since 1996 far outnumbered that of international observers, international observers were present for the 2008 general elections to confirm that international standards would be met. Seven groups of international observers were present: the European Union (EU), the African Union (AU), the Commonwealth, the Economic Community of West African States (ECOWAS), the National Democratic Institute (NDI), as well as the Carter Center. The Electoral Institute of South Africa (EISA) and Pan-African Parliament came to observe as one group. The Carter Center came earliest and was engaged in some pre-election observation (Larvie 2009, interview). The consensus among these seven groups of international observers was that despite some few incidents some of which have been enumerated above, the 2008 general elections were largely free, fair, and transparent. The international donor community also played an important supportive role in promoting free and fair elections and democracy in Ghana: USAID funded CODEO's 2008 election activities, while the British High Commission supported CODEO's observation of the 2 January 2009 Tain constituency presidential run-off elections.

Lessons Learned

From the above discussion, it is fair to say that domestic election observation is a better option than international election observation. Although international observers may still be needed in first time elections or in highly polarized countries, domestic election observers, if properly organized and prepared, have important advantages over international observers. They know the political culture, language and terrain, they can turn out in very large numbers, they establish organizations that stay even after the elections are over, and may be more cost effective because the cost of their hotel accommodation, transportation and other logistics would be relatively lower than that of international observers (Carothers 1997b; c.f. Squire 2012).

All in all, domestic election observers were respected by election officials, political party agents, and the public at large, as many of them were already known as independent and respectable members of their communities. Observers' relationship with election officials was therefore very cordial, and their presence could deter fraud and facilitate ownership of the electoral process. The cordial relationship extended to political party representatives during the collation of results in the 'strong room' of the EC at the Electoral Commission headquarters in Accra.

Political party representatives were fed by the EC and all the representatives ate together from the same table as they waited for results to come in. There were no fights; rather a lot of teasing jokes among themselves. When results came in through the facsimile machines, those who lost could only shake their heads. This is because they accepted the transparency of the entire process (Larvie 2009, interview).

Ghana has come a long way since the 1992 disputed elections, and the public's acceptance (to a large extent, although there were some reservations among some opposition party supporters) of the 2008 election results attests to the gradual trust they have developed in the transparency of the electoral process. Election observers, both domestic and international, must continue to strive for professionalism and adherence to high standards. They should work to counteract the diplomatic pressures that sometimes lead them to be too lenient in their assessment and take greater pains to ensure impartiality (Carothers 1997a). As the Ghanaian experience shows, the single most important indicator of a country's graduation to maturity regarding the conduct of democratic elections is a reduction in the number of international election observer groups (Carothers 1997b; c.f. Squire 2012).

Conclusion

One key finding is the importance of international donor funding for civil society activities and elections for Ghana and other African countries, at least in the short to medium term (and therefore for democratization). Civil society is increasingly able to support Ghana's democratic process due largely to the help of the donor community.

Second, the Ghanaian experience shows clearly that democracy can be consolidated, and democratic reversals pre-empted, when civil society organizations take the initiative to enhance domestic ownership of the electoral process through active observation and monitoring of elections. Success in performing these roles instils credibility and transparency in the electoral process, so that election results would be accepted by all (to a large extent) and post-election violence and conflict prevented. The advantages of a well-trained domestic observer and monitoring groups for elections and for the entrenchment of democratic norms have been emphasized in the Ghana Legal Literacy and Resource Foundation's (GLLRF) report on the 1996 elections:

> Local monitors have a better understanding of the culture, language, and local conditions and a better perception of subtleties in society. Local monitors are better able to sustain a monitoring presence in the community before, during, and after the election. Because of their numbers....more comprehensive reporting is done...The presence of local monitors provides a sense of confidence to the public and encourages the electorate to participate in the process. After the election, monitors can verify to their communities the validity, or otherwise, of the process

and results and influence public opinion by their judgment of the freeness and or fairness of the election. As indigenous groups, local monitors can bring pressure to bear on the legislature to amend the electoral laws if they observe lapses in them.... (GLLRF 1996:3-4).

Nonetheless, the fact is that local election observation and monitoring are necessary but not sufficient conditions for consolidating a democratic order. Electoral management reforms as have been carried out by the EC since 1996 as well as elite consensus on the rules of the democratic game, with the supportive role of the state or governments of the 4th Republic, have been very important in conferring credibility on the electoral process and enhancing the legitimacy of its outcomes.

International observers are also increasingly considered not enough to bring credibility and legitimacy to the election results. Increasingly the local public seeks affirmation from those usually numerous, respected, neutral and trusted members of their communities about the transparency and fairness of election proceedings. International observers, if professional and fair rather than diplomatic, are nevertheless helpful in ensuring that international electoral procedural and observation standards are adhered to, while they give a weight of support to the reports of local election observers and monitors. If political legitimacy, the authority to rule in accordance with law or with the established legal forms, is a necessary outcome of elections for a peaceful and well-functioning democracy, then domestic/civic election observation of Ghana's general elections since 1996 has been a critical factor in furthering the democratic process. It has given considerable credence to elections and election outcomes and legitimatized newly elected governments in the 4th Republic.

Notes

1. CODEO participating organizations included the Federation of Muslim Councils (FMC), Council of Independent Churches (CIC), Ghana Committee on Human and People's Rights (GCHPR), Ghana Bar Association (GBA), Civil Servants Association (CSA), Trades Union Congress (TUC), Ghana National Association of Teachers (GNAT), Ghana Journalists Association (GJA), Ghana Registered Nurses Association (GRNA), International Federation of Women Lawyers (FIDA-Ghana), National Union of Ghana Students (NUGS), Ghana Legal Literacy and Resource Foundation (GLLRF), Non-Violence International, Ghana National Chamber of Commerce and Industry, Center for the Development of People (CEDEP), International Prisons Watch (IPW), Health Watch International, and Institute of Democratic Studies (IDS) (CDD-Ghana/CODEO 2001:3).
2. Interview with Larvie (2009)
3. Interview with Larvie (2009)
4. Interview with Larvie (2009)
5. Interview with Larvie (2009)
6. Interview with Larvie (2009)

References

Agyeman-Duah, B., 2005, 'Elections and Electoral Politics in Ghana's Fourth Republic', *Critical Perspectives* 18. (July), Ghana Center for Democratic Development (CDD-Ghana).

Almond, G. and S. Verba, 1963, The *Civic Culture: Political Attitudes and Democracy in Five Nations,* Princeton, NJ: Princeton University Press.

Armijo, L.E., 1993, *Conversations on Democratization and Economic Reforms Working Papers of the Southern California Seminar* (ed.), Los Angeles, CA: University of Southern California, Center for International Studies.

Ayee, Joseph R. A. 1998. ed. *The 1996 General Elections and Democratic Consolidation in Ghana.* Accra: University of Ghana, Dept. of Political Science.

Bjornlund, E., 2004, *Beyond 'free and fair': Monitoring Elections and Building Democracy,* Washington: Woodrow Wilson Center Press.

Boafo-Arthur, K., 2001, 'Election Monitoring and Observation in Ghana: Problems and Prospects.' In Ayee, J.R.A. (ed.} *Deepening Democracy in Ghana: Politics of the 2000 Elections,* Vol. One, Accra: Freedom Publications.

Bratton, M., 1994, 'Civil Society and Political Transitions in Africa.' In Harbeson, J., D. Rothchild, and N. Chazan (eds.) *Civil Society and the State in Africa,* Boulder: Lynne Rienner Publishers.

Bratton, M., 1999, 'Second Elections in Africa'. In L. Diamond and M. Plattner (eds.) *Democratization in Africa,* Baltimore: The Johns Hopkins University Press.

Carothers, T., 1999, *Aiding Democracy Abroad: The Learning Curve,* Washington: Carnegie Endowment for International Peace.

Carothers, T., 1997a, *The Rise of Election Monitoring: The Observers Observed,* Journal of Democracy, Vol. 8, No. 3, July 1997, (pp. 19-31).

Carothers, T., 1997b, 'Democracy Assistance: The Question of Strategy', *Democratization* 4.3: 109-132.

Coalition of Domestic Election Observers (CODEO). 2008. *Final Report on the December 2008 Elections in Ghana.* Accra, Ghana: Ghana Center for Democratic Development (CDD-Ghana) and CODEO.

Coalition of Domestic Election Observers (CODEO), 2005, *Final Report on the December 2004 Elections in Ghana,* Accra, Ghana: Ghana Center for Democratic Development (CDD-Ghana) and CODEO.

Coalition of Domestic Election Observers (CODEO), 2001, *Final Report on the December 2000 Elections in Ghana,* Accra, Ghana: Ghana Center for Democratic Development (CDD-Ghana) and CODEO.

Dahl, Robert A. 1971. *Polyarchy: Participation and Opposition.* New Haven: Yale University Press.

Daily Graphic, 30 December 2000.

Darkwah, A., N. Amponsah and R.E. Gyampo, 2006, *Civil Society in a Changing Ghana: An Assessment of the Current State of Civil Society in Ghana,* CIVICUS: Civil Society Index Report for Ghana.

De Tocqueville, A., 1835 and 1840 (two parts), *Democracy in America,* edited and abridged by R. Heffner, New York: New American Library.

Diamond, L., J.J. Linz, and S.M. Lipset, 1995, *Politics in Developing Countries: Comparing Experiences with Democracy*, Boulder, CO: Lynne Rienner Publishers.

Diamond, L., J.J Linz, and S.M. Lipset, 1990, *Politics in Developing Countries: Comparing Experiences with Democracy*, Boulder, CO: Lynne Rienner Publishers.

Drah, F.K., 1993, 'Civil Society and the Transition to Pluralistic Democracy'. In Ninsin, K.A. and F.K. Drah (eds.) *Political Parties and Democracy in Ghana's Fourth Republic*, Accra: Woeli Publishing Services.

Electoral Commission of Ghana, 2007, *Framework for Domestic Election Observation*, Accra: Electoral Commission.

Ghana Legal Literacy and Resource Foundation, 1996, *Document on Election Observation*. Accra.

Gyekye-Jandoh, M.A.A., 2006, *Explaining democratization in Africa: the case of Ghana*, Doctoral dissertation, Temple University.

Gyimah-Boadi, E., 1999, 'Ghana: The Challenges of Consolidating Democracy.' In R. Joseph (ed.) *State, Conflict and Democracy in Africa*, Boulder, CO: Lynn Rienner.

Gyimah-Boadi, E., M. Oquaye and K. Drah, 2000, *Civil Society Organizations and Ghanaian Democratization*. Accra: CDD-Ghana.

Gyimah-Boadi, E., 2001, 'Democratizing Africa: Halting Progress, Outstanding Problems and Serious Dilemmas', inter-faculty lecture, Accra: Ghana Universities Press.

Havel, V., 1985, *The Power of the Powerless* (ed. J. Keane), New York: M. E. Sharpe.

Hegel, G.W.F., 1821, *The Philosophy of Right* (English Translation 1942), Berlin.

Linz, J. and A. Stepan, 1978, *The Breakdown of Democratic Regimes: Crisis, Breakdown and Reequilibration*, Baltimore: Johns Hopkins University Press.

Lipset, S.M., 1960, *Political Man: The Social Basis of Politics*, New York: Doubleday.

Marx, K. and F. Engels, 1932, *The German Ideology*, Moscow: Marx-Engels Institute.

Meyns, P., 1993, 'Civil Society and Democratic Change in Africa: The Cases of Cape Verde and Zambia.' In Wohlmuth, K. and F. Messner (eds.) *Recent Developments in the Region 1992 and 1993 African Development Perspectives Yearbook*, Vol. 3.

Network of Domestic Election Observers (NEDEO), 1997, *Report of NEDEO*, Accra, Ghana, 28 February.

Ninsin, K.A., 2006, 'Institutional Development and Democratic Consolidation.' In Boafo-Arthur, K. (ed.) *Voting for Democracy in Ghana: The 2004 Elections in Perspective*, Vol. 1, Accra: Freedom Publications.

Potter, D., D. Goldblatt, M. Kiloh, and P. Lewis, 1997, *Democratization (Democracy from Classical Times to the Present, 2)*, UK: Blackwell Publishers.

Schumpeter, J.A., 1950, *Capitalism, Socialism, and Democracy*, New York: Harper.

Squire, P., 2012, *ICTs and Election Observation in Ghana*, unpublished manuscript, University of Ghana, Master of Philosophy thesis.

Stepan, A., 1988, *Rethinking Military Politics, Brazil and the Southern Cone,* Princeton, NJ: Princeton University Press.

Verclas, K., 7 December, 2008, MobileActive.org.

Interview

Larvie, John, Program Director, Coalition for Domestic Election Observers (CODEO), 21 July 2009.

3

The Regional Balance of Presidential Tickets in Ghanaian Elections: Analysis of the 2008 General Elections

Ziblim Iddi

Introduction

Ghana's Fourth Republican Constitution prescribed a hybrid of the presidential and parliamentary systems of government to be practiced in a multi-party democracy. This is a clear departure from the country's previous attempt at constitutional government in the first three republics. The country experimented with the presidential system of government in the first and third republics, and practiced the parliamentary system under the second republic. It is reported that the constitutional experts assembled by the Provisional National Defense Council (PNDC) government to produce a draft constitution for the fourth republic were guided by the lessons learned under the first three republican constitutions. For example, the requirement that the majority of ministers of state shall be appointed from among members of Parliament as prescribed by Article 78 of the 1992 constitution was recommended because of lessons learned under the third republican constitution. The president, under the third republic, failed to get his budget passed by parliament in 1981. This was largely blamed on the fact that no member of parliament was a minister of state under the 1979 constitution. The framers of the 1992 constitution, therefore, recommended hybridization to cure the mischief of members of parliament of the ruling party sabotaging the president's agenda. Nonetheless, Ghana's current hybrid system of government could easily pass for a presidential system (Ninsin 2008).

The institutional arrangement and power dynamics between the executive and the legislature sanctioned by the 1992 constitution has inadvertently created what is gradually becoming an 'imperial presidency' in Ghana. The 'hybridization of the parliamentary and presidential system has given the executive a huge and unequivocal presence in parliament' (Ninsin 2008:2). It is, therefore, not uncommon to find Ghana listed among the countries practicing a presidential system of government in comparative studies literature (Van De Walle 2003:309). Like most other countries with presidential constitutions, political power in Ghana is highly concentrated in the presidency. This makes the office of the president a highly coveted prize. Consequently presidential contestations are always highly competitive. Presidential candidates running for election, therefore, meticulously explore and exploit every opportunity that can enhance their electoral fortunes. The selection of a running mate by a presidential candidate is undoubtedly one of the major decisions that can make or break the political ambition of a presidential candidate and the dream of a political party.

The conventional wisdom in Ghana's elections is that northerners are likely to vote for a party that has a northerner on its presidential ticket. This has guided presidential candidates in the selection of a running mate since 1992. With the exception of Rawlings who contested the 1992 and 1996 elections with a running mate who did not hail from the northern part of Ghana, all presidential candidates from the two major parties have had a northerner as running mate. As discussed in detail below, both the NPP and the NDC have followed this convention. This paper focuses exclusively on these two major parties, NDC and NPP, because they are the ones that have won a presidential election and formed a government since 1992.

This paper will do a qualitative analysis of the 2008 elections to determine whether the conventional practice of balancing a presidential ticket by partnering a southern presidential candidate with a northern politician as a running mate has the potential to enhance the electoral fortunes of the party. The study relied on secondary literature and primary data on electoral strategy, political behaviour and voting outcomes during the 2008 elections. The primary data are election figures obtained from the Electoral Commission (EC). A questionnaire was not administered and formal interviews were not conducted for data collection. Nonetheless, the study benefitted from information obtained by the author in his interactions with some key players in the December 2008 elections as a consultant for the Center for Democratic Development (CDD-Ghana) and the Institute of Economic Affairs (IEA). The author analyzed the election results of the Northern region[1] with the objective of finding out which of the two running mates – Bawumia of the NPP and Mahama of the NDC – added more value to his party's ticket in terms of votes. The study shows that the conventional wisdom alluded to above may be true in some elections, but not in all elections. That is, northerners do not always vote along ethnic lines.

The study is divided into six main sections. Following the introduction is a discussion on the office of vice president; section three presents the regional balance in Ghanaian elections. The fourth section is devoted to the drama of running mate selection in the 2008 elections. Section five examines ethno-clientelist politics in the northern region, while the last section is devoted to the findings and conclusions of the study.

The Office of Vice-President

The 1992 constitution stipulates that 'a candidate for the office of Vice-President shall be designated by the candidate for the office of President before the election of the President' (Article 60:2). Even though some commentators and politicians have questioned the relevance of the position of Vice President in most democracies, the selection of presidential running mates has always generated interest and inflamed passions within certain political parties and the country in general. It would seem that the choice of a presidential running mate is of some consequence only if it engenders controversy in the political discourse. However, Article 60: 6 of the 1992 constitution makes a vice president only a heartbeat away from presidency. This article states that 'whenever the President dies, resigns or is removed from office, the Vice-President shall assume office as President for the unexpired term of office of the President with effect from the date of the death, resignation or removal of the President.' Accordingly, political parties and their flag bearers have always taken the search for a running mate very seriously. Several factors often come into play in any consideration of a potential candidate for the position of a running mate.

One major factor that normally weighs heavily on the minds of presidential candidates in selecting a suitable person to partner with in an election is the need to balance the presidential ticket by expanding its appeal across ethnic, ideological, gender, religious and geographical boundaries. Other critical factors in the selection process include the voting behaviour of the electorate of the prospective running mate's traditional base (region); the need to unite the party by selecting someone who was a viable rival to the flag bearer at the party's primaries; and the need to select someone who can compliment the candidate's age by bringing on board someone younger to partner an older candidate and vice versa.[2] Above all, the competence of the potential running mate and his ability to step into the presidency in the event of the absence of the substantive president is paramount in the consideration (Frempong 2010; Goldstein 1982; Hiller and Kriner 2008). Various presidential candidates may put more emphasis on a different set of factors depending on their own strengths and weaknesses.

Regional Balance in Ghanaian Elections

The political map of Ghana has over the years been conventionally categorized into 'north' and 'south'. The three regions of the savannah belt (Northern, Upper-

East and Upper-West) are lumped into what is commonly referred to as 'the north', while the seven coastal and middle-belt regions (Greater Accra, Western, Central, Volta, Eastern, Ashanti and Bron Ahafo) are categorized as 'the south'.[3] The major political parties in the Fourth Republic have so far seriously factored the need for regional balance in the equation in the selection of a running mate. It is believed that having a partnership between a southerner and a northerner on a presidential ticket brings a broader appeal to the ticket and has the potential to win votes across ethnic groups all over the country.

Since 1992, the New Patriotic Party (NPP) has religiously followed this convention in all the elections in which it has contested for the presidency. The only time the issue of regional balance was not up for consideration was when the party went into alliance with other opposition parties to contest the 1996 Presidential elections.[4] In 1992, the party had Adu Boahen, an Akan from the Ashanti region and Issifu Alhassan, a Dagomba from the northern region on its ticket. In 2000 and 2004 the party had Agyekum Kufuor, an Akan from the Ashanti region, and Aliu Mahama, a Dagomba from the northern region on its ticket. In 2008, the NPP had Akufo Addo, an Akan from the eastern region, and Bawumia, a Mampruga from the northern region, on its ticket. Out of the four elections the party contested with a south/north-balanced ticket, it won two and lost two.

The NPP argued in *The Stolen Verdict* (1993) a publication chronicling election malpractices during the 1992 elections, that victory was stolen from them by the incumbent president Rawlings and his NDC party. They concluded that the irregularities of the 1992 elections were so grave that the conduct of the elections could not be described as free and fair. The party boycotted the 1992 parliamentary elections to protest the conduct of the presidential election. In the 2008 elections the NPP took a commanding lead in the first round of voting, but lost in the second round of voting, albeit with a narrow margin. But, for the constitutional requirement of 50% plus one vote for presidential elections, the NPP candidate would have been declared the winner of the 2008 elections in the first round. It, therefore, appeared that the north/south partnership had served the party well at the polls.

The National Democratic Congress (NDC) has had a south/north partnership on its presidential ticket in three out of five elections since 1992. The party's founder and its presidential candidate for the first two elections (1992 and 1996) did not comply with this convention of regional balance on presidential tickets. For both elections, he ignored competent and good candidates from the north as a running mate and opted for an Akan from the Central region. The founder and leader of the NDC, Jerry John Rawlings, could afford to go without a northern partner because he did not need a politician from the area to help him win votes in the three regions. Rawlings had played clientelist politics in the area as the country's Head of State from 1982 to 1992, and had won the hearts and minds of the people of the north for three major reasons. First, as Chairman of the PNDC, Rawlings sanctioned the creation of a third region (Upper West) out of the hitherto two regions of the political north. Second, his government launched the Northern Electrification project which extended hydropower to the three northern regions. This, some have argued, put the north on the path of modernization and development. Finally, the establishment of the University for Development Studies (UDS), the first and only university in the north, by the Rawlings' government, with its campuses spreading across the three administrative regions of the political north was highly regarded by the people as a significant share of the 'national cake'.

Rawlings maximized the dividends from this political capital in the form of electoral votes. His name and picture alone on the ballot was enough to win the votes of most of the electorate from the north. Rawlings could, therefore, take the northern votes for granted and rather go after Akan votes, in order to weaken the electoral support of his opponents in their strongholds. Nonetheless, the NDC, without Rawlings, had to factor into the political equation the conventional regional balance thesis when considering a presidential running mate. Hence, in all three elections that he contested as the NDC's presidential candidate, Atta Mills partnered with northerners as his running mate. In the 2000 elections he had Martin Amidu, a Builsa from the Upper East region as his running mate; in 2004 candidate Mills partnered with Mohammed Mumuni, a Dagomba from the northern region; and in the 2008 elections he chose as his running mate, Mahama, a Gonja from the northern region. The party's presidential candidate has won one out of the three elections it contested with a south/north ticket.

The Selection Drama: Who Gets the Nod?

The selection of presidential running mates has always generated interest within the political class. Political parties in democracies across the world have a different mode of selecting a candidate to partner their flag bearer at general elections. In Ghana, most of the major political parties have very similar rules and regulations (with minor variations) on the selection of a running mate. The constitutions of both the NDC and the NPP clearly stipulate the procedure to follow in selecting the presidential running mate. In both cases, the flag bearer has the prerogative to select a running mate in consultation with, and upon the approval of, the party's National Executive Committee (NEC). Even though the presidential candidate has discretionary powers in the selection process, it is often the case that various competing interests within the party vigorously mobilize party activists in support of potential candidates perceived to represent their group interest. Intensive lobbying of the presidential candidate by power brokers within the party for their preferred candidate normally takes place.

It is usually during the selection process of a party's running mate that intra-party factional interests emerge and seriously threaten or undermine party unity and cohesion. The internal party democratic institutions and structures are challenged and the management of potential cleavages within the party becomes paramount at this time.

Mills and the Trinity

For the 2008 elections the NDC was the first party to initiate the process of selecting a presidential running mate. There were various groups and power blocs within the party championing the candidature of the three short-listed persons. The only woman among the three, Betty Mould Iddrisu, had the blessing and support of the founder of the party, Rawlings, and his wife Agyeman Rawlings. Moslem and northern groups within the party preferred Mumuni and campaigned for him. Some splinter northern groups and youth movements within the party favoured Mahama as the running mate of Mills. All three personalities are very successful and accomplished professionals in private life. Iddrisu is a lawyer of international repute. Mumuni is a legal practitioner and former Member of Parliament. He had the added advantage of being the running mate of the presidential candidate in the 2004 general elections. Mahama was a Member of Parliament and former Minister of Communication.

As the date scheduled by the party for the flag bearer to submit his choice to the National Executive Committee drew closer, it became clear that the candidate was leaning toward a north/south ticket. It was widely reported that the race was between Mumuni and Mahama. On the other hand, the former first lady continued to push for the choice of Iddrisu as Mill's running mate. Commenting on the prospects of the NDC flag bearer choosing a northerner over a woman, the former first lady expressed her displeasure on various Accra-based radio stations (Joy fm, Peace fm, and Radio Gold) on Tuesday, 1 April 2008.[5] She threatened that there would be trouble in the party if her favourite candidate was dropped from the list. Uncharacteristic of her stature as a former first lady, she warned that the presidential candidate would not be 'treated with kid gloves' this time around as was the case in 2004. According to her, the 2008 election was too crucial to be left to the whims and caprices of the candidate.

Making her case for Iddrisu, the former first lady argued that there is no political merit in choosing a northern candidate to partner the flag bearer. She contended that politics is a game of numbers and that Iddrisu was likely to pull more votes for the NDC from the Ashanti region because of her ethnicity and gender. In her estimation, the northern votes, for which one may choose any of the two gentlemen to partner the candidate, was nothing compared to the votes Iddrisu was capable of pulling from Ashanti and other Akan speaking areas. What the former first lady failed to appreciate was that it was equally possible for the young and affable Mahama to also pull votes from the youth across the country, including Akan youth. It was estimated that over sixty per cent of the country's population would be below the age of 45 years by 7 December 2008 (Daily Dispatch, 31 March 2008). This translated into a large segment of potential voters being within the youth bracket. It was clear therefore that selecting a youthful candidate to attract the youth vote was a compelling reason in the mind of the presidential candidate.

The youth factor notwithstanding, it must be emphasized that northern votes have always been crucial for an NDC victory in all general elections since 1996. For the 7 December 2008 first round ballot, the NDC had 763,541 valid votes from the three northern regions, representing 19 per cent of the party's total valid votes of 4,056, 634 (EC 2008). This figure is by no means insignificant in the general scheme of NDC votes in the election. It was clear in the first round that, but for the wide margin between the NDC and NPP votes in the three northern regions, there would not have been the need for a second round.

Even when it came down to choosing between two northerners, the NDC presidential candidate was confronted with the need to take cognizance of religious alignments in that part of the country. Some NDC youth in the northern regional capital, mobilized by the Azorka boys[6], vehemently protested the likely selection of Mahama because of his religious background. The group expressed support for Mumuni because he is a Moslem. Mahama, a practicing Christian, was forced to extol his association with the Islamic religion by invoking his relationship with his godfather, a highly respected Moslem mallam in Kumasi and also emphasizing the fact that his mother is a practicing Moslem.[7] In the end, the presidential candidate was not swayed by pressures from all the vociferous interest groups. He selected Mahama as his running mate for the 2008 elections. Clearly, the two most compelling factors in the NDC flag bearer's decision were the need for regional balance and the youthful appeal of Mahama.

NPP's Selection Quagmire

Contrary to what most political pundits had predicted, it was rather the flag bearer of the then ruling NPP who had the most difficult task in selecting his running mate. The academic question today is whether his final selection was a calculated surprise or a desperate move by a candidate trying to prove to party and country that he was his own man. After openly expressing his preference for selecting a woman and a northerner to partner him in the December 2008 elections at a forum organized by the Institute of Economic Affairs (IEA), the candidate was greeted with loud protests from strong and powerful voices within the party. The target of the protests was the person of Alima Mahama, a member of parliament and a minister of state for Women and Children Affairs – who was strongly rumoured by people close to the presidential candidate to be a preferred choice. Alima Mahama did not help matters when she allowed women groups to champion her bid by openly campaigning and putting pressure on the party and candidate to select her as the running mate.

The pressure from both sides of the divide on the potential selection of Alima Mahama was so unbearable that the candidate succumbed and reverted to 'plan B'. An infamous letter by a former national chairman and founding member of the party, B.J. Da Rocha, was the final nail in the coffin of Alima Mahama's candidature. In the confidential letter addressed to the flag bearer, the party's National Chairman and other leading members of the NPP, Da Rocha said that Alima Mahama did not have what it takes to be a running mate. According to him, it would be difficult, particularly in the north, to sell an unmarried woman to the voters. Rejection of her potential nomination by powerful women in the party such as the then first vice chairperson of the party, Ama Busia, did not help her case. Some Moslem groups within the party also protested against her potential selection on grounds that Alima Mahama was a single woman and could not be a good role model to young Moslem women in the country.

The candidate soon realized that his 'plan B' was no less problematic for some party leaders than his first preference. Staying with the NPP's tradition of presenting a north/south regional balanced ticket, the candidate turned his eye on the then second deputy speaker of parliament and MP for Yendi, Malik Alhassan Yakubu.[8] The problem with Yakubu was that he was a Dagomba and a leading member of the Abudu gate. Incidentally, the NPP had selected a Dagomba to partner a southerner as a running mate in all three preceding general elections. There was therefore a visible 'Dagomba fatigue' in some NPP circles. There were those who believed that other ethnic groups from the three regions should be given the opportunity this time to be selected as the running mate of the party's flag bearer.

There was also a school of thought within the NPP that held the view that the Dagbon conflict had negatively affected the electoral fortunes of the Party in the north. According to this group, selecting a Dagomba as running mate would rather compromise the party even further, and would affect the electoral fortunes of the party in the area. This contention is contradicted by the famous words of Tip O'Neal (former Speaker of the U.S. House of Representatives,) that 'all politics is local'. Those who believed that the Dagbon conflict negatively impacted the NPP's electoral fortunes in the north were mostly southerners who erroneously thought of 'the north' as a geographical region inhabited by one homogeneous group of people. On the contrary, Dagombas are only one of the several ethnic groups inhabiting the three northern regions, and the Dagbon conflict is limited largely to what is commonly described as the Dagbon Traditional Area. The Dagbon Traditional Area has only 12 out of 49 constituencies in the political north. Also the Abudus/Andanis divide in the Dagbon conflict has a zero effect on the voting pattern of the Gonja, Wala, Kusasi or Frafra as it is on the Asante, Fanti, Ga or Ewe. No Dagati or Sisala voter will cast his or her vote based on the Dagbon conflict, just as no Akyem or Nzema voter will cast a vote for one party or the other because they support the Abudus or the Andanis.

In sum, the impact of the Dagbon conflict, in terms of the electoral fortunes of political parties, is limited largely to the Dagbon Traditional Area and some settler communities in the south populated by Dagombas. Moreover, even in the Dagbon Traditional Area, the conflict has only reinforced the two strategic voting blocs that have traditionally dominated Dagbon politics. The voting pattern of Dagombas since independence has been that the Abudus and Andanis have always voted in the opposite direction on national elections. Traditionally, the Andanis have demonstrated their loyalty to the CPP/Nkrumaist tradition while the Abudus have placed their loyalty in the United Party (Danquah/ Busia) tradition (Staniland 1973; MacGaffey 2006; and Tonah 2012). Even in non-partisan elections, the two factions have consistently pitched camps with opposing candidates. In the UNIGOV referendum, for example, the Abudus voted largely 'No' while the Andanis voted 'Yes'. Furthermore, in all four national elections under the Fourth Republic, the Abudus have consistently voted for the NPP while the Andanis have consistently voted for the NDC or any Party other than the NPP. All things being equal, the Andanis will always vote against the NPP for 'ideological utility value', irrespective of what the Party's performance in government has been, or what the other Party's probability of winning is. Admittedly there are some swing voters among the two factions, but they are of marginal significance.

Nonetheless, the pressure to drop Yakubu in the selection of a running mate for Akufo Addo was so great that the NPP presidential candidate had to change his mind at the eleventh hour. The candidate was in South Africa with Yakubu a week to the day he was to announce his running mate. He reportedly informed Yakubu that he was his preferred choice and that when they returned to Ghana his name would be presented to the NEC[9]. On his return to the country, the flag bearer was confronted with serious lobbying and maneuvering by surrogates of the then sitting President, J.A. Kufour, to select one Zakaria Adam as his running mate. Adam was a member of the party, a Gonja from the northern region and the then Principal of Bagabaga Training College in Tamale. The candidate vehemently resisted this move to impose an unknown party member on him as a running mate. He, however, could not overcome the growing opposition to his preferred choice (Yakubu). At this juncture, Akufo Addo was getting more desperate and frustrated by the day. With the rejection of his first two preferences by NPP power brokers, he was inadvertently creating the impression of a waffling leader who suffers from indecision. To prove to all that he was his own man and that he was too big for others to push around, the flag bearer made up his mind on his vice-presidential candidate and kept the decision secret. On a fateful August night at the Alisa Hotel, Accra, in a room packed with the top brass of the NPP, Akufo Addo surprised a lot of the party stalwarts in the room with his announcement of the young Bawumia as his running mate.[10] The candidate prefaced his announcement by informing the august party members in the room that his preferred choice was Yakubu. Akufo Addo assured the NEC of the party that his selection of Bawumia over Yakubu was influenced by his determination to unite the party and the country behind him. Hence, it was prudent for him to select someone who would not be perceived as a divisive figure in the Dagbon conflict. A debate ensued among members of the party assembled in the room, with an overwhelming majority speaking in favour of Yakubu. It was reported by sources at the NEC meeting that if the process was purely democratic and put to a vote, then Yakubu would have carried the day over Bawumia who was not known in the party. The then sitting president, J.A. Kufour, had the final word, and he reminded party members that it was under the watch of Yakubu, as his interior minister, that the unfortunate events of 25-27 March 2002 that led to the assassination of the king of Dagbon happened. He, therefore, supported the candidate's decision not to select Yakubu and endorsed his choice of the young Bawumia.

Ethno-Clientelist Politics in the Northern Region: Counting the 2008 Votes

Does ethnicity and regionalism still play a significant role in Ghanaian voting behaviour? Is the Rawlings factor a rare exception or compelling evidence that clientelism weakens ethnic voting in Ghana? There is debate in comparative scholarship as to whether ethnicity is still a driving force in the voting behaviour of most of the African electorate. There are those who argue that ethnic groups in Africa are not primordially fixed, but are constructed in the course of social, economic, and political interaction (Mozaffar, Scarritt and Galaich 2003:379). Arguing from this perspective, Anebo concludes that ethnicity is becoming less significant in Ghanaian politics. In his analysis of the 2004 elections, he argued that Ghanaian voters were largely influenced by the issues at stake in the elections, but were not voting simply on ethnic grounds. According to Anebo, 'the process of societal modernization and heightened political awareness are strenuously eroding the traditional social identities, based on ethnicity, dialect, tribe, region, and religion that had predicted the mass basis of party support in Ghana during the earlier decades' (Anebo 2006:107). In his opinion, 'geographical mobility and urbanization have engendered crosscutting cleavages based on location, occupation, and communication, thereby weakening linkages with tribal groups...' (Anebo op. cit.). This assertion may be true to some extent in the case of the 2004 elections. There is, however, no preponderance of evidence to support the decline of ethnicity in Ghanaian elections. Even in the 2004 elections, there was documented evidence of the electorate in some regions voting solely on the basis of ethnicity.[11] According to Ben Ephson, between four and five per cent of Ghanaian voters base their choice of who to vote for on ethnicity (The Daily Dispatch 2009).

The other side of the argument is those who believe that primordial ethnic cleavages reinforce group solidarity in Africa. They believe that politicians will continue to maximize the advantages derived from group identity, including winning votes by manipulating group interest and grievances. Group identity is still the basis of most voting in poor countries. It is by far the easiest basis for political mobilization (Collier 2009:26). According to Ake, 'ethnicity has a preponderant influence on voter choice. This is because in the conception of primordialism, ethnicity serves to bond a particular group together and it is within such primordial cleavage that they [the group] realize its identity' (Ake 2003:93). In Ake's opinion, 'ethnic groups are real, at least in the limited sense of solidarity, of consciousness, however misguided or spurious' (ibid.). Commenting on ethnicity in Ghanaian politics, Boafo-Arthur observed that notwithstanding the effort by Ghana's first president, Nkrumah, in dealing with ethnicity by 'the promulgation of the Avoidance of Discrimination Act ...the 'ghost' of ethnicity and ethnic influence in voting, especially in the Volta and Ashanti Regions of Ghana have refused to die as the general elections of 1969, 1992, 1996, 2000, 2004 portrayed' (Boafo-Arthur 2008:63).

In this section, we will examine the role of ethnicity and clientelism in the 2008 elections in the home region of the two gentlemen selected to partner the presidential candidates of the NPP and NDC. We will rely on election results from the region to determine the voting pattern in some selected constituencies. Ethnicity played a significant role in the Gonja traditional area of the northern region in the 2008 general elections. The major tribes in the northern region include Dagombas, Mamprusis, Nanumbas, Gonjas and Konkombas. The first three tribes belong to the Mole-Dagbani group and are known to be descendants of one great-grandfather (Naa Gbewaa).[12] In the 2008 elections, the NDC's running mate was a Gonja from the Guan-speaking group, while the NPP's presidential running mate was a Mamprusi from the Mole-Dagbani-speaking group. The NDC's campaign strategy in Gonjaland was reduced to using ethnic/tribal sentiments to rally Gonjas behind a 'son of the soil' in the elections. They told the Gonja people that the Mole-Dagbani group had their vice-president in the person of Aliu Mahama, and that it was their turn to produce the next vice-president. Gonjas were constantly reminded that the NPP by-passed two prominent Gonjas (Abubakari Sadique Boniface and Nurudeen Jawula) for a Mamprusi. The NDC was touted as a party that listened to the concerns of Gonja chiefs to select a running mate from Gonjaland. The voters were, therefore, asked not to let their chiefs down by coming out in their numbers to vote massively for the NDC. Some leading members of the Gonja Youth Association and the Gonja Students Union who are NPP members were recruited from Accra to join the NDC campaign team in the area to help win votes for Mahama in NPP strongholds. As far as they were concerned, the general good of Gonjaland was over and above their individual interest and ideology. They concluded that an NDC government with a Gonja as its vice-president was good for Gonjaland.[13]

The results of the 2008 elections in all the constituencies of Gonjaland clearly indicate that the voters in the area did not disappoint their favourite son and his party. The NDC swept all six constituencies, including constituencies previously won by the NPP. The NDC's victory in Salaga and Damongo/Daboya – the two largest constituencies – was a big blow to the NPP in the area. These constituencies were represented in parliament by NPP members and the MP for Salaga (Saddique Boniface) was a Minister of State and a leading member of the NPP campaign team. In three of the six constituencies (Bole/Bamboi, Sawla/Tuna/Kalba, and Yapei/Kusawgu) the NPP parliamentary candidate had more votes than the party's presidential candidate. This suggests that some NPP voters in these constituencies indulged in what is now commonly known in Ghanaian political parlance as 'skirt and blouse'; that is, they voted for the NPP parliamentary candidate based on their party ideology, but turned around and voted for the NDC presidential candidate based on ethnicity. In the Kpandai constituency, the NDC presidential candidate obtained 15,126 valid votes while the party's parliamentary candidate received 10,391 valid votes (EC 2008). This suggests that about 4,729 Gonjas in the constituency voted for the NDC presidential candidate for reasons other than party membership: they voted on the basis of ethnicity. For the first time since 1996, all six Gonja MPs in the country's legislature were members of the NDC.

Ethnicity was apparently not a factor in the voting in constituencies populated by the Mole-Dagbani tribes. By selecting a Mamprusi to partner their presidential candidate, the NPP were probably expecting to do well in the northern region. If one were guided by Ake's conceptualization of ethnicity and voting behaviour in Africa (Ake 2003:93), or Collier's theory of group identity as the basis for political mobilization (Collier 2009: 26), the selection of a member of the largest ethnic group in the region (mole-dagbani) as a running mate was an excellent strategy for the NPP to carry the region. Out of 894,342 registered voters in the northern region for the 2004 general elections, the 17 constituencies of the Mole-Dagbani ethnic group alone recorded 624,220 voters (EC 2004). This represented seventy per cent (70%) of total registered voters in the region. Based on election results from the 2004 elections, 189,197 of the total NPP valid votes of 273,897 in the northern region came from the 17 constituencies of the Mole-Dagbani ethnic group (ibid.). This represented 69 per cent of NPP votes in the region. It is not, therefore, surprising that since 1992 the NPP has always selected a running mate from the Mole-Dagbani group.

As in previous elections, the selection of Dr. Bawumia was not enough to change the voting behaviour of the people in the Mole-Dagbani constituencies. Since 1992, the voters in the 17 Mole-Dagbani constituencies have voted on the basis of considerations other than ethnicity. The Rawlings factor (clientelism), as discussed above, and chieftaincy have been significant factors determining voting outcomes in these constituencies.[14] In the 2008 elections, the NDC presidential candidate won 12 of the 17 constituencies in the area, including all the three large constituencies of Tamale South, Central, and North. The difference between the votes obtained by the presidential candidates of the NDC and the NPP in the three Tamale constituencies alone was 81,897 valid votes during the 7 December first round ballot (EC 2008). This figure is significant against the backdrop of the number of votes needed by the NPP to reach the magic 'fifty-plus-one vote' for a first round victory. Out of the 8,465,834 total valid votes cast for the first round of the December 2008 elections, the NPP presidential candidate recorded 4,159,439 valid votes. This was only 73,479 votes less than the 4,232,918 votes needed to win the election (ibid.). What is more, The NPP could only manage to win 3 of the 17 parliamentary seats in the Mole-Dagbani traditional area. The party lost in all three constituencies of the Mamprugu area, including Bawumia's own constituency (Walewale), which had been previously won by the NPP.

From the outset, it was clear that Bawumia faced an uphill battle in his bid to win votes from his ethnic group for the NPP. Even members of his own family were sharply divided between the NDC and the NPP.[15] The clientelist politics of Bawumia's father and his NDC party consolidated voter support for the NDC. As pointed out by Bratton and Van de Walle (1994 and 1997), electoral politics in most African societies is inherently clientelist. The patriarch of the Bawumia family, Mumuni Bawumia, built a political empire in the area through his many years of public service as a politician. For over a period of five decades, the elder Bawumia delivered private and public goods to the people through his association with almost all post independence governments in Ghana. His political influence in the region is unparalleled in the history of Ghana. The last political association of the elder Bawumia before he passed away was with the NDC. He was the chairman of the Council of State and a stalwart of the party in the northern region.

The Akufo Addo campaign team did not make things easy for Bawumia in his effort to win the northern votes. Even though his selection was hailed by northerners in the party as a great honour,[16] the campaign team had a different agenda. The strategy was not to market the running mate as a northern candidate, but as a generational candidate and a successful professional to attract the votes of the youth and the middle class voters. To this end, every effort was made to distance him from northerners who were already managing his day-to-day affairs. A campaign specialist, Yofi Grant, was tasked with the responsibility of managing the candidate. His itinerary was prepared by Grant and the Akufo Addo campaign team, thus his campaign tour was heavily skewed in favour of southern appearances. Bawumia's presence was not felt in the northern sector in the days closer to the elections. The NPP in the northern region did not organize the usual last big rally in Tamale before election day because the running mate was shipped out of town to be with the presidential candidate in Accra for the party's last rally. The marginalization of northerners closer to the candidate and the trivialization or sometimes outright disdain for northern protocol demonstrated by Grant, Yonny Kulendi, and Ofori Atta negatively impacted the electoral fortunes of the party in the north.

While the NPP vacillated between marketing their running mate as a 'northern boy' or a generational candidate, the NDC's Mahama was consistent and comfortable with the image he presented to the electorate. He obviously had the advantage of being a known public figure and a seasoned politician. The NDC used him to attract northern votes for the party, marketing himself to the people of the north as one of their own.

For the 2008 elections, it is safe for one to conclude that clientelism and loyalty to the 'big man of northern politics' weakened ethnicity in the three constituencies of the Mamprugu traditional area. Unlike the six constituencies of the Gonja traditional area where the electorate voted overwhelmingly for the NDC's presidential candidate because of Mahama, the voters in the three constituencies of the Mamprugu traditional area disappointed the 'son of the soil' and his NPP presidential candidate. They voted for the NDC's presidential candidate because of their loyalty to his father's legacy and clientelism.

Voting outcomes in the other fourteen constituencies of the Mole-Dagbani ethnic group was largely influenced by a combination of chieftaincy and clientelism. The Abudu/Andani chieftaincy conflict heavily influenced the voting trend in the 12 constituencies of the Dagbon Traditional Area (DTA). Just as in the 2004 general elections, the voting pattern in the area was highly skewed in favour of the then opposition NDC. The NPP continued to suffer electoral defeats in Dagbon constituencies because of the alleged involvement of some leading members of the party in the gruesome murder of the overlord of the Dagbon kingdom (MacGaffey 2006). The NPP only managed to win 2 of the 12 constituencies in the Dagbon Traditional Area with a very slim margin. The NDC has been very astute in using the Dagbon conflict to energize its base and win more votes from undecided voters in the Dagbon Traditional Area. Faced with the daunting challenge of overcoming his father's legacy to win votes for the NPP from his people, the younger Bawumia failed the test.

Findings and Conclusion

The excitement of the 2008 elections was not limited to the presidential candidates alone; it permeated the entire trajectory of political party electoral activities – from the choice of their running mates to party parliamentary primaries and finally to voting. The wait-and-see strategy adopted by the two major political parties in the selection of a running mate ended with the NDC presidential candidate making the bold selection of Mahama as his running mate. This was against the preferred choice of the founder of the party and it came as a disappointment to the former president and founder of the NDC. Mills demonstrated to the Ghanaian electorate that he is decisive, and that he is his own man and not the 'poodle' of the founder of his party. The NPP candidate, on the other hand, had to contend with a creeping perception of indecisiveness and lack of control over his preference for a running mate in the selection process. In the end, Akufo Addo had to settle for his third option.

This paper revealed that presidential elections in Ghana subject presidential candidates to considerable pressure during the selection of a running mate. Second, it has argued that, contrary to the claim of direct correlation between ethnicity and voting in Africa, the determinants of voting behaviour are complex. Using the voting pattern in the 2008 general elections among Gonjas and Mamprusis in northern Ghana, it has been shown that in Gonjaland the people voted overwhelmingly for the NDC. The fact that NDC's presidential running mate was a son of Gonjaland played a decisive role in voter choices and enabled the party to sweep all the parliamentary seats in the area and substantially increase the presidential votes for the NDC. The story was not quite the same for the NPP and its running mate in his home base of Mamprugu and the extended Mole-Dagbani traditional area. The selection of a true son of Mampruguland was not compelling enough to change the voting pattern in the area. Party loyalty, not necessarily ideological, was much stronger than ethnic loyalty. Loyalty to the NDC in the area has been natured over the years through the clientelist politics of the elder Bawumia. The strong perception by the electorate in the area that the NDC is the party most likely to deliver both personal and public goods than the NPP has been developed through the politics of Mumuni Bawumia. His son fought an uphill battle against a party that invokes the memory of the father. The result was that the NPP lost all the three parliamentary seats in the area, including the constituency where the running mate voted.

It is, however, noteworthy that the presidential running mates selected by the NDC and NPP in the 2008 elections to complete a north/south balance pulled additional votes from the three northern regions to their respective parties. The NPP made significant gains in terms of the percentage of votes it obtained in 2004 and 2008. The party increased its votes by 5 per cent, 3 per cent, and 1 per cent in the Upper West region, Upper East region, and Northern region respectively.

What is more, the party gained two parliamentary seats in the Upper West region, the first time in the Fourth Republic that the NPP had won a parliamentary seat in that region. Above all, it was only in the three northern regions that the NPP's presidential candidate obtained more votes than President Kufour had obtained for the party in 2004.

The NDC also enhanced its performance in the north during the 2008 elections. The party had carried the three regions in all the elections under the Fourth Republic. However, its performance in the north in 2008 was spectacular and crucial to the party's chance of winning. The party recorded an increased number of votes across the three regions, with very high figures coming out of the three constituencies of the Tamale metropolis. It was evident that between the two presidential running mates, Mahama was the most valuable partner in terms of winning votes. The freestyle, three-pronged campaign (with the three Johns) adopted by the NDC allowed Mahama to do intense grassroots campaigning in the north to win the heart and minds of the people for the NDC. The party had the luxury of keeping him up north to campaign while Mills and Rawlings concentrated on taking votes away from the NPP in the south.

The fact that the Dagbon conflict was still a big campaign issue in the Dagbon traditional area also benefitted the NDC. The running mate himself did not make it his campaign mantra, but some NDC parliamentary candidates in the area exploited the sentiments of the people on the conflict to their party's advantage. The Mahama factor in winning votes for the NDC in the region was equally profound in Dagbon constituencies highly populated by Abudus who are traditionally aligned with the NPP. In the Tamale Central constituency for example, a stronghold of the Abudus in the Dagbon chieftaincy divide, the NDC obtained 40,640 valid votes, representing 64 per cent of total votes in the constituency. The NPP presidential candidate obtained only 21,136 valid votes (EC 2008). This election victory in the constituency was a great feat for the NDC considering the fact that the party was running against an NPP parliamentary candidate who was the sitting Tamale Metropolitan Chief Executive. The cumulative effect of the total votes from the three Tamale constituencies was very significant in tilting the outcome of the 2008 general elections in favour of the NDC.

Notes

1. Home region of the two personalities selected to partner the presidential candidates of the two largest parties in the 2008 elections – John Dramani Mahama and Mahamudu Bawumia.
2. One of the compelling factors considered by both the NPP and the NDC candidates in their selection of a running mate for the 2008 election was the youthful appeal of their respective choices. At 47 and 50 respectively, Bawumia and Mahama were better

positioned to attract the vote of the youth for their party than the two septuagenarian politicians.

3. It must be noted that this north/south geographical divide can be varied in some other considerations. For example, some parts of the Brong Ahafo and Volta regions are sometimes conveniently classified with the three northern regions.

4. In the 1996 presidential elections, candidate J.A. Kufour from the Ashanti region partnered with fellow Akan and sitting Vice President Nkensen Arkah from the Central region on the ticket of the opposition alliance.

5. These interviews were widely reported and carried by ghanaweb on its General News of Wednesday, 2 April 2008.

6. The Azorka boys is a notorious gang of young unemployed market boys who are organized by Azorka, a leading member of the northern regional branch of the NDC. They have been variously associated with acts of election-related violence in the area. The group gained notoriety at the NDC's national congress in Koforidua when they attacked NDC members perceived to be opponents of their preferred candidate (Atta Mills) and prevented some leading members of the party (including the then chairman, Obed Asamoah, and Wayo Seini, a then NDC member of parliament) from leaving the congress hall, not even to attend to nature's call.

7. What the Hon. Mahama failed to add about his affinity with the Islamic religion is the fact that he had his secondary education at a Moslem dominated school where most of his friends and classmates were practicing Moslems. He had both his G.C.E. Ordinary and Advanced level education at Ghana Secondary School in Tamale where he was year mates with the likes of Sulley Gariba; Alhassan Yakubu, MP for Mion; Prince Imoro Andani, former northern regional Minister and presidential advisor under the Kufour administration; as well as Mosses Asaga, former MP for Nabdam.)

8. Malik Yakubu was the party's first national youth organizer in 1992 and later the Minister of Interior under the first Kufour administration. He served with the flag bearer at the party's national secretariat when Akufo Addo was the party's national organizer. It is reported that Akufo Addo sponsored Yakubu to contest for the party's presidential ticket in 1998 as a strategy to take the northern votes away from Akufo Addo's main challenger in that contest, Agyekum Kufour.

9. Interview with Malik Alhassan Yakubu Yakubu

10. Bawumia's selection did not completely come 'out of left-field' (to borrow a baseball terminology). The only people who knew about the bombshell were a select group of the candidate's closest advisors who for a long time had been quietly canvassing for the young banker and deputy Governor of the Bank of Ghana. This group of mostly young financial securities and investments wizards was championed by Ken Ofori Atta, a cousin of the flag bearer. As the one entrusted with the enviable responsibility of controlling the campaign purse of the candidate, Ofori Atta had the ear of the flag bearer and he never stop trumpeting and extolling the virtues of his banker friend to the candidate. It was reported that Ofori Atta made a compelling case for the next president to have a strong economic management team with the young accomplished banker as head of the economic team working with himself (Ofori Atta) as the finance minister. Many were those who heard the rumours and ruled it out as impossible. In the end, as they say, 'money talks' – he who pays the piper calls the tune.

11. In Ghana, the Ashanti and Volta regions are noted for voting largely along ethnic lines. The Akan votes in the Ashanti region largely go to the NPP, while the Ewe votes in the Volta region go to the NDC. This has been the voting pattern in the two regions since 1992. This phenomenon of voting has led to the regions being euphemistically refer to in Ghanaian political parlance as the 'World Banks' of the two parties.

12. Dagombas, Mamprusis, and Nanumbas are descendants of the three sons of Naa Gbewaa – Sitobu, Tohugu, and Mantambu respectively. The three tribes speak the same dialect and practice the same customs and traditions. The Gonjas are Guan-speaking and have had historical battles with the Mole-Dagbani group for territorial dominance.

13. In an interview with Braimah I. Awaisu, a former president of Gonja Students Association, Legon chapter, he bemoaned how most of his NPP colleagues on the Legon campus joined the NDC campaign solely because the party's presidential running mate was a Gonja.

14. Rawlings and his NDC specialized in neo-patrimonial politics in the three northern regions. That is, they capitalized on the poor socio-economic environment in the area and engaged in 'vote-buying' through the use of private interest delivery.

15. Bawumia's elder brother, Mandeya Bawumia, openly campaigned for the NDC in the area. Some family members of the running mate felt that it was a betrayal of the Bawumia legacy for the younger Mahamudu Bawumia to run against the NDC. Mandeya Bawumia has since been rewarded by the NDC with an ambassadorial position for campaigning and supporting the party in the area during the 2008 elections. Some have argued that there was a sibling rivalry in the house of Bawumia between half-brothers in the polygamous family.

16. The northern Region NPP issued a press statement to the effect that they were 'grateful to the NPP for always taking into consideration the religious and geographical divides of our country in matters of the selection of running mates' (GNA 21 August 2008).

References

Ake, C., 2003, *The feasibility of democracy in Africa*, Dakar: CODESRIA (reprint).

Anebo, F.K.G., 2006, 'Issue Salience Versus Ethnic Voting in the 2004 Elections', in K. Boafo-Arthur (ed.) *Voting for Democracy in Ghana: Ghana's 2004 Elections in Perspective*, Vol. 1, pp. 187-210, Accra: Freedom Publications.

Boafo-Arthur, K., 2008, 'Democracy and Stability in West Africa: The Ghanaian Experience,' Uppsala: Universitetstryckeriet.

Bratton, M., and N. van de Walle, 1994, *"Neopatrimonial regimes and political transitions in Africa"*, *World Politics* 46 (3): pp. 453-89.

Bratton, M. and N. van de Walle, 1997, *Democratic experiments in Africa: regime transitions in comparative perspective*, Cambridge: Cambridge University Press.

Collier, P. 2009. Wars, Guns, and Votes: Democracy in Dangerous Places, New York, NY: Harper Collins.

Daily Dispatch, 31 March 2008 and 2009

Electoral Commission (EC), 2010, 2008 Presidential and Parliamentary Results, accessed July 2010. www.ec.gov.gh/page.php?page=396&section=51&type=1

Frempong, K.D.A., 2010, Playing the Second Fiddle: Reflections on Running Mate Selection and the Vice Presidency in the Fourth Republic of Ghana, *Ghana Social Science Journal,* Vol. 7, No. 2, pp. 119-144.

Ghana News Agency 21 August 2008

Goldstein, J.K., 1982, The Modern American Vice Presidency: The Transformation of a Political Institution, Princeton, NJ: Princeton University Press.

Hiller, M, and D. Kriner, 2008, Institutional Change and the Dynamics of Vice President Selection, *Presidential Studies Quarterly,* Vol. 38, No. 3, pp. 401-421.

MacGaffey, W., 2006, Death of a King, Death of a Kingdom? Social Pluralism and Succession to High Office in Dagbon, Northern Ghana, *The Journal of Modern African Studies,* Vol. 44, No 1, pp. 79-99.

Mozaffar, S., J. Scarritt, and G. Galaich, 2003, "Electoral institutions, ethno-political cleavages and political parties in Africa", *American Political Science Review 93(3).*

Ninsin, K. A., 2008. *Executive-Parliament Interface in the Legislative process (1993-2006): A Synergy of Power?* Accra: WOELI PUBLISHING SERVICES.

Republic of Ghana, 1992, Constitution of the Republic of Ghana, Tema: Ghana Publishing Corporation.

Staniland, M., 1973, The Manipulation of Tradition: Politics in Northern Ghana, *Journal of Development Studies.*

Tonah, S., 2012, The Politicisation of a Chieftaincy Conflict: The Case of Dagbon, Northern Ghana, *Nordic Journal of African Studies* 21(1), pp. 1-20.

The Stolen Verdict, 1993 (Accra: New Patriotic Party)

Van de Walle, N., 2003, 'Presidentialism and clientelism in Africa's emerging party systems', *Journal of Modern African Studies* 41(2).

http://ndc.org.gh/docs/ndc_constitution_webver.pdfhttp://www.newpatrioticparty.org/index.php/who-we-are/our-party/constitution

4

Manifestos and Agenda Setting in Ghanaian Elections[1]

Joseph R. A. Ayee

Introduction

There is a longstanding scholarly debate over the factors that influence electoral outcomes or voter behaviour in elections globally (Downs 1957; Blais 2000; Schram 1991; Butler & Stokes 1974; Kanazawa 1998:974-995; Geys 2006:16-35; Kiewiet & Mattozzi 2008:313-326; Caplan 2007). In his seminal work in 1957, Downs, for instance, argued that voters in established democracies choose a party or candidate on the basis of the benefits that they are likely to enjoy when that party or candidate wins power. This is the 'rational-choice' perspective. In other words, electoral choices are based on the policies, ideologies and philosophies of the parties. Other factors that are known to influence voter behaviour include party identification, social background and psychology, lifelong attachment to parties and candidates' or parties' records (Butler and Stokes 1974). With regard to elections in Africa, however, many scholars (Bates 1974:457-484; Horowitz 1985 and 1991; Lonsdale 1994; Chabal & Daloz 1999; Young 2002; Posner 2005) have attributed the voting behaviour of the electorate to ethnicity or what Lonsdale (1994) referred to as 'political tribalism'. Emphasizing the role of identity politics and ethnicity, Horowitz (1985 and 1991) referred to elections in sub-Saharan Africa as ethnic 'censuses'.

As a contribution to the debate over the factors that influence electoral outcomes in Ghana, this chapter examines how manifestos of political parties have influenced their electoral fortunes. The paper uses the manifestos of the two dominant parties in Ghana's Fourth Republic – the National Democratic Congress

(NDC) and the New Patriotic Party (NPP) – as case studies. The emphasis on manifestos is important because they have played an important role in elections all over the world (Caplan 2007 and Kiewiet & Mattozzi 2008:313-326). To win an election political parties prepare manifestos and espouse ideologies. Manifestos are documents outlining in more or less detail the policies or programmes a party proposes to pursue if elected to power, while ideologies are more or less coherent sets of ideas that provide the basis for some kind of organized political action. The policies and programmes contain the blueprint for the development strategy the party will pursue if it wins power. Elections are like a political market[2] with several competitors in which voters are in a position to demand the delivery of certain goods mainly social welfare policies and programmes, while politicians are under pressure to provide some kind of policy responses to such requests, if they are to win elections. To operate in the political market, one needs to have political products that include personalities, manifestos, ideology, past performance, and reliability. As a key political product, therefore, manifestos create the platform for political parties and politicians, who are looking for the mandate, particularly in poor democracies such as Ghana, to envision responses to social needs and demands from the electorate (see, for example, Lake and Baum 2001:587-621; de Mesquita, Morrow, Silverson and Smith 2002:559-590; Henneberg 2004). In other words, manifestos are generally responses to popular demands that seek to articulate societal issues and challenges and how to overcome them.

This chapter is divided into seven parts. Part one defines agenda setting, which serves as our framework, because we regard manifestos as important agenda drivers. Part two is devoted to understanding the Ghanaian context. Part three gives a brief review of the literature on elections in Ghana. Part four is devoted to the history of elections and manifestos with special reference to the 1951 manifestos of the Convention People's Party (CPP) and the United Gold Coast Convention (UGCC). As the maiden manifestos in modern Ghanaian politics, they bequeathed a legacy for subsequent manifestos. Part five examines the manifestos of the NDC and NPP in the Fourth Republic following our discussion of the institutional context and the ideologies underlying these manifestos; the analysis focuses on a comparison of the two manifestos. Part six analyses the interests of societal actors; the debates by presidential candidates; the campaigns; and finally the influence of manifestos on the electorate. Part seven summarises the lessons learned from this analysis.

Agenda-setting Defined

Agenda-setting is about the recognition of a problem on the part of government (Kingdon 1984). In the words of Cobb, Ross and Ross (1976:126), agenda-setting is the 'process by which demands of various groups in the population are translated into items vying for the serious attention of public officials'. Problem recognition is essentially a socially constructed process. It involves definitions of normalcy and what constitutes an undesirable deviation from the norm. Hence problem recognition is not a mechanical process, but a sociological one that sets the 'frames' within which governments operate and consider to be of critical importance. The 'problems' that are the subject of agenda setting are constructed in the realm of public and private discourses (Rochefort and Cobb 1993; Spector and Kitsuse 1987). As Edelman (1988:12-13) has argued:

> Problems come into discourse and therefore into existence as reinforcements of ideologies, not simply because they are there or because they are important for well-being. They signify who are virtuous and useful and who are dangerous and inadequate, which actions will be rewarded and which penalized. They constitute people as subjects with particular kinds of aspirations, self-concepts, and fears, and they create beliefs about the relative importance of events and objects. They are critical in determining who exercise authority and who accept it. They construct areas of immunity from concern because those areas are not seen as problems. Like leaders and enemies, they define the contours of the social world, not in the same way for everyone, but in the light of the diverse situations from which people respond to the political spectacle.

These frames, of course, are not always widely, or as strongly, held by all the important policy actors, meaning that the agenda-setting process is very often one in which there is a clash of frames (Bleich 2002). The resolution of this conflict is related more to the abilities and resources of competing actors than to the elegance or purity of the ideas they hold (Surel 2000).

The idea that agenda-setting is a process in which policy makers react to objective conditions in a rational manner is misleading. Rather, policy makers are involved in the same discourses as the public and in the manipulation of the signs, sets and scenes of a political play or theatre. According to the script of these ideological discourses, different groups of policy actors are involved and different outcomes prescribed in the agenda-setting process (Muntigl 2002). According to this view, then, the agenda of politics or policy making is created out of the history, traditions, attitudes and beliefs of a people encapsulated and codified in terms of its political discourse. Symbols and statistics, both real and fabricated, are used to back up one's preferred understanding of the causes of the problem. Ancient and contemporary symbols are discovered or created to make one's case. Convenient statistics are put together to bolster one's case. In such statistics, one finds what one is looking for (Howlett and Ramesh 2003). Hence to understand agenda-setting, it is important for us to comprehend how demands for a policy are made by individuals and/or groups and responded to by government, and vice versa. In addition, the conditions must be understood under which these demands emerge and are articulated in prevailing policy discourses. Towards this end, we need to understand the material interests of social and state actors as well as the institutional and ideological contexts in which they operate (Spector and Kitsuse 1987; Thompson 1990).

Furthermore, it should be noted that the agenda of politics or policy making also includes the contemporary socio-economic and political conditions; the nature and level of education of that society, and the role of organic intellectuals; the socio-psychological, emotional and kinship interests as well as history and class, feelings, attitudes, and emotions (Scheufele & Tewksbury, 2007; McCombs 2005; Gramsci 1982). Gramsci (1982:9), for instance, discussed the role of intellectuals in society. Even though he stated that all men are intellectuals, in that all have intellectual and rational faculties, he at the same time pointed out that not all men have the social function as intellectuals. He saw modern intellectuals not as talkers, but as practically-minded directors and organizers who produced hegemony by means of ideological apparatuses such as education and the media.

Understanding the Ghanaian Context

In 1957, Ghana became the first country in colonial Africa to gain independence from Britain. It is considered one of the most successful democracies in Africa and has one of the continent's fastest growing economies, which is supported by the discovery of oil in commercial quantities. It is one of the few countries in Africa that has had significant experiences with democratic political life. It was governed under a democratic regime during the period of internal self-rule 1951-1957, during the early post-independence period 1957-1960 before succumbing to one-party rule, and during two brief renewals of civilian, constitutional rule in October 1969-January 1972 and September 1979-December 1981 (see Table 1). Ghana has experienced prolonged military rule[3] under the National Liberation Council (NLC) in February 1966-October 1969, the National Redemption Council/Supreme Military Council (NRC/SMC) in January 1972-June 1979, the Armed Forces Revolutionary Council (AFRC) in June 1979-September 1979 and the Provisional National Defence Council (PNDC), December 1981-January 1993 (see Table 1). Despite prolonged periods of military rule, there were important social and political forces embedded in the fabric of Ghanaian society that believed deeply in democratic government (Chazan 1983).

Table 4.1: Post-Independence Governments and Constitutions in Ghana, 1957 to Date

Year	Event	Basic Law	Legislative Body	Executive Body
1957	Independence (Convention People'sParty Government)	Independence Constitution	Parliament	Queen + Prime Minister + Cabinet

1960 (Jan-June)	Constituent Assembly (CPP Government)	Independence Constitution	Constituent Assembly	Queen + Prime Minister + Cabinet
1960 (1st July 1960)	1st Republic (CPP Government)	1st Republican Constitution	Parliament	President + Cabinet
1966 (24th February)	1st coup d'etat (NLC Government)	NLC (Establishment Proclamation)	National Liberation Council (NLC)	National Liberation Council (NLC)
1969 (August)	2nd Republic (Progress Party Government	2nd Republican Constitution	Parliament	President + Prime Minister + Cabinet
1972 (13th January)	2nd coup d'etat (NRC Government)	NRC (Establishment Proclamation)	National Redemption Council (NRC)	National Redemption Council (NRC)
1975	Revised composition and renaming of the NRC	SMC (Establishment Proclamation)	Supreme Military Council (SMC)	Supreme Military Council (SMC)
1978 (July)	Palace coup	SMC (Establishment Proclamation)	Supreme Military Council (SMC)	Supreme Military Council (SMC)
1979 (4th June)	Military Uprising (3rd coup d'etat) AFRC Government	AFRC (Establishment Proclamation)	Armed Forces Revolutionary Council (AFRC)	Armed Forces Revolutionary Council (AFRC
1979 (24th September)	3rd Republic (PNP Government)	3rd Republican Constitution	Parliament	President + Cabinet
1981 (31st December)	4th coup d'etat) PNDC Government	PNDC (Establishment Proclamation)	Provisional National Defence Council (PNDC)	Provisional National Defence Council (PNDC)
1993 (7th January)	4th Republic (NDC Government)	4th Republican Constitution	1st Parliament of the 4th Republic	President + Cabinet
1997 (7th January)	4th Republic (NDC Government)	4th Republican Constitution	2nd Parliament of the 4th Republic	President + Cabinet
2001 (7th January)	4th Republic (NPP Government)	4th Republican Constitution	3rd Parliament of the 4th Republic	President + Cabinet
2005 (7th January)	4th Republic (NPP Government)	4th Republican Constitution	4th Parliament of the 4th Republic	President + Cabinet

2009 (7th January)	4th Republic (NDC Government)	4th Republican Constitution	5th Parliament of the 4th Republic	President + Cabinet
2012 (24th July)	President John Mills dies in office. Succeeded by Vice President Mahama	4th Republican Constitution	5th Parliament of the 4th Republic	President + Cabinet
2013 (7th January)	4th Republic (NDC Government)	4th Republican Constitution	6th Parliament of the 4th Republic	President + Cabinet

Source: Institute of Economic Affairs (IEA) 2008. 'Democracy Consolidation Strategy Paper' *An Issue Paper*, June 2008 and updated by the author to cover the period 2012-2013.

Since the establishment of the Fourth Republic in 1992, majority control in parliament has shifted between the NDC and NPP parties. Other parties, such as the People's National Convention (PNC) and Convention People's Party (CPP), have won a small number of seats in each election. While the NPP party is viewed as more conservative and the NDC is socially progressive, they both strongly advocate issues such as better education, modernized agriculture, good governance, basic service delivery and equitable distribution of oil revenue. These and many other issues were prominent in the 2012 election and proved to be crucial in the closely contested race.

Elections and Manifestos in Ghana's Politics

Since independence, there have been several studies on elections in Ghana (including Gyimah-Boadi 1994:75-86 and 1997:78-91; Ayee (ed.) 2001a and 2001b; Ohman 1999:1-43 and 2002; Apter 1963 and Austin 1964). These studies have focused largely on the outcomes and challenges of the elections, voter alignments, ethnicity, legal and institutional frameworks, campaign issues, party financing and abuse of incumbency, elite consensus, candidates' selection, election management, managing conflicts, and the transition to and consolidation of democracy. A few have argued that manifestos are without political significance. For instance, Dunn has stated that 'policy' programmes (or manifestos) and ideologies have played a strikingly insignificant role in shaping voters' choice' (Dunn 1975:191). Chazan, in a similar tone, emphasizes that 'once issues were set, politicization during elections tended to occur around social groups, local interest, and personalities and not around contents' (Chazan 1983:67). This chapter contributes to the debate on the influence of manifestos on the electoral fortunes. It focuses on the two main political parties that have been in government under the Fourth Republic, namely, the National Democratic Congress (NDC) and the New Patriotic Party (NPP).

Elections and manifestos have been part of government and politics in Ghana just before and after independence and remain so. This is evidenced by the number of both national and local government elections, by-elections, plebiscite and referenda held and the manifestos that have been formulated (see Table 2). The interest in and enthusiasm for elections may be attributed to the faith of Ghanaians in elections as a key means of promoting socio-economic development and improvement in their standard of living.

Table 4.2: Number of National and Local Elections and Referenda, 1951-2008

Period	National Elections	Local Elections	Referenda/Plebiscites
Pre-independence	3 (1951; 1954; 1956)	–	1 (1956) – Trust Territory of Trans-Volta Togoland (for union or separation)
Post-independence	9 (1965; 1969; 1979 & run-off; 1992; 1996; 2000 and run-off; 2004, 2008 and run-off; 2012)	8 (1958; 1978; 1988/89; 1994; 1998; 2002; 2006; 2010)	4 (1960 – 3 days; electorate voted twice; one for or against the draft constitutional proposals and again for Nkrumah or Danquah; 1964 - 2 amendments to the 1960 constitution; 1978; 1992)
Total	12 & 3 run-offs	8	5

Source: Compiled by the author

The table shows that since 1951, Ghana has had a total of 12 national or general elections and three presidential run-offs, in 1979, 2000 and 2008; 8 local elections and 5 referenda or plebiscites[4]. The first elections, which were held in 1951, that is, before independence in 1957, were contested by the Convention People's Party (CPP), the United Gold Coast Convention (UGCC) and independent candidates. The CPP and UGCC produced what have become the first manifestos[5] in Ghanaian elections; they were entitled, 'Towards the Goal' and 'Plan for the Nation' respectively (see Boxes 1 and 2). The initial elections, from 1951 to 1957, were very critical as their materiality, morality and ideologies derived from anti-colonialism and Pan-Africanism.

Box 4.1: CPP Manifesto 1951: 'Towards the Goal'

> 1. **Constitutional:** The Coussey Committee let the country down by prolonging white imperialism. The CPP will fight for self-government NOW.

2. **Political:** An upper house of the Legislature, known as the Senate, shall be created for the Chiefs. Universal adult suffrage at the age of 21. Direct elections with no property or residential qualifications for candidates.

3. **Economic:** A five-year Economic Plan... (i) Immediate materialization of the Volta hydro-electric scheme; (ii) Railway lines to be doubled and extended; (iii) Roads to be modernized and extended; (iv) Canals to join rivers; (v) Progressive mechanization of agriculture; (vi) Special attention will be given to the swollen shoot disease; farmers will be given control of the Cocoa Industry Board funds; (vii) Industrialization will be carried out with all energy.

4. **Social:** Education: (i) a unified system of free compulsory elementary, secondary and technical education up to 16 years of age; (ii) The University College to be brought up to university status; (iii) A planned campaign to abolish illiteracy.

5. **Social:** Family Assistance: (i) A free national health service; (ii) A high standard housing programme; (iii) A piped-water supply in all parts of the country; (iv) A national insurance scheme.

Source: Austin, *Politics in Ghana, 1946-1960*, p. 130.

Box 4.2: UGCC Manifesto 1951: 'Plan for the Nation'

1. **Constitutional:** The present constitution is a watered-down version of the Coussey recommendations; it is 'a step, but not our last step, in the struggle for self-government', which must be achieved 'by all legitimate and constitutional means'.

2. **Political:** The chiefs must, in spite of themselves, be saved for the Gold Coast, by removing the Governor's power to grant or withdraw recognition from Chiefs recognized by their people.

Remove civil servants from the top level of 'field administration' and place the character and structure of the civil service under the control of the Assembly. Civil servants must cease to be the 'Civil Masters' of the country.

3. **Economic:** A Ten-Point Programme – to ensure that the optimum diffusion of private enterprise and ownership of property shall be developed alongside the maximum attainment of personal liberty, within the framework of the WELFARE STATE: (i) an end to Government's extravagant spending and appointments, and to the lowering of the dignity of the Chiefs; (ii) An end to the political officers system and to the 'Go-Slow' policy in education; (iii) A reduction in the importation of light manufactured goods, which should be manufactured locally under a five-year plan; (iv) A national bank; (v) An

active and adequate road building programme; (vi) Scholarships for industrial and technological training to show results, within five years; (vii) The raising of the standard of living, improvements in housing, water supply, primary education, health, lighting, clinics, literacy and culture; (viii) The safeguarding of agriculture and land products, a rationalized cocoa industry, diversified agriculture, development of the Volta and of base metals; (ix) Development of the rural life of the people.

Source: Austin, *Politics in Ghana, 1946-1960,* p. 136.

A number of lessons can be drawn from these two early manifestos, which have influenced subsequent manifestos. First, they were concerned with challenges in the political, social and economic sectors that the political parties pledged to address if voted to power. Since then successive manifestos have emulated this format. For instance, the areas of infrastructure (good roads and railways), industrialization, mechanized agriculture and service provision in education, water and health care delivery have engaged the attention of all manifestos in subsequent elections. Secondly, as we shall see in subsequent manifestos, there is little to choose between the two manifestos. In the words of Austin (1964:138), 'in general, there was very little difference (except in the language used) between the CPP 'Goal' and the UGCC 'Plan'.' Thirdly, the two manifestos made promises that could not be fulfilled given the resources and the political climate at the time. For instance, according to Bourett (1959:175), the CPP manifesto 'made sweeping promises – industrialization, jobs for all, free primary education, national health service, the equal opportunity of a socialist state... Stress was laid on materialistic advantages and there was no mistaking the secular spirit embodied in the slogan 'Seek ye first the political kingdom and all things will be added to it'.'

Fourthly, even though, they were designed to draw the electorate to the two parties and brighten their chances of winning the 1951 elections, they 'blended emotion with self-interest ... and promised immediate material benefits' (Austin 1964:131). In other words, the manifestos showed the demand, or claim-making interests of both the politicians and voters. Hence, the argument that agendas are socially constructed. The CPP's manifesto, for instance, promised a 'return to a market price for kerosene, cloth, matches, rice, yam, plantain, and tinned fish, as to enable the ordinary man to live within his income while he enjoined the amenities of pipe-borne water, free schooling, cheap houses, smooth roads, and more hospitals' (Austin 1964:131).

Fifth, the manifestos recognized the problems that faced Ghanaian society and set the agenda for debate and discussion and largely shaped voter behaviour whether rationally or irrationally. Sixth, and very important, there is no evidence that the manifesto gave the CPP its electoral victory when it won 34 of the

38 popularly contested seats. The main reason for the CPP's victory was its nationalist fervour and crusade, the sympathy vote for Nkrumah who was in prison and the weak opposition challenge from the UGCC with its 'half-hearted attempt to compete' and being led by 'elder statesmen of more moderate views who were unwilling to enter the rough and tumble of (Ghanaian) politics' (Austin 1964:144). In other words, the manifesto had little influence on the electorate in the elections. It reveals a reversal of roles. Instead of leading or guiding the people, the manifesto was led by the popular interests. Manifestos did not shape popular attitudes on the anti-colonial struggles but their consequences. This is a very important point that will be revisited later as we examine the manifestos of the NDC and NPP in the Fourth Republic.

It must be noted that 'knife and fork' issues and the provision of basic amenities have been manifesto targets as far back as 1951, and they still formed a large chunk of the political agendas in 2012. This shows that little progress has been made in fulfilling such manifesto promises.

The Constitutional and Institutional Context of Political Party Manifestos in the Fourth Republic

The 1992 Constitution provides the legal and institutional framework for the role of political parties in interest articulation and aggregation. Article 55(3) provides that a political party is 'free to participate in shaping the political will of the people, to disseminate information on political ideas, social and economic programmes of a national character'. In this regard Chapter Six of the Constitution (*The Directive Principles of State Policy*) provides a strategic policy direction to 'guide all citizens, Parliament, the President, the Judiciary, the Council of State, the Cabinet, political parties and all other bodies or persons in applying or interpreting the Constitution for the establishment of a just and free society'. The President is required under this constitutional directive to report to Parliament at least once a year all the 'steps taken to ensure the realization of the policy objectives contained in Chapter Six, and in particular, the realization of basic human rights, a healthy economy, the right to work, the right to good health care and the right to education'. In furtherance of these, the chapter further lists political, economic, social, educational, and cultural objectives which must be fulfilled in addition to the pursuit of international relations, duties and obligations expected of citizens vis-à-vis their exercise and enjoyment of rights and freedoms. Thus Chapter Six – The *Directive Principles of State Policy* – provides the basis for a social contract between the government and the governed. In the words of the Committee of Experts, the Directive Principles are not only the 'core principles around which national, political, social and economic life revolves' but also a 'set of fundamental objectives which a people expect all bodies and persons that make or executive public policy to strive to achieve' as well as a 'barometer which the people could measure the performance of their government. In effect, they provide goals for legislative programmes and a guide for judicial interpretation' (Republic of Ghana 1991:49).

Ghanaian political parties have sought to define the parameters of this social contract through their manifestos. A review of the manifestos of both the NDC and NPP since 1992 shows that even though the manifestos have tried to address some of the political, economic, social, educational and cultural objectives, they do not make direct reference to the *Directive Principles* as their source. In fact, the *Directive Principles* are not mentioned at all in the manifestos and thus linking the two becomes speculative. The result is that when a political party is in government there is little or no reference to the *Directive Principles* while the manifesto is expected to define public policy. As we will see later, political parties have shown poor commitment to fulfilling the objectives of their manifestos.

Furthermore, there is a need to separate intentions from the substantive or practical issues. Frankly, most parts of manifestos are more of intangible promises – or utopia – that are designed to woo the electorate into voting a party into power. In addition, they are written in English with no translation in the local languages. The question therefore remains as to how much they can influence the largely peasant population who constitute the vast majority of Ghanaian voters. Worst of all, the parties do not ensure that ordinary citizens can easily access their manifestos. There is an urgent need to transcend the educated middle class populations and to include the illiterate and semi-illiterate subalterns in the discourse on manifestos.

Ideological Context

In the view of Marx (Marx and Engels 1992) and Antonio Gramsci (1982; 1993), all meaning derives from the relation between practical human activity (or 'praxis') and the 'objective' historical and social processes of which it is a part. According to them, ideas cannot be understood outside their social and historical context, apart from their function and origin. The concepts by which societies or individuals organise their knowledge of the world do not derive primarily from their relation to things (to an objective situation), but rather from the social relations between the users of those concepts. Furthermore, philosophy and science do not 'reflect' reality that is independent of man. Rather, a theory is 'true' when, in any given historical situation, it expresses the real developmental trend in that situation. They conclude that ideology may be regarded as a mask for hiding reality. It is within this context that the ideologies of the political parties in Ghana can be viewed.

Chazan (1983:119) has noted that the 'range of formal political debate in Ghana since the late 1940s has revolved around seemingly opposing poles: the liberal western-oriented one espoused by J.B. Danquah and later by K.A. Busia, and the socialist-nonaligned pole put forward by Kwame Nkrumah and later elaborated by his self-proclaimed apostles'. This observation seems no longer valid in respect of the NDC and NPP since they were formed in 1992. This is because there is no clear ideological difference between them. The NDC regards itself as a social democratic party[6] and its brand of social democracy 'seeks to marry the efficiency of the market and private initiative with the compassion of state intervention to protect the disadvantaged and the marginalized and to ensure optimum production and distributive justice' (NDC Manifesto 2004:xiv). The NPP, on the other hand, is a liberal democratic capitalist party, and seeks to 'liberate the energies of the people for the growth of a property owning democracy in this land, with the right to life, freedom and justice, as the principles to which the Government and laws of the land should be dedicated in order to specifically enrich life, property and liberty of each and every citizen' (Danquah quoted in NPP Manifesto, 2000:i). Despite these declared differences, the two parties are known to follow largely:

> .... the same ideological line both in terms of manifestos and policies – neo-liberal economics and liberal democracy with a huge dose of populism. In fact, they hardly articulate any identifiable ideology on their policy platforms, other than a vague 'developmental ideology' aimed at improving the lot of the people. Moreover, the parties rarely mobilize electoral support on ideological platforms. Their manifestos and campaign messages do not reflect any clear ideological stance. Rhetorical shifts in ideological positions have been largely driven by changes in domestic politics and the contingencies of outmanoeuvring political competitors and dislodging the incumbent (Gyimah-Boadi and Debrah 2008:151-152).

Comparing NDC and NPP Manifestos

The two parties have produced six manifestos each between 1992 and 2012 (see Table 3). Each manifesto has a foreword written by the key functionaries of the two parties. For the NDC, the foreword was written by the chairman and presidential candidate of the party while the founder J.J. Rawlings wrote the message showing his importance and influence in the party. On the other hand, the foreword for the NDC manifesto for the 2012 elections was written by John Mahama, the presidential candidate and leader of the party. This is due to the fallout from the defeat of Nana Konadu Agyeman Rawlings in the presidential primaries, the subsequent formation of the breakaway National Democratic Party to contest the 2012 elections and Rawlings' own criticism of the leadership of the NDC especially under the late President John Mills. Unlike the NDC, the foreword to NPP's manifesto has always been written by its leader and presidential candidate.

Each manifesto focused on the intentions of the parties to promote development, introduce changes and make Ghana a better place for its citizens to enjoy the national 'cake' equitably. Even though the documents include short, medium and long-term plans, the manifestos are largely seen as promises and slogans rather than specific and strategic policy initiatives to be implemented within a four-year term. There is little time spent on how the policies and programmes in the manifestos would be financed, for instance, making each of them a wish list instead of a properly researched set of policy alternatives. This fact notwithstanding, the comprehensive and copious nature of the manifestos is evident in the increased page count over the years, especially from 2000.

Furthermore, the NPP and NDC manifestos of 2000 and 2008 intentionally castigated the policies and programmes of each other while in opposition. For instance, the NPP manifesto of 2000 was intended to bring about 'complete change from the NDC's shameful and depressing record that [had] led Ghana and Ghanaians into poverty and insecurity' (New Patriotic Party 2000:viii). The NPP stated further that Ghana, 'which is blessed so generously with natural and human resources, is still unable to feed itself – all because of the failed policies and confused leadership of the NDC government' (New Patriotic Party 2000:1). On the other hand, the 2008 manifesto of the NDC[7] noted that there was 'more than enough evidence to the fact that under the NPP Government, a whole generation [was] being bequeathed with hopelessness, despair, drugs, immorality and crime' (National Democratic Congress 2008:12) and expressed deep concern at 'the growing inequality and social exclusion in the Ghanaian society since 2001, primarily because of the policies of the NPP government', which the NDC claimed were 'divisive, and…utterly discriminatory' (National Democratic Congress 2008:14).

The manifestos did, however, usefully catalogue the problems and challenges facing the country and how they can be addressed. Some of the key recurring issues covered by the manifestos of both parties between 1992 and 2012, most of which have also featured in the manifestos of other political parties since independence, include the imperative for good governance, economic concerns, employment, the role of the private sector, challenges to agriculture, improving basic service delivery, the decentralisation question, securing peace and stability, fighting the narcotic menace, Ghana's international role and relationships, and the discovery of oil. Other issues include the environment, gender equality, crime, energy and chieftaincy. It is instructive to note that both the CPP and UGCC mentioned chiefs in their manifestos as far back as 1951. For the institution to feature in the manifestos of parties in the Fourth Republic shows its importance in governance at both the national and local levels.

Table 4.3: Main Features of NDC and NPP Manifestos, 1992-2012

Year	Theme: NDC	Theme: NPP	Contents NDC	Contents NPP	Pages NDC	Pages NPP
1992	Continuity and Stability	Development in Freedom	Introduction; The Economy; The Social Contract; Mind Body and Spirit, Security; Ghana and the World	Introduction; Positive Change; The Economy: Building Prosperity for All; The NPP's Policies for Selected Areas of the Economy; Developing and Managing Human Resources; Ghana and the World	36	46
1996	Always for People, Always for Development	Development in Freedom	Introduction; The Economy; The Social Contract; Mind Body and Spirit, Security; Ghana and the World	Introduction; Positive Change; The Economy: Building Prosperity for all; The NPP's Policies for Selected Areas of the Economy; Developing and Managing Human Resources; Ghana and the World	35	46
2000	Spreading the Benefits of Development	Agenda for Positive Change	Introduction; A Moral and Just Society; The Economy; The Social Contract; Mind, Body and Spirit; Security; Ghana and the World	Introduction; The Time for Positive Change is Now; The Economy: Building Prosperity for all; The NPP's Policies for Selected Areas of the Economy; Developing and Managing Human Resources; Ghana and the World	76	48
2004	A Better Ghana	Agenda for Positive Change: Chapter Two	Introduction; the Economy Bases; The Social Sector; A Fair and Just Society; The National Infrastructure; Law; Order and Society; Governance; Chieftaincy and Culture; Foreign Policy; Conclusion	Introduction; Achievements; The Economy: Building Prosperity for All; The NPP's Policies for Selected Areas of the Economy; Developing and Managing Human Resources; Ghana and the World	103	51

2008	A Better Ghana: Investing in People, Jobs and the Economy	Moving Ghana Forward: Building a Modern Ghana	Introduction; Governance; Economy; Investing in People; Infrastructure for Growth; Conclusion	Introduction; Achievements – Promise Delivered; Strengthening our Democracy; Law and Order; Structural Transformation of the Economy; Modernizing our Society; Regional and Continental Integration	97	64
2012	Advancing the Better Ghana Agenda: Jobs, Stability and Development	Transforming Lives, Transforming Ghana Building a Free, Fair and Prosperous Society: A Programme of Transformation	Theme 1: Putting People First; Theme 2: A Strong and Resilient Economy; Theme 3: Expanding Infrastructure; Theme 4: Transparent and Accountable Governance	Chapter 1: Building the Foundation for a Free and Fair Society; Chapter 2: Economic Transformation, Prosperity and Job Creation; Chapter 3: Public Investment to Provide Basic Amenities and Support Job Creation; Chapter 4: A Disciplined and Safe Society; Chapter 5: Creating Opportunities and Promoting Enterprise; Chapter 6: Ghana in a Wider World; Chapter 7: Moving Ghana Forward Together	76	116

Source: Compiled by the author.

Interests of Societal Actors

Social forces engaged in the political process showed interest in the manifestos of the political parties. For instance, the Institute of Economic Affairs (IEA) created a platform for presidential candidates to reach out to the electorate, and clarify and market their manifestos when it organized presidential debates in 2000, 2004, 2008 and 2012 and the evening 'Encounters'. It also provided funding for the printing of their manifestos in 2008 and 2012, which was duly acknowledged by the parties. There is, however, no evidence to show that the IEA's support did influence the content of the manifestos.

A more structured approach of societal actors' interest in the manifestos was manifested in April 2008. The Private Enterprise Foundation (PEF) organized a forum at which representatives of the various private sector associations interacted with the presidential candidates of the parties. The manifestos were to be enriched by the suggestions, ideas, concerns and statements emanating from the deliberations. After the launching of the manifestos by the parties in June and July, the PEF once again, with support from the Konrad-Adenauer Stiftung, organized a meeting for representatives of the private sector and political parties to deliberate more specifically on the policy initiatives as captured in the published manifestos of political parties and their expected impact on the productive sector of the economy. A similar meeting with the presidential candidates in the 2012 elections was held by the Association of Ghana Industries (AGI) at which the AGI laid out their vision for the private sector. Even though it is difficult to assess the real impact of such interactions between presidential candidates and business interests on their manifestos, the mere fact that they were consulted shows more goodwill and commitment on the part of the political parties to make the private sector participate in the discourses on manifesto formation than there used to be.

The sensitivity of the manifestos to gender equality, the disabled and youth empowerment arose from inputs and lobbying by these social forces. For instance, the publication of the Women's Manifesto for Ghana in April 2004 led to more space being devoted to gender issues in the manifestos in 2008 and 2012. For instance, in its 2008 manifesto the NDC not only accepted the objectives of the Women's Manifesto based on the 'achievement of gender equality and equity in national development' and promised to 'work with the sponsors of the Manifesto to incorporate its key demands in the NDC's 'Affirmative Action Policy for Women' document, first issued in 1999 which is to be revised and implemented upon assuming office in 2009' (National Democratic Congress 2008:75).

Influence of Manifestos on the Electorate

As pointed out above, the idea that manifestos influence the fortunes of political parties is based on a model of voting behaviour of voter rationality, insofar as it suggests that voters select parties on the basis of policies and issues and the benefits that are likely to accrue to them when the parties and their candidates come to power[8]. This line of argument has been questioned by other scholars who have pointed out that voters are not always the rational or well informed creatures that the doctrine of mandate suggests[9]. They can be influenced by a range of 'irrational' factors such as the personalities of the leaders, the images of the parties, habitual allegiances and social background, conditioning and psychology and identity politics and ethnicity especially in Africa (see for example, Bates 1974:457-484; Chabal & Daloz 1999; Horowitz 1985 and 1991; Joyce 1996; Young 1986:421-495; Oelbaum 2004:242-273.

Furthermore, we have noted that opinions differ on the influence of manifestos on the Ghanaian electorate. The first viewpoint, which is supported by the literature on Ghanaian politics, suggests that manifestos have little influence on the electorate in elections. Ghanaians have voted largely on party lines with varied reasons. Some voted based on the ideological inclinations of the parties they support whereas a large number voted for parties based on ethnocentric nuances associated with the party; ethnic identification either with the leader, some top leaders around the centre of power, personalities, party origin, local factors and last minute campaign tactics particularly directed to floating voters (for some of the reasons see for example, Asante 2006; Frempong 2001; Ayee 2005:82-100; Ayee 2008:185-214; Arthur 2000:34-58; Lindberg & Morrison 2005:565-586; Gyimah-Boadi & Debrah 2008; and Gyimah-Boadi & Asante 2006).

One major reason for the perceived poor influence of manifestos on the electorate is that voters doubted the credibility of their manifestos as promises made in previous elections were not fulfilled by the parties when it was in power. This led the Moderator of the Presbyterian Church to urge all the presidential candidates in the 2008 elections to 'faithfully keep their promises'[10], and the then running mate of the NDC and currently the President, John Mahama to caution all politicians to 'avoid empty promises they have made which have led to all politicians to be branded as people who make promises and do not deliver them. It is about time we change that trend to gain the confidence of the people'[11]. This failure of politicians to honour manifesto or electoral promises has been confirmed by the surveys conducted by the Department of Political Science, University of Ghana in 2000 and 2004 which showed the inability of the two parties in power to deliver on their electoral promises and manifesto objectives (Ayee 2001a;b and Boafo-Arthur 2006). This Ghanaian experience reflects the political agency problem whereby voters cannot demand accountability from their elected representatives, giving politicians ample political scope to pursue their personal agenda rather than that of their constituents (Jonah 1998).

However the second viewpoint, which is supported by this writer, acknowledges the influence of manifestos on the electorate and emphasizes that they cannot be easily ignored given that in every elections, political parties have developed manifestos and a large chunk of their campaign messages are based on them. Accordingly, like in any market environment, the campaign message that the parties send out must be clear, because it is a political product in a competitive political market designed to attract voters and win their votes. Clarity in the message of 'Positive Change', for instance, was one of the reasons that won the elections for the NPP in 2000 in contrast to the NDC's message of 'Spreading the Benefits of Development' (Ayee 2002:148-174 and 2008; Boafo-Arthur 2006; Gyimah-Boadi 2001:103-117). Similarly, the NDC's 'I care for you' manifesto message and making poverty reduction the main focus of its campaign promises, touting investment in people, jobs, the economy and making government more transparent and accountable were part of its trump card in the 2008 elections (Arthur 2009:34-58 and Daddieh 2009:642-647). The electorate saw this message more appealing and deliverable than the NPP's message which fought the elections on its record of eight years in office and focused on four thematic areas, namely, strengthening the country's democracy, structural transformation of the economy and industrialization, regional and continental integration and the modernization of Ghanaian society (Gyimah-Boadi 2009:138-152; Amoah 2009:12-21; Arthur 2009:34-58; Daddieh 2009:642-647; Whitfield 2009:621-641). Similarly, the NDC won the 2012 elections because the majority of the electorate thought it had a feasible and more attractive manifesto while the NPP's was considered complex and impossible to achieve.

Voting patterns in Ghana show that the influence of manifestos cannot be simply ignored because they contained policies and programmes of the parties that were being marketed to the electorate through campaigns, advertisements and debates by presidential candidates. Ayee, for instance, has pointed out that voting patterns in Ghana since 1992 have also been influenced by the quality of governance and poverty levels and the ideologies and programmes of the parties (Ayee 2008:185-214). Similarly, Arthur has emphasized that the 'characterization of ethnicity as the basis of electoral behaviour in Ghana is simplistic: other factors, such as perceived improvements in their socio-economic lot, issues concerning increased corruption, and other electoral messages that on the surface might appear ethnicity-driven, greatly influence the choices that Ghanaian voters have been making since 1992' (Arthur 2009:55). Alabi has also shown that manifestos as political products are salient in determining political marketing outcomes or fortunes of political parties in Ghana in addition to ethnicity, personality, perceived party image or identity of the political party and communication (Alabi 2007:39-52). Certainly, ethnicity only partly explains the voting behaviour of Ghanaians. In spite of the links that the Volta and Ashanti regions have with the NDC and NPP respectively, there is a number of areas in the country where competition is real and often close. Between the 1996 and the 2008 parliamentary elections, for example, five regions out of ten, namely, Greater Accra, Central, Western, Eastern and Brong-Ahafo, swung at least once from one party to the other (Arthur 2009 and Whitfield 2009). It is instructive to note that issues over poverty, governance, ethnicity, ideologies, socio-economic lots, and corruption were all contained in the manifestos of the parties thus making them issue-based and therefore influencing in one way or the other the electoral fortunes of the political parties. In the 2012 elections, for example, the NDC won eight regions while the NPP won the remaining two regions.

That policies and programmes in the manifestos influenced voting patterns and voter motivations were amply demonstrated in the 2008 and 2012 elections in Ghana. Some of the key issues include a strong and effective leadership, fighting corruption, education, agriculture, security and safety, unemployment, the economy, the drug menace, enforcement of sanctions, general conditions of living in the country and the record of the performance of the two governments, namely, the NPP and NDC, which were issues contained in the manifestos. For specific regions such as Greater Accra, the main issue was the return of land which was taken over by governments and which was not being used for the purpose for which it was acquired but was sold to some public officials, while in the coastal regions of Central and Western regions, the issue was the inability of the government to deal with foreign fishing trawlers operating in the shores of Ghana, therefore depriving local fisherman of their means of livelihood, and also the irregular supply of the pre-mix fuel used by fishermen (Gyimah-Boadi 2009:138-152; Arthur 2009:34-58; Daddieh 2009:642-647; Whitfield 2009:621-641). Even though these specific issues were not mentioned in the manifestos of the two parties, there was provision for addressing rural development and promoting good governance. In spite of undertaking popular policies such as the national health insurance policy, free health care for pregnant women and the capitation grant, the basic school feeding programme, the incumbent New Patriotic Party (NPP) government lost the elections because the opposition National Democratic Congress (NDC) campaign machinery used its manifesto to paint the government as being responsible for domestic economic mismanagement and high youth unemployment in large urban areas (Gyimah-Boadi 2009:138-152; Arthur 2009:34-58; Daddieh 2009:642-647; Whitfield 2009:621-641).

The elections were bitterly fought and the results show that they were a close match between the NPP's Nana Akufo-Addo and the NDC's John Atta Mills. Akufo-Addo had 49.13 per cent while Atta Mills had 47.92 per cent, a difference of 1.21 per cent (see Table 4). None of the candidates therefore secured the 50+1 constitutional requirement to win the presidency. Akufo-Addo needed an additional 0.88 per cent to avoid a run-off. In the parliamentary elections, the NPP lost 21 seats to the opposition NDC (see Table 4) and won seats in only three of the ten regions of Ghana. The NDC won the remaining seven regions.

The presidential run-off took place on 28 December 2008. The NPP lost because the majority of Ghanaians wanted a change. They had seen eight years of the NPP in power and even though the government had done well and brought some real improvements in the economy and in the provision of social services such as health, education and general infrastructure, most voters continued to complain that life was hard and that they could not see the 'prosperity' the government talked about in their pockets as there were not enough jobs to go around (Gyimah-Boadi 2009:138-152; Arthur 2009:34-58; Daddieh 2009:642-647; Whitfield 2009:621-641).

In the December 2012 presidential elections, the NPP's candidate, Nana Akufo-Addo lost again to the NDC's candidate, John Mahama, who, as the then Vice-President, had assumed the position of President after the tragic death in office of President John Atta Mills on 24th July, 2012. This time round there was no run-off as Mahama secured the 50+1 constitutional requirement to win the presidency (see Table 6). The NDC also won the parliamentary elections which were held the same day. Of the 275 seats, the NDC won 148 seats while the NPP won 123 seats. The PNC won one seat, while independent candidates won three seats (see Table 5).

Is there a link between the manifesto of the NDC and its electoral victory in 2008 and 2012? This is a difficult question. However, the fact that the NDC won based on its campaign slogan of 'Change for a Better Ghana', and 'Advancing the Better Ghana Agenda' in 2008 and 2012 respectively shows that the influence of manifestos in elections should not be ignored. The 'Change for a Better Ghana' agenda by the NDC as contained in its manifestos referred to policies and programmes to deal with corruption, the economy, security, employment, education, agriculture, energy, decentralization and infrastructure development. However, the NDC's victory may not be regarded as an endorsement of its manifestos by the electorate but rather the logical manifestation of manifestos as political products in a competitive political market and the arena for articulating policies and programmes on major national issues and challenges and for which the electorate were being asked to compare the NDC with the NPP and to hold them accountable should they win the elections (Gyimah-Boadi 2009:138-152; Amoah 2009:12-21; Arthur 2009:34-58).

Table 4.4: The 7 December 2008 Presidential Elections Results

Party	Name of Candidate	Votes Received	% of Votes Received
New Patriotic Party (NPP)	Nana Akufo-Addo	4,159,439	49.13
National Democratic Congress (NDC)	John Atta Mills	4,056,634	47.92
Convention People's Party (CPP)	Papa Kwesi Nduom	113,494	1.34
People's National Convention (PNC)	Edward Mahama	73,494	0.87
Democratic Freedom Party (DFP)	Emmanuel Ansah-Antwi	27,889	0.56
INDEPENDENT	Kwesi Amoafo-Yeboah	19,342	0.33
Democratic People's Party (DPP)	T.N.Ward-Brew	8,653	0.10
Reformed Patriotic Democrats (RPD)	Kwabena Adjei	6,889	0.08

Source: Electoral Commission of Ghana

Table 4.5: Parliamentary Seats of Parties, 1996-2012

Parties	Number of Seats (1996)	Number of Seats (2000)	Number of Seats (2004)	Number of Seats (2008)	Number of Seats (2012)
NDC	133	89	94	115	148
NPP	61	103	128	108	123
CPP	5	1	3	1	-

PNC	1	3	4	2	1
Independent	-	4	1	4	3
Total	**200**	**200**	**230***	**230**	**275**

Source: Electoral Commission of Ghana

*The number of parliamentary seats was increased in 2004 from 200 to 230 and then to 275 in 2012.

Table 4.6: 2012 Presidential Election Results

Candidates	Votes	Vote Share
John Mahama	5,573,572	50.63
Nana Akufo-Addo	5,263,286	47.81
Paa Kwesi Nduom	64,267	47.81
Henry Herbert Lartey	38,250	0.35
Hassan Ayariga	24,621	0.22
Dr Abu Sakara	15,156	0.14
Jacob Osei Yeboah	15,156	0.14
Kwasi Addai	8,909	0.08

Realizing Manifesto Objectives/Targets

To enable both the NDC and the NPP to achieve the objectives of their manifestos, they formulated development plans and strategies when they won power. The NDC's strategies were contained in Vision 2020: The First Step: 1996-2000 and the First Medium-Term Development Plan, 1997-2000. The NPP, on the other hand, adopted the Highly Indebted Poor Countries (HIPC) initiative in 2001 and published the Ghana Poverty Reduction Strategy, 2003-2005 and the Growth and Poverty Reduction Strategy, 2006-2009. The extent to which their manifesto objectives were realized can be gleaned from the State of the Nation Address when they were in power. For the NDC, its achievements included the following: (i) an improved macro-economic environment characterized by growth, savings and investment; (ii) an expanded and improved national infrastructure, especially in roads, port rehabilitation, electricity generation and distribution especially in the rural areas, and a vastly improved radio and telecommunications network; (iii) the restoration of incentives for exports through the abolition of import licensing and liberalization of the foreign exchange regime, the establishment of the export retention scheme and the introduction of the export finance scheme; (iv) a solid health infrastructure with a network of teaching, regional and district hospitals and health centres, and a pilot health insurance project; (v) a more reliable water delivery and sanitation system that had appropriately distinguished between the water needs of urban and rural dwellers together with systems to reflect those needs; (vi) the introduction of the Ghana Education Trust Fund (GETFund) to support the financing of education and education-related expenditure; (vii) an agricultural policy and programme that had resulted in the acclamation of Ghana's Food Production Index of 148% as 'the third largest achievement on record after Jordan (157%) and China (156%)', according to the World Bank's 1999-2000 Development Report; (viii) the introduction of the Minerals and Mining Act in 2006 with improved incentives; (ix) a lowering and harmonization of tariffs and special taxes and rationalization of the public sector through divestiture and the introduction and monitoring of performance benchmarks; (x) the empowerment of local communities through the introduction of a decentralized local government system and the District Assemblies Common Fund (NDC Manifesto 2004).

The NPP, on the other hand, took refuge in the following legacy: (i) bringing back the dignity of the Presidency; (ii) an internationally recognized good governance regime which has enlarged the freedoms of the individual citizen, institutions and the press through the repeal of the Criminal Libel Law; (iii) an enlarged mechanism of representative government through the institution of the People's Assembly concept whereby the President met the people and took questions and queries from the public; (iv) passing of the Procurement Act, Whistleblower Act and other legal instruments to ensure public accountability and tackle corruption; (v) earning US$547 million from the US government through the Millennium Challenge Account because of good governance; (vi) an increase of the District Assemblies Common Fund from 5 per cent to 7.5 per cent; (vii) in nominal GDP terms, the economy grew from US$3.9 billion in 2000 to US$16.3 billion in 2008 while per capita income rose from US$300 in 2000 to US$600 in 2008; (vi) the introduction of the National Youth Employment Programme in 2004 which created 108,000 jobs; (vii) the introduction of the National Health Insurance Scheme in 2003 to replace the 'cash-and-carry' system, School Feeding Programme, Capitation Grant and a Metro Bus System; (viii) the creation of the Ministries of Women and Children Affairs, and Public Sector Reform Programme (NPP Manifesto 2008).

Similarly, for the 2012 elections, the NDC recounted its achievements. According to the manifesto of the party, the government made significant progress in attaining and ensuring that Ghana would become a middle-income country for the first time in the history of the country. In addition to this, the government maintained a sustainable rate of growth rate and reduced inflation to a single digit. There were also robust public and private policies and programmes that had successfully laid the foundation for sustained prosperity. The manifesto promised to build on these achievements through the following strategies: (i) to deepen and diversify economic performance for the provision of basic human needs;

(ii) to decentralize governance for citizens access to resources and to demand accountability for services; (iii) to develop infrastructure to accelerate and transform Ghana into a full middle-income status; (iv) to modernize agriculture through the promotion of partnership between private agricultural investors and peasant smallholders in a manner that will introduce capital, technology and expand local and international access; and (v) to expand educational assets to provide equitable access for every child to enter and complete basic education and enter and complete secondary school (NDC 2012).

The NPP, on the other hand, reiterated that its eight-year rule from 2001-2008 had brought relief, dignity, hope and promise to many Ghanaians. It promised to extend free education to the Senior High School level, build public universities in regions without one and raise the quality of education at all levels with more and better facilities, teaching and equipment. It castigated the rule of the NDC as 'four wasted years' and one which had made Ghanaians live in desperate and trying times, and promised to replace despair with hope, and promise where the NDC bequeathed 'helplessness, desolation and hardships' (NPP 2012:xiii-ix). It emphasized the retrogression under NDC rule which lacked purpose with an unprecedented weak, bungling inept leadership, backsliding economy, rising cost of living, falling standard of education, collapsing healthcare and unprecedented corruption being the order of the day (NPP 2012).

Notwithstanding these modest achievements by the parties while in government, the realization of manifesto objectives in eight years seems to be an uphill task for them and largely contributed to the two parties being in and out of government in the election cycle. An examination of the 2008 manifestos of the NDC and NPP shows that most of the manifesto objectives of previous elections were not achieved; they were 'recycled' into their 2008 manifestos. They include areas such as poverty (Ghana ranks 11th out of 45 sub-Saharan African countries on the Human Development Index), inequality, inequitable distribution of national resources, poor revenue mobilization, ethnicity, corruption, unemployment, slow pace of industrialization and mechanization of agriculture, inadequate diversification of the economy, reliance on external donors to finance about 40% of the annual budget, grossly inadequate public sector wages and salaries resulting sometimes in worker unrest, and the generally slow progress in achieving economic prosperity and the eight Millennium Development Goals[12] – all of which have sought to undermine the legitimacy of the parties while they were in government and contributed to their defeat: the NDC in 2000 and the NPP in 2008 (Ayee 2009).

As a result of the inability of governments to improve their standards of living since independence in 1957, some Ghanaians, especially those in the rural areas, have become more and more cynical about politics (for a good overview see Daddieh 2009:642-647; Arthur 2009:34-58; Amoah 2009:12-21; Gyimah-

Boadi 2009:138-152). In the popular mind, politics is closely associated with the activities of politicians or political parties. Politicians are often seen as power-seeking hypocrites who conceal personal ambition behind the rhetoric of public service and ideological conviction. They are seen as self-serving, two-faced people rather than serving the public interest. This perception has become common probably as result of the intensified media exposure of the incidence of corruption, dishonesty and other rent-seeking activities as well as abuse of power (Daddieh 2009:642-647; Arthur 2009:34-58; Amoah 2009:12-21; Gyimah-Boadi 2009:138-152). This rejection of the personnel and machinery of conventional political life has led to the use of derogatory phrases such as 'machine politics', 'politicking' and 'office politics'. This image of politics held by some Ghanaians may be traced back to the writings of Niccolo Machiavelli, who, in *The Prince*, developed a strictly realistic account of politics which drew attention to the use by political leaders of cunning, cruelty and manipulation. Such a negative view of politics reflects the essentially liberal perception that as individuals are self-interested, political power has become corrupting, because it encourages those in power to exploit their position for personal advantage and at the expense of others (Machiavelli 1961).

Authenticity of Manifestos

Both parties have levelled accusations against each other over the authenticity of their manifestos. For instance, the NDC in a 56-page document entitled 'The NPP Manifest o – A Set of Stolen Policies' (dated November 2000) accused the NPP of plagiarizing its manifesto on such issues as tax identification numbers, ECOWAS monetary union, government partnership with the private sector, neighbourhood watch schemes, prison farms and additional roles to armed forces in national development. The NDC further described the NPP manifesto 'Agenda for Positive Change' as a document full of 'lies, insults and unrealistic promises' and one which insulted the NDC in a 'language that is uncouth, indecent, provocative and inflammatory'. The NPP, on the other hand, responded that it produced a credible manifesto that posed a great challenge to the dominance of the NDC in Ghanaian politics (Ayee 2002). In February 2009, the NPP minority caucus in Parliament also accused the NDC of dusting off its previous manifesto and publishing it as the 2008 manifesto. The NPP referred to the NDC's 2008 manifesto as the 'The New King James Version'.

The matter of the two contrasting manifestos became a subject of acrimonious debate on the floor of Parliament when the NPP MP for Bimbilla attempted to quote a section from the manifesto on education while contributing to the debate on the State of the Nation address by President Mills. His NDC colleagues asked him to use the new version of their manifesto because, according to them, the old one had been withdrawn (Parliamentary Debates February 2009). No reason was given for the withdrawal of the original manifesto. It has, however, been speculated that the NDC realized it could not fulfil most of the promises in that manifesto.[13] One is therefore tempted to question the parties whether they based their manifestos on thorough consultations and research. It is believed that quite often manifestos appeared to be the product of a small committee of the party elite rather than a product of extensive consultations with the rank and file of members down to the branch level. Contrary to this suspicion the NDC has pointed out that its 2008 manifesto 'was created by Ghanaians from all walks of life and regions who spoke to Prof. Mills during the door-to-door tours. The policies and pledges it contained are built upon the difficulties and challenges Ghanaians find most important' (NDC Manifesto 2008: 5). Similarly, in the run up to the 2012 elections, the National Youth Organiser for the New Patriotic Party, Anthony Karbo, said that the party delayed its manifesto for the 2012 elections based on lessons from the 2008 elections when he claimed the National Democratic Congress copied portions of the NPP manifesto. He said, for instance, the NDC's Savannah Accelerated Development Authority (SADA) was copied from the NPP's proposed Northern Development Authority (NDA), a programme he said the party intended to implement if it had won power.[14]

Conclusion

This chapter has shown that even though there are several factors or variables that have influenced elections in Ghana, the electoral successes and failures of the two main political parties, namely, the NDC and NPP may be linked to their manifestos because they are political products showcasing their policies and programmes and how they planned to deal with national priorities in the political market. There is evidence to suggest that some progress has been made in fulfilling some of the manifesto objectives. However, there is still more room for improvement judging by the fact that issues concerning poverty reduction, the economy, environment, corruption, safety and security, employment, education, agriculture, water, electricity and equitable distribution of national resources have remained key objectives in manifestos since 1992, and they continue to set the policy agenda.

Four main lessons can be distilled from the paper. First, there is no doubt that manifestos of political parties can make and unmake their political fortunes. No serious and credible party can enter elections without a manifesto. It has become more or less a 'trademark' for political parties. This is evident by the fact that both the major and minority parties in Ghana's history have written manifestos to contest elections. Consequently, it is important that political parties in Ghana and other African countries take their manifestos more seriously than is currently the case. In other words, politicians need to show more commitment in fulfilling their manifesto objectives. They must know what is in the kitty before developing their manifestos. In this connection, it might be useful for political parties to use research that is available on policy matters, both locally and globally, to prepare their manifestos. They should develop their own research units or think tanks to investigate policy options and keep abreast of relevant research findings and international trends between elections.

Secondly, manifestos will have to be owned by the party members and invariably the voters. Consequently, the parties should ensure that manifesto proposals are discussed at meetings that are representative of the party membership, especially the grassroots activists. In addition to this, more platforms other than the current campaigns and debates of presidential candidates should be created for the parties to market their manifestos and engage with more voters. Parties must listen carefully to what those outside their parties are saying, particularly the floating voters. They should also consider holding focus group discussions with groups of potential voters to gauge their views on possible policy options in their manifestos.

Thirdly, all the manifestos are written in English. The majority of the Ghanaian voting population is unable to speak, read, understand or articulate issues in English. Given that the manifestos are in English it becomes difficult for the majority of the voting population to understand and digest the issues in them. The political parties in their campaign messages have sought to deal with some of the salient issues in the manifestos but they have not achieved the desired impact. This is why it is important for the parties and the agencies of public education in Ghana such as the National Commission on Civic Education (NCCE) to organize more proactive and coordinated public education programmes in the local languages to educate more Ghanaians on the manifestos. Even though this may be expensive, it might be worth trying it.

Fourthly, one should ask why politicians in Ghana and other countries spend resources to design manifestos or revise them for elections if there is no link between them and electoral outcomes? Is the development of manifestos a public relations hoax or a window-dressing venture by the political parties? To some it is, but to the author of this chapter it is certainly not, given that manifestos are not only political products in a highly competitive political market but also avenues for cataloguing the nation's priorities, and that they also constitute a record of promises that the electorate could use to press for change.

Notes

1. This is a revised and updated version of an article published by the author as "Manifestos and Elections in Ghana's Fourth Republic", *South African Journal of International Affairs*, Vol. 18, No. 3 (December) 2011: pp. 367-384.
2. The theory of political marketing refers not only to the spin and campaigns of political parties but also the role of market intelligence in policy, leadership and organization of political parties. See Lees-Marshment (2001); and Newman (1999).

3. The forces that enabled the military to intervene several times in Ghanaian politics include the colonial legacy; the weak political system and leadership; US imperialism through the CIA; greed for power; inadequate economic resources; and absence of a strong civil society. Morris Janowitz and Samuel Huntington have emphasized the importance of the military elite in spearheading modernisation in the former colonies. See Huntington (1957); Hutchful (1979:35-55); and Hutchful and Bathily (1997).

4. A referendum or plebiscite is a vote in which the electorate can express a view on a particular issue of public policy, unlike an election that is a device for filling an office or post through choices made by the electorate. See Heywood (2000:199-201).

5. The manifesto according to Bourett (1959) drew heavily from the 1946 Colonial Development and Welfare Plan.

6. In 2002, the NDC published a policy document entitled A Social Democratic Agenda for Ghana to define the ideological basis of its existence as a political organization. In 2003, it was accepted as a member of the worldwide Socialist International at a meeting held in Sao Paulo, Brazil.

7. The 2008 NDC manifesto developed on the theme 'Building a Better Ghana' has four themes, namely, investing in people, jobs, the economy and ensuring a transparent and accountable government. This is in contrast to the 2008 NPP Manifesto which had the theme 'Moving Ghana Forward – Building a Modern Ghana'. It is broken into five chapters, namely, 'Achievements – a Promise Delivered'; 'Strengthening our Democracy'; 'Structural Transformation of the Economy'; 'Modernizing our Society'; and 'Regional and Continental Integration'.

8. The idea of voter rationality was first popularized in Downs (1957).

9. A more elaborate dissenting view on voter rationality is found in Caplan (op. cit.), Kiewiet & Mattozzi, (op. cit.:313-326); Eubank (1986:253-266).

10. Rt. Rev. Dr Yaw Frempong-Manso, Moderator of the General Assembly of the Presbyterian Church in Ghana addressing the Eighth General Assembly of the Church at the auditorium of the Sunyani Polytechnic on 22 August 2008. See Daily Graphic, 29 August 2008, p. 13.

11. John Mahama, then running mate of the NDC presidential candidate addressing the student wing of the NDC, the Tertiary Education Institutions Network (TEIN) at the Takoradi Polytechnic on 29 August 2009. See Daily Graphic, 1 September 2009, p. 14.

12. The eight MDGs are: eradication of poverty and hunger; reduction in child mortality; universal primary education; promotion of gender equality and empowerment; improvement in maternal health; combating HIV/AIDS, malaria and other diseases; ensuring environmental sustainability; and developing global partnership for development. Admittedly, there has been some progress in the achievement of at least one MDG and some effort at addressing the other MDGs in Ghana. For instance, 'the number of undernourished people in Ghana has decreased from 34 percent to eight percent over approximately fifteen years' while the Ghana Strategy Framework for Food Security and Action Plan was designed under the NPP government in 2005. The plan focuses on large scale water development, rural road infrastructure and market development, enhancement of crops, as well as small scale livestock and aquaculture within a comprehensive food security strategy (http://www.fao.org/countries/55528/en/gha/ accessed 10 November 2013).

13. On p. 78 of the 2008 NDC manifesto, the party pledged to build a 50,000-seat capacity stadium for each regional capital and a 7,000-seat capacity stadium in every district. It was however, pointed out by the NDC caucus in Parliament in February 2008 that the figures quoted were typographical errors.
14. See NPP 2012 manifesto tactically delayed to prevent NDC copying - Anthony Karbo http://politics.myjoyonline.com/pages/news/201203/82427.php (accessed 10 November 2013).

References

Agyeman-Duah, B., 2008, "Elections Management and Electoral Politics", in Agyeman-Duah, B. (ed.) *Ghana: Governance in the Fourth Republic*, Accra: CDD-Ghana, Chapter 7.

Alabi J., 2007, "Analysis of the Effects of Ethnicity on Political Marketing in Ghana", *International Business & Economics Research Journal*, Vol. 6, No. 4 (April): pp. 39-52.

Amoah, M., 2009, "The Most Difficult Decision Yet: Ghana's 2008 Presidential Elections", *African Journal of Political Science and International Affairs*, Vol. 3, No. 3 (April): pp. 12-21.

Asante, R., 2006. "Local Factors that Shaped the 2004 General Elections in the Ejura-Sekyedumase, Mampong and Effiduase-Asokore Constituencies", in K. Boafo-Arthur (ed.), *Voting for Democracy in Ghana – 2004 Elections in Perspective*. Accra: Freedom Publications.

Apter, D., 1963, *Ghana in Transition*, New York: Atheneum.

Arthur, P., 2009, "Ethnicity and Electoral Politics in Ghana's Fourth Republic", *Africa Today*, Vol. 56, No. 2: pp. 34-58.

Austin, D., 1964, *Politics in Ghana, 1946-1960*, Oxford: Oxford University Press.

Ayee, J.R.A., 2001a (ed.), *Deepening Democracy in Ghana: Politics of the 2000 Elections: Thematic aStudies*, Vol. 1, Accra: Freedom Publications.

Ayee, J.R.A. (ed.), 2001b, *Deepening Democracy in Ghana: Politics of the 2000 Elections: Constituency Studies*. Vol. 2. Accra: Freedom Publications.

Ayee, J.R.A., 2005, "Voting Patterns in Ghana's 2004 Elections", in Friedrich Ebert Foundation, *Elections 2004: Ghana Parliamentary and Presidential Elections*. Accra: Electoral Commission of Ghana/Friedrich Ebert Foundation.

Ayee, J.R.A, 2008, "The Evolution of the New Patriotic Party in Ghana", *South African Journal of International Affairs*, Vol. 15, No. 2 (December): pp. 185-214;

Ayee, J.R.A., 2002, "The 2000 General Elections and Presidential Run-off in Ghana: An Overview", *Democratization*, Vol. 9, No. 2 (Summer): pp. 148-174.

Ayee, J.R.A., 2009, Signpost to Healthy Politics in Ghana, paper presented at the Ghana Academy of Arts and Sciences Annual Lecture in the Humanities held at the British Council Hall, Accra, 23 April.

Ayee, J.R.A., 2011, "Manifestos and Elections in Ghana's Fourth Republic", *South African Journal of International Affairs*, Vol. 18, No. 3 (December), pp. 367-384.

Bates R., 1974, "Ethnic Competition and Modernization in Contemporary Africa", *Comparative Political Studies*, Vol. 6, No. 4: pp. 457-484.

Blais A., 2000, *To Vote or Not to Vote: The Merits and Limits of Rational Choice Theory*. Pittsburgh: University of Pittsburgh Press.

Bleich, E., 2002, Integrating Ideas into Policy Making Analysis: Frames and Race Policies in Britain and France, *Comparative Political Studies*, Vol. 35, No. 9: pp. 1054-1076.

Boafo-Arthur, K., 2006, *Voting for Democracy in Ghana: The 2004 Elections in Perspective*, Thematic and Constituency Studies, Volumes 1 & 2. Accra: Freedom Publications.

Butler, D. and Stokes, D., 1974, *Political Change in Britain*. London: Macmillan.

Bourett, F.M., 1959, *Ghana: The Road to Independence, 1919-1957*, London: Oxford University Press.

Caplan, B., 2007, *The Myth of the Rational Voter: Why Democracies Choose Bad Policies*. Princeton: Princeton University Press.

Chabal, P. and Daloz, J-P., 1999, *Africa Works: Disorder as Political Instrument*. Bloomington, Indiana University Press.

Chazan, N., 1983, *An Anatomy of Ghanaian Politics: Managing Political Recession, 1969-1982*, Boulder, CO: Westview.

Cobb, R., Ross, J.K. and Ross, M.H., 1976, Agenda Building as a Comparative Process, *American Political Science Review*, Vol. 70, No. 1: pp. 126-138.

Edelman, M., 1964, *The Symbolic Uses of Politics*. Chicago: Chicago University Press.

Daddieh C,, 2009, "The Presidential and Parliamentary Elections in Ghana, December 2008", *Electoral Studies*, Vol. 28, No. 4: pp. 642-647;

de Mesquita, B.B., Morrow, J., Silverson, R. and Smith, A., 2002, "Political institutions, policy choice and the survival of leaders", *British Journal of Political Science*, Vol. 32, No. 4: pp.559-590.

Downs, A., 1957, *An Economic Theory of Democracy*. New York: Harper and Row.

Dunn, J., 1975, "Politics in Asunafo", in D. Austin and R. Luckham (eds.) *Politicians and Soldiers in Ghana*. London: Frank Cass.

Eubank, W. L., 1986, "Voter Rationality: A Retest of the Downsian Model." *Social Science Journal*, Vol. 23, No. 3, (Fall): pp.253-266.

Frempong, A.K.D., 2001, "Ghana's Election 2000: The Ethnic Undercurrent", in J.R.A. Ayee (ed.) *Deepening Democracy in Ghana: Politics of the 2000 Elections*. Accra: Freedom Publications.

Geys B., 2006, "Rational Theories of Voter Turnout: A Review", *Political Studies Review*, Vol. 4: pp. 16-35.

Gramsci, A. ,1982, *Selections from the Prison Books*, London: Lawrence and Wishart.

Gramsci, A., 1993, *Historical Materialism and International Relations*, Cambridge: Cambridge University Press.

Gyimah-Boadi, E., 1994, "Ghana's Uncertain Political Opening", *Journal of Democracy*, Vol. 5: pp. 75-86.

Gyimah-Boadi, E., 2001, "A Peaceful Turnover in Ghana", *Journal of Democracy*, Vol. 12: pp. 103-117.

Gyimah-Boadi, E. and E. Debrah, 2008, "Political Parties and Party Politics", in B. Agyeman-Duah (ed.) *Ghana: Governance in the Fourth Republic*. Accra: CDD-Ghana.

Gyimah-Boadi, E. and R. Asante, 2006, "Ethnic Structure, Inequality and Public Sector Governance in Ghana", in Y. Bangura (ed.), *Ethnic Inequalities and Public Sector Governance*. Basingstoke: Palgrave Macmillan.

Gyimah-Boadi, E., 2009, "Another Step Forward for Ghana", Journal of Democracy, Vol. 20, No. 2 (April): pp. 138-152.

Henneberg, S.C., 2004, "Political Marketing Theory: Hendiadyoin or Oxymoron" *Working Paper Series*, No. 19, School of Management, University of Bath, United Kingdom.

Heywood, A., 2000, *Key Concepts in Politics*, London: Palgrave.

Howlett, M. and Ramesh, M., 2003, *Studying Public Policy: Policy Cycles and Policy Subsystems*, 2nd edn. Oxford/New York: Oxford University Press Canada.

Horowitz, D., 1985, *Ethnic Groups in Conflict*. Berkeley & Los Angeles, University of California Press.

Horowitz, D. 1991, *A Democratic South Africa: Constitutional Reengineering in a Divided Society*. Berkeley & Los Angeles, University of California Press.

Huntington, S., 1957, *Soldier and the State*. Cambridge: Harvard University Press. Hutchful, E., 1979, "A Tale of Two Regimes: Imperialism, the Military and Class in Ghana", *Review of African Political Economy*, Vol. 6, Issue 14: pp. 35-55.

Hutchful. E. and Bathily, A., 1997, *The Military and Militarism in Africa*. Dakar, CODESRIA.

Jonah, K., 1998, "Agency and Structure in Ghana's 1992 and 1996 Elections", in Ayee JRA (ed.) *The 1996 General Elections and Democratic Consolidation in Ghana*. Accra: Department of Political Science.

Joyce, P., 1996, *Politics*, London: Hodder Headline.

Kanazawa, S., 1998, "A Possible Solution to the Paradox of Voter Turnout", *Journal of Politics*, Vol. 60, No. 4: pp. 974-995;

Kiewert, D.R and Mattozzi, A., 2008, "Voter Rationality and Democratic Government", *Critical Review*, Vol. 20, No. 3 (September): pp. 313-326

Kingdon, J.W., 1984, *Agendas, Alternatives and Public Policies*, Boston: Little, Brown.

Lake, D.A. and Baum, M.A., 2001, "The Invisible Hand of Democracy: Political Control and the Provision of Public Services", *Comparative Political Studies*, Vol. 34, No.6: pp. 587-621.

Lees-Marshment, J., 2001, *Political Marketing and British Political Parties*. Manchester: Manchester University Press.

Lindberg, S. and Morrison, M.K.C., 2005, "Exploring Voter Alignments in Africa: Core and Swing Voters in Ghana", *Journal of Modern African Studies*, Vol. 43, No. 4: pp. 565-586.

Lonsdale, J., 1994, "Moral Ethnicity and Political Tribalism", in Kaarsholm & J Hultin (eds) *Inventions and Boundaries: Historical and Anthropological Approaches to the Study of Ethnicity and Nationalism* Occasional Paper 11. Roskilde: Department of International Development Studies, Roskilde University.

Machiavelli, N., 1961, *The Prince*. Hammondsworth: Penguin (translation, G. Bau).

Marx, K. and F. Engels, 1992, *Selected Works of Karl Marx and Frederick Engels*, New York: International Publishers.

McCombs, M., 2005, "A look at agenda-setting: Past, present and future". *Journalism Studies* 6 (4): 25-45.

Muntigl, P., 2002, "Policy, Politics and Social Control: A Systematic Functional Linguistic Analysis of EU Employment Policy", *Text*, Vol. 22, No. 3: 393-441.

National Democratic Congress (NDC) Manifestos, 1992, 1996, 2000, 2004, 2008 and 2012, Accra: National Democratic Congress.

Newman, B., 1999, *The Mass Marketing of Politics: Democracy in an Age of Manufactured Images*. Beverley Hills, CA: Sage Publications.

New Patriotic Party (NPP) Manifestos, 1992, 1996, 2000, 2004, 2008 and 2012, Accra: New Patriotic Party.

Oelbaum, J., 2004, "Ethnicity Adjusted? Economic Reform, Elections and Tribalism in Ghana's Fourth Republic", *Commonwealth and Comparative Politics*, Vol. 42, No. 2: pp. 242-273.

Ohman, M., 1999, Elite Consensus in a Ghanaian Context – the Inter-Party Advisory Committee and the 1996 Elections, Minor Field Study, No. 69 (Spring): 1-43.

Republic of Ghana, 1991, *Report of the Committee of Experts (Constitution) on Proposals for a Draft Constitution of Ghana*, Tema: Ghana Publishing Corporation.

Parliamentary Debates, February 2009.

Posner, C., 2005, *Institutions and Ethnic Politics in Africa*. New York: Cambridge University Press.

Rochefort, D.A. and Cobb, R.W., 1993, "Problem Definition, Agenda Access, and Policy Choice", *Policy Studies Journal*, Vol. 21, No. 1: 56-71.

Scheufele, D. A. & Tewksbury, D., 2007, "Framing, agenda setting, and priming: The evolution of three media effects models", *Journal of Communication*, 57(1), 9-20.

Schram, A., 1991, *Voter Behaviour in Comparative Perspective*. Berlin: Springer-Verlag. Spector, M. and Kitsuse, J.I., 1987, *Constructing Social Problems*, New York: Aldine de Gruyter.

Surel, Y., 2000, "The Role of Cognitive and Normative Frames in Policy-Making", *Journal of European Public Policy*, Vol. 7, No. 4: 495-512.

Thompson, J.B., 1990, *Ideology and Modern Culture: Critical Social Theory in the Era of Mass Communication*. Cambridge: Polity Press.

Young, C., 2002, *Ethnicity and Politics in Africa*. Boston: Boston University Press.

Whitfield L, 2009, "Change for a Better Ghana': Party Competition, Institutionalization and Alternation in Ghana's 2008 Elections", *African Affairs*, Vol. 108, No. 433: pp. 621-641.

5

Elections and Representation in Ghana's Democracy

Kwame A. Ninsin

Introduction

An *electio*n constitutes an important principle in liberal democratic ideology; on it hinges the very notion of democracy as a form of government that embodies the rights and freedoms of the citizen, and affirms their capacity to make decisions after careful reflection of alternatives regarding what is good in the long run and what is for the good of society. As David Held (2006) has pointed out, this notion of democracy raises many questions, including the 'categories of people who might be entitled to participate in politics', and the 'many substantive areas where democracy might be legitimately extended.' The challenge facing democratic practice is rather to implement procedures that would facilitate the formulation of reasonable alternatives that reflect the will of the people and constitute the basis for 'a sound and reasonable political judgment' (Held 2006:233). An election has become the framework within which citizens are expected to exercise such reasonable judgment as well as the moment when they assert their sovereign power for self-government.

Logivally therefore it could be argued that by turning out in their numbers to vote at general elections since the country returned to democratic rule under the 1992 Constitution, Ghanaians are demonstrating their capacity to make rational choices between policy alternatives, and mandating their elected representatives to govern in accordance with their policy preferences. Indeed, voter turnout in Ghana's presidential elections since 1996 has surpassed the 50 per cent mark: 1996 – 78.2 per cent; 2000 – 61.7 per cent; 2004 – 85.1 per cent; and 2008 –

72.91 per cent. In a liberal democracy, where the traditional *promissory form of representation* prevails, the vote defines a dyadic relationship between the voter and the representative (Mansbridge 2003).[1] The electorate use the power of the vote to demand accountability from their representatives whose responsibilities are embedded in the promises they make either explicitly during the election campaigns or implicitly when the representative accepts the trust of the voter expressed through the ballot. Periodic elections provide an opportunity for voters to exercise the legal and moral power inherent in the right to vote to control their representatives by demanding accountability from them. Failure to give satisfactory account is punished. Does such a dyadic relationship govern elections in Ghana? Further, does the fact that Ghanaian voters turn out in impressive numbers at the polls suggest that Ghanaians believe in the efficacy of elections as the expression of their sovereign power to choose and change who is to govern them?

Earlier studies of Ghanaian electoral politics pioneered by the veteran student of Ghanaian politics, Dennis Austin, have consistently drawn attention to the predominance of peasant and small town society culture in Ghana's political economy and how this affects political behaviour, particularly electoral choices.[2] More recent studies, including those conducted by the Department of Political Science at Legon from 1996, shift the explanatory variables from local or community factors to the rationality of the voter who punished the National Democratic Congress (NDC) in the 2000 elections for failure to keep the electoral promise of growing the economy and improving their living conditions, and rewarded the New Patriotic Party (NPP) with 56.90 per cent of their vote, and again voted to retain it in power in the 2004 presidential elections with 52.45 per cent of the votes.[3] Lindberg and Morrison (2005:1-22) have made a similar claim, arguing that the electoral choices of the Ghanaian voter are shaped by a mixture of objective socio-economic factors such as level of education, income, occupational status,as well as rural/urban factors. In my view, the Ghanaian voter may exhibit a measure of rationality at the polls; however being rational does not mean that they vote on the basis of the policies of the competing political parties.

Jonah (1998:229-257) on the other hand has argued that ethnicity is a salient factor shaping voter choices at the polls more than socio-economic factors. According to him, ethnicity is a major explanatory factor in what he describes as 'structural shifts in voting patterns' in 1992 and 1996, which became pronounced in the 2000 and 2004 elections. The growing saliency of ethnicity in Ghana's electoral politics prompted Gyimah-Boadi (2001:67-68) to warn against the potentially destabilizing consequences of ethnic voting, especially when ethnic voting appeared progressively to coincide with regional voting. Fridy (2007:281-305) does not dispute the saliency of socio-economic influences in the choices made by the Ghanaian electorate. He nonetheless assigns a determinate role to ethnicity. According to him many voters take 'ethnocentric information about the parties behind the polling station security screens than anything resembling socioeconomic distinctions' (ibid.: 300; see also Frempong 2006).

In this chapter, I argue that existing studies of why Ghanaians enthusiastically vote have generated explanations and conclusions that are formal, often contradictory and most of all reduce a complex relationship between citizens and their representatives to the usual *authorization and accountability functions*. As Friday (2007:298) has argued, such conclusions that are based on responses to questionnaires and observations of trends in voting behaviour, and concerned about the meaning of elections and representation, are 'notable for their dearth of content.' Indeed the essence of electoral politics, which is the expression of the rights and freedoms of sovereign citizens to choose their representatives, is mediated by a number of social, political and economic factors and developments within and outside their immediate environment. Such factors may distort the meaning of representation and the processes leading to electoral outcomes. To gain a better understanding of the relationship between citizens and their representative, as expressed through elections, would require that we depart from the study of formal structures by which the electorate choose their representatives to 'a more abstract and normative evaluation of the institutional forms' that representation may take. 'The norm (of representation) should be divorced, at least in the first instance, from any particular institutional arrangement, so it is possible to identify representative relationship within a variety of possible institutions and practices, and then to judge them in terms of their contributions to democracy' (Castiglione and Warren 2006:3).

In Ghana, factors mediate the relationship between the citizen and the representative. First is the domination of the capitalist state and economy over a largely peasant economy and society. The two dominant instances (the state and economy) shape the latter's norms and attitudes at the level of politics where the interface between the electorate, who operate largely in a peasant based society, and the political class who control the capitalist economy and the state, is mediated by poverty.

Poverty is a major feature of Ghana's social structure, and remains a powerful determinant of the attitudes of the mass of the electorate toward the political class. Even during the 1950s and 1960s when the country experienced accelerated socio-economic development, it was only the minority of workers engaged in administration, manufacturing and commerce who recorded improvements in their material conditions: the rest experienced 'lower income levels and average standards of living'. In 'the late 1970s and early 1980s absolute poverty', according to a UNICEF study, 'rose from around 60/65 per cent to 65/75 per cent in rural areas'. The UNICEF study further 'showed that the deprivation was significantly worse for people who lived in those parts of the country ... that are characterized by structural and endemic poverty, difficult environmental conditions, and poor social infrastructure and services...' More recent studies affirm that poverty is pervasive, and though the people in all the ecological zones of the country experience pockets of poverty, those living in rural savannah, rural forest, and rural coastal areas, export crop farmers, food crop farmers, and non-farm self-employed workers (those in the informal sector) fall within the bracket of the poor and very poor. In all these areas people engaged in agriculture, especially food agriculture, and in informal sector activities are the poorest: they live below the poverty line[4]. It is this pervasive poverty that defines the relationship between the electorate and the political class, and is the supreme determinant of the dependency relationship of the electorate with the political class generally, and their elected representative in particular. In this era of democratic politics elections provide the institutional and ideological framework for legitimising this relationship.

The second mediating factor is the community or ethnic identity. Austin, Chazan Dunn, and Twumasi, for example have argued that local factors and similar considerations influence the choices voters make at the polls.[5] At any particular time an individual belongs to multiple territorial boundaries – the nation, region, tribe and local community - within which she functions as a citizen capable of exercising her democratic rights. The local or community factors constitute a local tradition that is re-lived during each election period. During elections the boundaries of the local community tend to become coterminous with the ethnic group or region, depending on the group's definition of which citizenship identity promises greater material advantage in accessing public goods. Ultimately the choice of membership of a particular political territory depends on the citizens' perception of the domain where decisions about access to public goods benefit her most.[6] For Ghanaians, especially the poor who live in rural communities, access to public goods such as piped water, health facilities, schools, tarred roads and jobs are crucial for improved quality of life. An election is about choices of immense public import because its outcome impinges on the wellbeing of the local community or ethnic group insofar as its outcome shapes the distribution of public goods. I would argue in this regard that the pervasive poverty among rural dwellers induces a strong community/ethnic solidarity and identity that determine who the members of the collective should vote for.

Elections and Elite Interest

Do elections produce parliamentary representatives who act to promote the interest of those who elected them, including facilitating their participation in the choices made at various levels of the governance structure; that is, the people's participation in the decision-making process such that policy outcomes would be seen to benefit them? For Ghana's political class elections have become a very lucrative arena for competitive politics. It has become a business sector where the return on investment is usually good. Consequently, the number of candidates competing in parliamentary elections has been increasing since 1992 (see Table 1 below.)

Table 5.1: Candidates Competing in Constituencies 1992 - 2012

Election Year	No. of Candidates	Increase	Percentage Increase	No of Constituencies	Increase	Percentage Increase
1992	463	–	–	200	–	–
1996	778	315	68.03	200	0	0.0
2000	1074	296	38.05	200	0	0.0
2004	951	-123	- 11.45	230	30	15.0
2008	1060	109	11.46	230	0	0.0
2012	1332	272	25.64	275	45	19.57

In the 2012 parliamentary elections the numbers, according to provisional figures released by the Research and Monitoring Department of the Electoral Commission (see *Daily Graphic and Ghanaian Times* of 29 October 2012), show an increase in the number of candidates contesting the 275 parliamentary seats to 1,332. On the surface of things the increase does not look substantial, especially given the fact that the number of constituencies has increased from 200 in 1992 to 230 in 2004 and to 275 in 2012. These increases do not show the intense scramble for nomination to contest parliamentary seats that occurs during the primaries of the various political parties. On the other hand, the record of contestants for parliamentary seats since 1992 shows how aggressive the competition for parliamentary seats has become: 1992 = 463 (for 200 seats); 1996 = 778 (for 200 seats); 2000 = 1,074 (for 200 seats); 2004 = 951 (for 230 seats); 2008 = 1,060 (for 230 seats); and 2012 = 1,332 (for 275 seats). In 1992 the average number of candidates per constituency was 3. For the 2008 and 2012 elections the average number of candidates per constituency was 5. Table 2 shows how the political class has intensified the competition for parliamentary seats.

Table 5.2: Regional Breakdown of Candidates Vying for Parliamentary Seats in 2012

Region	No. of Candidates	No. of Parliamentary seats
1. Ashanti	228	47
2. Greater Accra	202	34
3. Eastern	152	33
4. Northern	155	31
5. Brong Ahafo	129	29
6. Western	111	26
7. Volta	125	26
8. Central	107	23
9. Upper East	63	15
10. Upper West	60	11

Why has the Ghanaian political class shown exceptional interest in *politics as a vocation?* I would argue that the rising level of elite competition for parliamentary seats is due to the prevailing view of elections as a means to control the state for accumulation of private wealth, and a market place where the electorate exchange their vote for material benefits: small gifts but primarily for development projects in their community or their ethnically defined territory where the benefits will accrue to all the members (citizens) equally. A relationship of exchange between citizens and their elected representatives, described by Clapham as patron-client relationship,[7] is forged. The notion of patron-client relationship immediately modifies the voter-representative relationship that is implied in democratic elections, and poses the question as to what the elected representative represents.

The elected representative functions at two levels. First, he represents himself at the highest level of the state to promote his private material interests in conjunction with other representatives. It is significant that since the attainment of political independence, not a single faction of this class has left office without being tainted with corruption.[8] Politics has become a theatre of accumulation of private wealth. Second, he represents his constituents by lobbying for development projects according to their expressed needs and interests, or as framed and articulated by him during the election campaign.

Because politics has become business, parliamentary candidates invest huge sums of money in it just to get elected to parliament; and their political parties spend astronomical amounts of money to win the presidency. The 2008 and 2012 elections dramatized the overwhelming power of money in Ghanaian politics. Political parties, especially the leading ones, organized lavish campaign activities. They mobilized and bussed people from one constituency to another to register to vote or transfer their vote; they organized expensive campaign rallies to mobilize electoral support; party primaries and congresses were characterized by conspicuous buying of votes. According to the Centre for Democratic Development (Ghana), money was splashed about to influence people at various levels of their campaigns, but more openly during both presidential and parliamentary primaries.[9] Much greater extravagance was evident in campaign advertising by political parties: the leading ones went to every length to outdo each other in print and radio or television advertising. The use of expensive campaign billboards underscored the determination of each of these political parties to win electoral votes over the other. It was clear from the huge sums of money which the political parties poured into their electioneering campaigns that wining political power had become an obsession, and each of them would use every means to win it.

The heavy financial investments that the two leading political parties made in the last elections, and of course in previous ones, and the ferocious competition for votes, which would start about a year before the election month, were driven by the expectation that victory would bring with it the right to pillage the state for themselves, and for the benefit of family members and friends as well as party supporters. According to J.L.S. Abbey the business associates of the political class also invest substantial sums of money in the campaign activities of their affiliate political parties. In fact, the private sector accounts for much of the spending during an election year. For them also politics has become business, and their expenditure on elections is an investment from which they expect profitable returns. Abbey elaborates his claim in the following terms.

> In 2008 we borrowed 25% more than the previous year …. Twenty five (25) per cent was borrowed by the private sector not to invest but to support their political parties. When you see these huge rallies, they say politics is a game of numbers. Everybody knows that the swing voter wants to be with the likely winner; so the politicians will endeavour to show huge numbers at every rally, with every one of them claiming to be a winner. All the parties, even the smaller ones, will bus people from far places to one venue. […] so everybody has enough numbers; and petrol will be bought for a fleet of vehicles, drivers must be paid; … and then food will be bought and wasted. … People will be given out of pocket allowances for coming at all, apart from the selected drinking places which will serve those attending the rallies. So the people attending the rally go out and spend.[10]

Being a President, Cabinet Minister or Member of Parliament promises huge financial benefits, in terms of monthly salary and as ex-gratia award after four years in any of these positions, either elective or appointive. On Wednesday 31 October 2012, that is barely a month to the next general elections, MPs decided at a closed session to approve an increase in the monthly salary for the President (GH¢12,000), Vice President (GH¢10,500), Ministers of State and their Deputies (between GH¢8,000 and GH¢9,000) effective 2009. A few months earlier the President had approved a monthly salary of GH¢7,200 for MPs. For the 2009-2012 period, they would earn roughly the following hefty income: President (GH¢5.76 billion cedis), Vice President (GH¢5.04 billion), Ministers (about GH¢4.52 billion), and MPs might take about GH¢3.45 billion each) for the 4-year period. Some sources have calculated the gross payment for their four-year service (2009-2012) at GH¢1115.2 billion.[11] These colossal monthly salaries exclude the controversial ex-gratia payments that have also become the subject of public fury and remonstrations. The ex-gratia awards proposed by the Chinery-Hesse Committee (CHC), which were generally regarded as lavish, naturally provoked much public outcry. The Committee had recommended that

> former presidents should be provided with 6 fuelled and chauffer-driven vehicles to be replaced every 4 years; offices and residential accommodation in and out of the capital; 3 professional assistants; annual all-expenses paid overseas travel/vacation; a non-taxable ex-gratia award plus pension benefits; entertainment of guests at the expense of the state, and US$1 million for a foundation; twelve months consolidated salary for each full year of service, and where the ex-president served 2 consecutive

terms he should be paid an additional non-taxable resettlement grant equivalent to 6 months of consolidated salary for each full year of service, plus a non-taxable ex-gratia payment equivalent to 12 months of consolidated salary for each year. There were also miscellaneous benefits, including medical and dental care, police escort during his drive in town and the provision of 24 hours security. [12]

The CHC Report was caught in another quagmire. Was there a document that could be legitimately called the CHC Report? Was there one version of it or several versions? etc.[13] Was *the* CHC Report approved by Parliament as required under Article 71 of the Constitution? The fact that, as late as 6 January 2009, hours before Parliament was dissolved, MPs in the 2004-2008 parliament deemed it appropriate to allegedly approve such extravagant awards for ex-presidents when millions of Ghanaians did not enjoy access to basic social services to enhance their human dignity, was another source of public concern. For many Ghanaians, the MPs' behaviour spoke volumes about how they perceive their role as representatives of the citizens of the country.

Beyond salaries, allowances and other perks which factions of the political class within Parliament and the Executive organs of state are privileged generally to enjoy, MPs, top party executives and private sector business allies of the political party in power further have infinite access to various avenues, including membership of boards of public corporations, management of state enterprises, commissions and committees, and public contracts which rake in huge incomes as salaries, allowances, profit and other forms of income. For example, a new president has power to appoint people to fill offices listed under Article 71 of the Constitution. An equally important avenue where the spoils for the victorious party are rich and rewarding is appointments: appointments to membership of state/public boards, corporations, commissions, and ambassadorial posts. Between May and July 2009 alone the newly elected President made appointments to 59 such public boards, corporations, commissions, councils, etc. More appointments, including those he made to diplomatic posts followed later in the year. The number of appointments varied from one in a few cases to as many as ten in at least one instance.

Table 5.3: List of State/Public Boards, Corporations, Commissions, Councils, etc. to which the President made Appointments: May–July 2009 (Excluding Ambassadorial Appointments).

1. Agricultural Development Bank Board	8. Export Development Investment Fund
2. Bank of Ghana	9. Fair Wages and salaries
3. Bulk Oil Storage and Transportation Company Limited	10. Food and Drugs Board
	11. Free Zone Authority
4. Central Tender Review Board	12. GAMA Film Company Limited
5. Council of Technical Education and Vocational Training	13. Ghana Aids Commission
	14. Ghana Airport Company Ltd.
6. Driver Vehicle Licences Authority	15. Ghana Cylinder Manufacturing Company
7. Energy Commission	16. Ghana Education Service Council

17. Ghana Education Trust Fund	38. National Identification Authority
18. Ghana Institute of Management and Public Administration	39. National Investment Bank
19. Ghana Investment Fund for Electronic Communications	40. National Pensions Regulatory Authority
	41. National Population Council
20. Ghana Investment Promotion Centre	42. National Road Safety Commission
21. Ghana Maritime Authority	43. National Service Board
22. Ghana Oil Company Limited	44. National Vocational Training Institute
23. Ghana Ports and Harbours Board	45. Plantation Development Board
24. Ghana Railway Development Authority	46. Public Procurement Board
25. Ghana Shippers Authority	47. Public Service Commission
26. Greater Accra Regional Lands	48. Public Utilities Regulatory Commission
27. Institute of Journalism	49. Revenue Agencies Governing Board
28. Institute of Professional Studies	50. Securities and Exchange Commission
29. Irrigation Company of Upper Region (ICOUR) Limited	51. Social Security and National Insurance Trust
	52. Statistical Service Board Limited
30. Korle Bu Teaching Hospital	53. Students Loans Scheme
31. Labour Commission	54. Tema Oil Refinery
32. Law Reform Commission Board	55. The Lands Commission
33. Legal Aid Board	56. University of Cape Coast Council
34. Legal Service Board	57. University of Development Studies Council
35. Millennium Development Authority	58. University of Education Winneba Council
36. Minerals Commission	59. University of Mines Council Venture Capital Trust Fund
37. Ministry Tender Review Board	

Source: Compiled from *myjoyonline.com*)

A key aspect of economic management is an efficient procurement system. 'Public procurement accounts for about 50 per cent -70 per cent of total government expenditure, represents 14 per cent of Gross Domestic Product (GDP) and accounts for about 24 per cent of total imports' (Ministry of Finance 2003; quoted in Adu Sarfo 2011). Despite attempts to reform the public procurement system, the process has been tainted by widespread corruption usually implicating a network of politicians, top party leaders who have business connections and must have bankrolled the party during the electioneering campaigns, bureaucrats in strategic positions within the state bureaucracy, and political cronies in business. The construction sector which includes roads and buildings for educational institutions and health facilities, as well as the supply of various materials for public works and the provision of services for public use have become popular breeding grounds for corruption.[14] According to The Auditor-General's Report for 2009 the nation lost GH¢2.5 billion in that year 'as a result of financial irregularities in the various ministries, departments and agencies'.[15] The losses were incurred through payroll irregularities, 'store/procurement irregularities' and 'procurement irregularities. At the Ministry of Water Resources, Works and Housing, 114 contractors who received funds totalling GH¢1.2 million as mobilization fund did not execute their projects.' The persistence of such irregularities had become a source of concern to the Auditor-General: 'The irregularities have been recurring and they run through my report annually, a situation which I continue to find very disturbing. Finding lasting solutions to the problems can save the nation millions of cedis to improve service delivery to taxpayers and strengthen public confidence and trust in the accountability process within the public sector.'

The spectre of 'judgment debt', that has emerged to haunt the nation, the political class their accomplices in the state bureaucracy, and local as well as their international business associates, illustrates the severity of the epidemic of corruption and highlights the extensive web of actors who are engaged in fleecing the country of its resources. Between 2001 and 2011 the government incurred GH¢642.0 million in judgment debt.[16] GH¢117.0 million of this debt was paid in 2009, GH¢276.0 million paid in 2010 and GH¢231.0 million paid in 2011. The debt arose from diverse causes, but payments for breach of contract formed the majority. In 2010 alone 86 institutions and individuals, including Alfred Abgesi Woyome and CP, benefited from such payments. The payment of GH¢52 million to Alfred Agbesi Woyome would appear to capture the intricate web of public and private officials who collude either consciously or unconsciously to plunder the nation. For example, according to media reports GH¢52 million was paid to Woyome as judgment debt emanating from a business agreement entered into between the Republic of Ghana and Watervile Holdings (BVI) on 26 April 2006. Implicated in this judgment debt debacle are individuals; public and private institutions, both local and private; previous governments during whose tenure the contracts were signed; a former Attorney-General who allegedly 'stood by' when the case was brought against the Republic at the High Court; the High Court judge who in spite of the 'glaring facts entered a default judgment against the Republic of Ghana';[17] a Deputy Minister and civil servants in the Attorney-General's Office, and civil servants in the Ministry of Finance and Economic Planning; also Astro-Invest Management Ltd. who, together with Woyome, had sued the Republic for breach of contract. The proceedings of the Justice Apau Commission on judgment debt continue to reveal sordid cases of complicity by Ghanaian politicians, officials in the state bureaucracy and corporate executives operating in the country or abroad to defrauding the nation of huge sums of money.[18]

Another object of plunder by the network of politicians, their relatives, cronies and friends, bureaucrats and foreign accomplices is state lands. Recent reports[19] have revealed that public servants operating at the Lands Commission, Ministry of Works and Housing, and the Town and Country Planning operated a scheme for allocating state lands and government bungalows to politicians, other government officials and their friends. This scheme was operated outside an official one initiated by the Rawlings government in 1996 and continued by the Kufuor government. Plots of land in prime areas of especially the capital city were sold for a paltry sum of money, and did not take into account the public interest to preserve land for future use.

The provision of public goods such as houses has also become the object of appropriation by the political class and their associates. On Thursday 8 November 2012 Enoch Tei Mensah, Minister of Water Resources, Works and Housing, reported at a news conference that 'About 10% of the (completed houses built under so-called low-income housing projects) were allocated free of charge to persons close to the NPP administration while huge sums were paid to the contractors with very little or no work done.'[20] This is not an isolated practice. Because of corruption and other malpractices in the housing sector the country's housing deficit has become almost intractable: it currently stands at about 1.6 million and is projected to double in 10 years if not addressed immediately. This situation has left the poor in urban towns like Accra, Kumasi, Tema, Sekondi-Takoradi and Tamale to rely on 'make-shift facilities – kiosk, tents, cargo containers, attachment to shops and offices for shelter.' There are also the homeless who live on the streets, lorry parks and markets (Addai-Boamah 2010).

In general, the distribution of the spoils of victory within the rank and file of the victorious political party is done disproportionately. At the lowest levels of state i.e., the district and community levels, the local elite (also called 'foot soldiers') fight for control over markets and toilet facilities from which they could generate an income;[21] district level appointments at the NHIS, NADMO, National Youth Employment Scheme, and others are also appropriated by this local elite of the victorious political party. Small procurement as well as construction and building contracts become the preserve of such elite.   The ruling class distributes the leftover of the 'war booty' to the masses in the form of jobs and other material benefits as reward for their support (see Lindberg 2010).

Political Power and the Vote

Politics has not just become a moneymaking vocation. It is the means to control state power for purposes of gaining access to public resources by which 'small boys' could transform themselves into 'big men' (Nugent 1995:4-6)[22]. The lucrative nature of political power, for either MPs or members of the President's team (ministers and a host of other political appointees) has transformed electoral politics into an intense competition in which fair or foul tactics are freely employed just to gain political advantage over the opponent. I have noted above the growing intensity of the scramble for parliamentary seats. In this competition money has become a major weapon; violence is another. It is the growing menace of violence in electoral politics, as an instrument for winning political power that prompted one Minister of State to warn that 'Elections are not about head-cutting but head counting'.[23] The fact is that politics has been divorced almost entirely from its moral purpose; and elections have become a means for securing the authorization of the citizens to become elected representatives. This is why the overriding impetus of elections is for a political party to secure the highest possible number of votes, and why electoral competition has been reduced to a game of numbers in which the number of votes that each party would win in the elections is the most salient in the power calculus. The controversy that surrounds the voters' register during each election year underscores this point. In 2008, for example, midway through that election year, the National Democratic Congress (NDC), which was in opposition, alleged to the Electoral Commission (EC) that the voters' register for 13 constituencies in the Ashanti Region was bloated while the registered voters' population for 3 constituencies in the Eastern Region had declined in both instances since it was last updated in 2006. One of the smaller political parties made similar allegations in respect of the voters' register in the Ashanti Region. The NDC implicated unnamed staff of the EC and immediately raised doubts about the integrity of the EC. The New Patriotic Party (NPP) entered the fray on the side of the EC, and in doing so politicized an allegation about the credibility of the voters' register for a few constituencies, which normally the EC is able to rectify administratively. The matter became the subject of a heated partisan dispute between the two leading political parties: the NDC and NPP, and between the NDC and the EC. This controversy over the bloated register did not subside even after the EC's investigative committee had cleared the air about the allegation.

Two election-related activities organized by the EC exposed the intentions of the two leading political parties in the unfolding electoral contest to win power in the 2008 elections by any means. The first was the decision to update the existing voters' register through a limited voters' registration exercise, which was held from 31 July to 12 August 2008, to enable those who missed the last registration exercise to register for the 7 December elections. Rather than allowing qualified citizens to register voluntarily as their civic duty, the political parties, especially the NPP and NDC, mobilized their supporters: adults (including persons who had already registered), under-aged persons, and aliens, to register. Their direct intervention mobilized a large number of unqualified people to register. The result was a total registered voter population of 12,822,515, an increase of about 50 per cent over the EC's projected total of between 600,000-1,000,000 new voters. The second event was the period set aside for the transfer of votes from a voter's previous constituency to his or her current constituency. On this second occasion, the two leading political parties bussed their supporters from one constituency to another; some including university students were allegedly paid per diem for transport and a day's expenses to enable them to transfer their votes. The mobilization for 'transfer votes' was often done to influence voting in one or the other constituency. It was virtual gerrymandering, and could change the configuration of the voting population in a constituency. The outcome of the 2008 and 2012 presidential elections that the NPP contested on the strength of its overwhelming electoral support in just two regions (Ashante and Eastern) out of 10 shows the value of numbers in Ghana's electoral politics. This is partly why intense voter mobilization has become a permanent feature of Ghanaian politics.

Democracy and the Poor

Can 'electoral' democracy bring improvements to the life of the poor? Michael Ross (2006: especially 860-865) has reviewed the literature on democracy and pro-poor spending by the state. This literature emphatically correlates the citizens' freedom to choose their own representatives with pro-poor spending by the state. The analysis of 44 African countries by Stasavage (2005) corroborates this claim. He argues with particular reference to access to education that recent democratic regimes in Africa have increased spending on education to benefit the poor whose children had hitherto not had access to basic education implying, as Halperin, Siege and Weinstein (2005) do, that democracy has the inherent advantage to promote prosperity, welfare, and peace.[24]

Recent election studies by the Department of Political Science, Legon also seem to give credence to these views that in liberal democracies the electorate use their voting power to punish governments that do not manage the economy well enough to improve their material conditions.[25] Claims such as these are premised on the assumption that the universalization of political rights empowers the poor to exercise such rights purposely to influence government policies.

Earlier studies on Ghanaian elections contradict such claims: they do not attribute substantive rationality to Ghanaian voters. Rather they postulate a link between the electoral fortunes of a candidate and the development expectations of the community or the region of the ethnic group. For example, Naomi Chazan claims that 'Elections essentially have to do with linkages: with the connection between state and society, between the local community and the national arena, between the economy and the polity, and between the non-formal processes and formal institutions' (Chazan 1987:62). The choice of the voter may be described as the exercise of bounded rationality: bounded by a number of subjective factors. A recent study by Lindberg would appear to confirm the exercise of bounded rationality by the Ghanaian electorate. That study concluded that 'a vast majority of voters put the main emphasis (regarding why they voted) on a narrow form of what are nevertheless collective goods; that is, local development goods for the community' (Lindberg 2010:7). In fact Lindberg considers elections as an exchange between two parties (the electorate and the political class) and that the 'rational politicians in an era of free and fair elections (know that they) gain many more votes seeking to further constituency development (a collective good) than they lose by disengaging from clientelism' (Lindberg 2010:14). Lindberg's conclusion is corroborated by a reported statement by the Paramount Chief of the Aflao Traditional Area, Togbui Amenya Fiti V, that the people of Ketu South Constituency voted for the NDC in the 2012 elections as 'a bargaining chip' for the development of the area.[26] It may thus be argued that in the developing countries democracy has rather provided the institutional mechanism for brokering an agreement between the political class and the masses to enable the former to exercise political hegemony over society. This hegemonic position enables the political class to control not just society but also its resources. The exchange relationship between voters and their representatives would naturally benefit the representatives than the voters, and what accrues to the latter would have little or no impact on their material wellbeing. The rules of democratic politics legitimize this transaction between citizens and their elected representative, and its outcome.

The exercise of political power to dominate society rather than govern has implications for distributional politics. The faction of the political class, acting in their capacity as representatives of the people, distributes public goods in two ways both of which are in accordance with the logic of their relationship as briefly described above. The first is symbolic distribution, which purports to improve the material conditions of the poor when it is rather intended to merely mitigate their appalling material conditions. After all, governments pursue pro-poor policies under compulsion by development partners and to meet the standards set by international declarations such as the UN Millennium Development Goals, and not out of conviction. As Michael Ross (2006) points out, the pro-poor policies (in education, health, agriculture, employment, etc.) invariably benefit the ruling fraction of the political class and their allies.

Since the coming into force of the 1992 Constitution governments have initiated several pro-poor policy interventions aimed at addressing the crunching poverty of the masses. Between 1992 and 2003 not less than nine (9) poverty alleviation policy initiatives were launched (see Ninsin 2007:98), in particular from 2001 when the Government acceded to a HIPC status major policy frameworks such as Ghana Poverty Reduction Strategy I and II and the Millennium Development Goals have given policies a pro-poor content and direction. The Free Compulsory Universal Basic Education (FCUBE), Capitation Grant, and School Feeding Programme have been implemented in the education sector; the High Impact Rapid Delivery (HIRD) and several others have been supplemented with the National Health Insurance Scheme to improve access to quality health care and achieve the MDGs. Investment in housing, slum upgrading and affordable housing projects have also been initiated to ensure access to safe and affordable housing; and a low income workers housing project aimed at providing 4,792 affordable houses in selected regional capitals was initiated in 2007. The National Youth Employment Programme (renamed Ghana Youth Empowerment and Entrepreneur Development Agency – GYEEDA) was designed to tackle youth unemployment; and the Livelihood Empowerment Against Poverty programme was designed to assist selected poor households with small amounts of money. However, as ISSER (2008) has pointed out the issue is not about government intentions, but the outcomes of such policy initiatives. Despite increased budgetary allocations towards various poverty alleviation interventions the poverty of the poor has not gone away. And the problems of education, access to potable water, health and environmental hygiene, unemployment and a severe housing shortage continue to scourge the nation.[27] Eugene Yirbuor[28] is right in arguing that the problem of failed pro-poor policies is due largely to implementation bottlenecks. Recent reports attest to this. For example, the 2008-2010 reports on the School Feeding Programme and the National Health Insurance Scheme revealed that massive corruption has played a big role in the failure of such pro-poor policies.[29] Even HIPC funds were misapplied despite the strict monitoring systems which the donors put in place, and so it failed to achieve its intended purpose of reducing poverty in the target communities.[30] In 2008 reports of widespread corruption led to the dismissal of the administrator of the school feeding programme. A participatory study of the programme in selected communities throughout the country which was undertaken by SEND Foundation Ghana also exposed widespread corruption and patronage in the implementation of the programme.[31] Naturally, corrupt officials find policy implementation the most fertile arena to indulge themselves profusely and frustrate the efficient implementation of policies. They are encouraged by the failure of accountability institutions, such as Parliament, which have to ensure the implementation of the Auditor-General's findings and punishment for corrupt public officials (Ninsin 2009:70-71).

Leo Ocran (then Minister for Education) was reported in The Ghanaian Times (Saturday, September 19 2009 page 9) as saying: 'Politics is like war ... when you win there are spoils to share.' This statement summarizes the second aspect of the politics of distribution that is embedded in Ghana's electoral politics, which is notoriously described as the 'winner takes all' rule. As the discussion in the section captioned *Elections and elite interest* above shows, the political class benefit disproportionately from the distribution of the 'spoils of war'. This is consistent with the proprietary culture that drives the political class to secure election to parliament or to the highest executive office of the land. The masses are unable to restrain the political class because this patron-client relationship weakens the power to demand accountability from their leaders – the political class which is embedded in their citizenship and expressed in various form of political participation, including voting. In a democratic society where political transactions are governed within the framework of patron-client relations, an election simply legitimizes the exercise of this kleptocratic culture of power, and gives members of the victorious political parties justification to employ state power to plunder resources of society for themselves and their supporters.[32]

Conclusion: A Vote for Democracy?

The starting point of this essay is that existing election studies have been premised on the assumption that elections give legitimate authority to state-centred representative institutions to govern, as well as affording citizens the means to demand accountability from such representatives. Accordingly, once the integrity of an election is guaranteed as having performed these functions, citizens are deemed to have voted for democracy.[33] I have argued that in Ghana a number of factors have reshaped the meaning of citizenship and *de-centred* the political frameworks within which citizens could seek their interests. Citizens see themselves in different identity frameworks, as belonging to the local community or ethnic group or region, depending on their perception of the issues pertaining to their wellbeing and the delivery of public goods to meet their interests. This has in turn affected the political relations between citizens and their representatives. Both the political class and the citizens have constructed a patron-client relationship that enables the representatives to satisfy their material interest and at the same time meet the public goods expectations of the citizens. To this extent members of the political class, as candidates in an election, deal with voters who are not the usual citizens able to exercise sovereignty and enforceable rights and entitlements. The elected representatives are mandated with a limited responsibility to address the poverty needs of those who voted them to power; yet the citizens have limited capacity to demand accountability.

The power of accountability of the citizens is circumscribed by the logic of patron-client relationship, which is dictated by poverty and lack of a learning process that enable the citizen to exercise 'rational' or 'enlightened' political judgment (Held 2006:232; paraphrasing Claus Offe and Ulrich Preuss). As argued by Castiglione and Warren (op cit:8), the transaction cost of accountability is high: 'it requires monitoring regimes' which fall far outside the reach of the citizen-voter; because he lacks the enlightened information necessary for effective performance. Therefore trust becomes a more efficient basis of the relationship between the citizens and the elected representative; and trusteeship becomes a more plausible 'feature of *democratic* representation'. Trusteeship is compatible with democratic governance because the socially constructed relationship between the citizens and their elected representatives is based on the 'congruence of interests and/or values between the truster and the trustee' (ibid.). There are other forms of democratic representation, but I would argue that Ghanaian voters elect representatives whom they trust would ensure that public goods would be distributed in a manner that would, more or less, address their own material concerns: they vote trusting that their representatives would pursue their interest. The problem with Ghana's democracy is that the political class, members of whom seek the mandate of the citizen-voter through periodic elections, is undermining the moral basis of the trust through unregulated monetization of politics in their insatiable quest to control state power, which has become central to the intra-class struggle for private accumulation of wealth.

Notes

1. See Jane Mansbridge's full article for a discussion of the different forms of representation.
2. The influence of local society – its politics, economy and mores – on the political choices of the Ghanaian citizen was a principal theme of his writings on Ghanaian politics, starting from his pioneering work *Politics in Ghana 1946-1960* Oxford: OUP, 1970. See also his introduction to Dennis Austin and Robin Luckham (eds.) (1975).
3. See for example Ayee (ed.) (2001) and Boafo-Arthur (ed.) (2006).
4. The data, some of which come from the UNICEF study, are taken from Kweku Appiah et al. (2000:306-310).
5. See for example, Austin (1975), Chazan (1987), Dunn (1975) and Twumasi (1975).
6. This is how Castiglione and Warren (2006) formulate this complex problem: 'Implied in this kind of boundary is a complex form of citizenship in which individuals have multiple memberships, depending upon the nature and domain of collective decisions' (page 4).
7. Refer to Clapham (1985: Chapter 3) for various levels at which this unequal exchange relationship is manifested.
8. See the reports of the various commissions and committees of enquiry appointed after the overthrow of each regime; for example, Ghana, 1965; Ghana, 1967; Ghana, 1968; Ghana 1975; also Ninsin 2000.
9. In 2008 the Centre for Democratic Development Ghana (CDD - Ghana) monitored the campaign activities of the various political parties; it found several cases where people had been induced with money to vote for particular candidates at the party primaries.
10. Dr Abbey was contributing extempore to a seminar on 'Economic Management During Political and Administrative Transitions' organized by the Institute for Democratic Governance (IDEG) on 11 April 2012. For a full report on this seminar see IDEG, *Policy Brief No 8 June 2012* page 13.
11. See *Public Agenda* No. 850 5 November 2012 Front Page continued at page 4.
12. I have paraphrased these awards from various sources listed on the internet.
13. For the various doubts cast on the CHC Report, see Masahudu Akilu Kunateh (2009).
14. Kwabena Amankwa, writing in *The Statesman* of 30 October 2012, alleges that because of rampant corruption in the award of contracts, the Minister for Finance and Economic Planning has not been able to submit reports of the operations of the Procurement Board to Parliament 'even though the Public Procurement Board has been submitting reports to' the Minister in accordance with Section 13 of the *Public Procurement Act (Act 663).*
15. The information from the Auditor-General's Report that is reported in this section is taken from http//:www.ghanaweb.com/GhanaHomePage/NewsArchives/artikel.php?ID=202145
16. The source of these judgment debt figures is the Deputy Minister of Information, Samuel Okudzeto Ablakwa as reported in Daily Graphic http://www.graphic.com.gh/dailygraphic/page.php?news=17774 dated 30 December 2011. See also the Auditor-General's Report 2010. In his testimony before the Justice Yaw Apau Commission on Judgment Debt on Wednesday 28 November 2010, the Chief Director of the Ministry of Finance and Economic Planning, Enoch H. Cobbinah, said that about GH¢158.269 million in judgment debt is awaiting payment by the state. The Auditor-General, Richard Kwatei Quartey, also reported that his office noticed the size of judgment debt payment

had increased in 2009, 2010 and 2011; hence the decision to highlight it in its report to Parliament. See *Daily Guide Thursday 29 November 2012*, pages 3 and 4; *Daily Graphic Thursday 29 November 2012* pages 1 and 3.

17. A former Attorney-General and Minister of Justice, Martin Amidu, had strong reasons to entertain such serious doubt about the payment of judgment debt to Alfred Abgesi Woyome that he filed a suite at the Supreme Court in which he asked the court to declare the payment of the judgment debt to Woyome null and void. In his Supreme Court suit the Attorney-General and Minister for Justice, Waterville Holdings (BVI) Astro-Invest Management Ltd and Woyome are parties. For details about the suit see a report in *The New Crusading Guide* 28 August 2012.

18. Reports of the proceedings of the Justiced Apau Commission on Judgment Debt have been carried in various issues of the Ghanaian print media since 2010.

19. See Timothy Gobah 'Politicians, Public Servants Connive' in *Daily Graphic* Wednesday 30 May 2012. Also CJA Press Conference on 'The Grabbing of Government Lands and Assets in Prime Areas by Individuals' http://www.ghanaweb.com/GhanaHome Page/NewsArchives/Artikel.php?ID=240414 dated 24 October 2012.

20. Reported by CitifmOnline.com/Ghana at www.citifmonline.com/index.php?id=1.1136424. Dated 9 November 2012 at 9.50 am

21. For a case study of such struggles to control local resources, see Joseph Ayee and Richard Crook 'Toilet wars': urban sanitation services and the politics of public-private partnerships in Ghana (December 2003) IDS Working Paper 213. See also Sodzi Sodzi Tettey, 'Long Live Human Waste' *Daily Graphic Monday 27 July 2009: 27* for a satirical essay on how these local elites struggle to control toilets which are considered a source of income at the local level.

22. Maxwell Owusu (2008) has argued that the Ghanaian political class employs money to win state power, which has become an instrument for private accumulation and for gaining access generally to state controlled resources.

23. This caution is attributed to Clement Kofi Humado, Minister for Youth and Sports. See *Daily Graphic* Wednesday 30 May 2012, page 22.

24. Herbert (2009) attributes such grand claims to Halperin et al. (2005).

25. See for example Ayee (2001) and Boafo-Arthur (2006).

26. See Victor Kwawukume, 'Our votes, bargaining chip for development – Togbui Fiti' *Daily Graphic* Saturday 14 December 2013, page 19.

27. For evidence on factors that undermine effectiveness of the education reform initiatives, see *Ghana: Effective Delivery of Public Services: Focus on Education* (a review by AfriMap and the Open Society Initiative for West Africa (OSIWA) (October 2009). The study was conducted for AfriMap and OSIWA by the Institute for Democratic Governance.

28. See his 'Electoral Promises on Pro-Poor Policies and Programmes: Implementation Fiasco' in *Citizens' Watch July-September 2012 Vol. 12 No. 25* Accra: A SEND Foundation Publication.

29. See *Whose Decision Counts? (A Monitoring Report on the Ghana School Feeding Programme* (2008).

30. See SEND Foundation, *Where Did Ghana's HIPC Funds Go? Assessing HIPC Expenditures on Poverty Alleviation 2002-2004. (Accra 2006).

31. SEND Foundation, *Whose Decision Counts? A Monitoring Report on the Ghana School Feeding Programme.* Accra, April 2008.
32. A recent case in which supporters of the New Patriotic Party (NPP) besieged the Bureau of National Investigation (BNI) (and later the courts) to protest the detention for questioning of Asamoah Boateng, former Minister of Information in the NPP government seems to suggest a previously unknown aspect of mass political culture, which is that the masses are now moving beyond voting to embark on political action (violent protest, in this case) to legitimize the use of state power for self-enrichment. Asamoah Boateng was being investigated by the BNI for allegedly breaching the Procurement Act in the awarding of contracts for the renovation of a section of the Ministry of Information building.
33. This is the principal claim in a recent publication by the Department of Political Science, University of Ghana, based on a study of the 2004 elections and titled *Voting for Democracy* Vols. 1 and 2 (Boafo-Arthur 2006).

References

Addai-Boamah, N., 2010, 'Housing Affordability in Ghana: A focus on Kumasi and Tamale' in *Ethiopian Journal of Environmental Studies and Management Vol. 3 No. 3.*

Adu Sarfo, P., 2011, 'Assessing the Effects of The Procurement Act (663) on Public Financial Management in Ashanti Region', thesis submitted to The School of Graduate Studies, Kwame Nkrumah University of Science and Technology, in partial fulfilment of the requirements for the degree of MSc in Development Policy and Planning, Department of Planning, College of Architecture and Planning, May 2011.

Appiah, K. et al., 2000, 'Poverty in a Changing Environment' in E. Aryeetey, J. Harrigan and M. Nissanke (eds.) *Economic Reforms in Ghana: The Miracle and The Mirage,* Trenton, NJ/Asmara, Eritrea: Africa World Press.

Austin, D. and R. Luckham (eds.), 1975, *Politicians and Soldiers in Ghana,* London: Frank Cass.

Ayee, J.R.A. (ed.), 2001, *Deepening Democracy in Ghana Volumes 1 & 2,* Accra: Freedom Publications.

Boafo-Arthur, K. (ed.), 2006, *Voting for Democracy in Ghana Volumes 1 & 2,* Accra: Freedom Publications.

Castiglione, D. and M.E. Warren, 2006, *Rethinking Democratic Representation: Eight Theoretical Issues,* paper delivered at Centre for the Study of Democratic Institutions, University of British Columbia, 18-19 May 2006.

Chazan, N., 1987, 'The anomalies of continuity: Perspectives in Ghanaian elections since independence' in F. Hayward (ed.) *Elections in Independent Africa,* Boulder, Co and London: Westview.

Clapham, C., 1985, *Third World Politics – An Introduction,* London: Routledge.

Dunn, J., 1975, 'Politics in Asunafo' in Austin and Luckham (eds.) *Politicians and Soldiers in Ghana.*

Frempong, A.K.D, 2006, 'Ethnicity, Democracy and Ghana's Election 2004' in K. Boafo-Arthur (ed.) *Voting for Democracy in Ghana* Vol. 1.

Fridy, K. 2007. "The Elephant, Umbrella, and Quarrelling Cocks: Disaggregating Partisanship in Ghana's Fourth Republic," African Affairs 106: 281-305

Gyimah-Boadi, E., 2001, 'The December 2000 elections and prospects for democratic consolidation.' in J.R.A. Ayee (ed.) *Deepening Democracy in Ghana: Politics of the 2000 Elections,* Vol. One, Accra: Freedom Publications.

Halperin, M.H., J.T. Siege and M.M. Weinstein, 2005, *The Democracy Advantage: How Democracies Promote Prosperity and Peace,* London: Routledge.

Held, D., 2006, Models of Democracy (3rd Edition), Stanford: Stanford University Press.

Herbert, H.W., 2009, 'The Case for Democracy: Remaining Questions', *J. of Developing Societies* (25).

Institute of Statistical Social and Economic Research, 2008, *The State of the Ghanaian Economy Report 2008.*

Jonah, 1998, 'Agency and structure in Ghana's 1992 and 1996 presidential elections' in J.R.A. Ayee (ed.) *The 1996 General Elections and Democratic Consolidation in Ghana*, Legon: Department of Political Science, University of Ghana.

Kunateh, M.A., 2009, 'Yamson Committee rejects Chinery Hesse Report' www.ghanadot. com/news.ghanad0t.kunateh.072109a.html posted July 21 2009

Lindberg, S.I., 2010, *Some evidence on the demand side of private-public goods provision by MPs,* Working Paper No. 8, Feb, Overseas Development Institute, London, UK.

Lindberg, S.I. and M.K.C. Morrison, 2005, 'Exploring Voter Alignment in Africa: Core and Swing Voters in Ghana', *Journal of Modern African Studies* 43(4): 1-22.

Ninsin, K.A., 2009, *How Parliament Decides: Decision-Making in Ghana's Parliament,* Accra: IDEG.

Ninsin, K.A., 2007, 'Markets and liberal democracy' in K. Boafo-Arthur (ed.) *Ghana: One Decade of the Liberal State,* Dakar: CODESRIA BOOKS.

Ninsin, K.A., 2000, 'The root of corruption: A dissenting view', reprinted in Rwekaza Mukandala (ed.), *African Public Administration – A Reader,* Harare: AAPS Books.

Nugent, P., 1995, *Big Men, Small Boys and Politicians in Ghana 1982-1994*, London: Pinter Publishing.

Owusu, M., 2008, *Money and Politics: The Challenge of Democracy in Ghana*, Accra: IDEG.

Republic of Ghana, 1967, *Report of the Commission of Enquiry into Irregularities and Malpractices in the Grant of Import Licences,* Nii A. Ollenu, Sole Commissioner.

Republic of Ghana, 1965, *Report of the Commission of Enquiry into Trade Malpractices in Ghana,* Chairman: W. E. Abraham.

Republic of Ghana, 1968, *Report of the Commission of Enquiry into the affairs of the Ghana Timber Marketing Board and the Ghana Timber Cooperative Union,* Chairman: R. S. Blay.

Republic of Ghana, 1968, *Report of the Commission of Enquiry into the Manner of Operation of the State Housing Cooperation,* Chairman: D. S. Effah.

Republic of Ghana, 1968, *Report of the Commission of Enquiry on the Local Purchasing of Cocoa,* Chairman: J. C. de Graft-Johnson.

Republic of Ghana, 1975, *Report of the Commission of Enquiry on Bribery and Corruption,* Chairman: P. D. Anin.

Ross, M., 2006, 'Is democracy good for the poor?', *American J of Political Science,* Vol. 50, No. 4, October.

Stasavage, D., 2005, 'Democracy and education spending in Africa', *American J. of Political Science,* Vol. 49, No. 2, April.

Twumasi, Yaw, 1975, 'The 1969 election' in Austin and Luckham (eds.), *Politicians and Soldiers in Ghana.*

6

Impact of Democratic Political Transition on the Economy of Ghana

Kwabena Asomanin Anaman

Introduction

In this chapter, we examine the impacts of democratic political transition on the economy of Ghana based on the assessment of the impacts on the macro-economy and industry groups. This examination is done from a human development perspective. Human development incorporates shared economic growth that ensures minimal adverse impact on the environment while protecting citizens against deprivation, securing for them peace and security as well as participation in economic and political governance processes. It is dependent on the attainment of peaceful democratic transitions given the rancour that is characteristic of the quadrennial national elections in Ghana. This is because democratic political transitions since 1992 have coincided with reduced focus on the socio-economic development of the country. The current winner-takes-all political system encourages the emergence of electoral winners and losers who are less likely to make efforts to develop a more inclusive governance structure to tackle the numerous socio-economic problems facing the country.

The rest of this chapter is organized along the following lines. The next section deals with the economic theoretical framework of the study. The macroeconomic analysis of impacts of democratic transitions are discussed next with emphasis on impacts measured on the bases of inflation, economic growth, money supply and exchange rate and government revenues, expenditures and budget deficits. This section is followed by a discussion of impacts on selected industries and the stock market. A few conclusions are reported at the end of the chapter.

Economic Theoretical Framework

The relationship between democratic transition, the economy and human development in Ghana is examined in this chapter. There is no doubt that these three areas are interlinked; however, the nature of the inter-connections must be teased out. How do democratic transitions impact on the economy? How is this impact transmitted into the spheres of human development? Democratic political transition refers to a process that establishes a democratic political regime that is based on the rule of the party or parties that get most votes in contested elections. This is different from democratic consolidation, which refers to the process by which democratic norms, rules and institutions are progressively incorporated in the workings of the political order. Successive peaceful democratic transitions lead to democratic consolidation.

Human development is a multi-faceted concept. However, for the purpose of this chapter, the definition of human development is based on the framework provided by Sen (1993). Human development is envisioned as a process that leads to the broadening of human choices in society. Similarly the central proposition of Welzel and Inglehart (1999:6-7) suggests that human development is based on three important factors that are all linked to the growth and expansion of human choices in society. These three factors are (1) physical and cognitive human resources (2) a culture that gives high priority to aspirations for liberty, and (3) democracy and institutionalization of human rights. The three factors derive from three spheres of social reality that are economic structure, political structure and a regime of freedoms and human rights. These three spheres interact to expand human choices. In the economic sphere, economic development increases the productivity and stock of human resources through the expansion of human capital and physical capital. Human resources increase with economic development and vice versa. Growth of human resources favours a culture of rising aspirations for liberty, and rising aspirations for liberty produce increasing pressures to establish and preserve broad-based democracy that then institutionalizes human freedom and rights.

There is a wealth of literature on the relationship between the economy, specifically economic development, and democracy. Lipset's (1959) research on the social requisites for democracy poses economic development as a central requirement for the establishment of democracy. Other authors, including Cutright and Wiley (1969), Winham (1970), Bollen and Jackman (1985), Helliwell (1992) and Burkhart and Lewis-Beck (1994) have demonstrated a significant causal link between economic development and democracy. This view is supported by evidence from economic development in countries such as South Korea and Taiwan over the last 40 years.

The political business cycle literature emphasizes the link between democratic political transition and the general state of the economy. The work of Nordhaus (1975) underscores the tendency for incumbent political parties to spend excessively during an election year (refer also to more recent works such as Acemoglu and Robinson 2001; Gonsalez 2002; Rodrik and Wacziarg 2005; Libich et al. 2010). This theory suggests that government expenditure typically increases on activities with short-term payoffs during election years. The higher expenditure is then hard to cut once the elections are over. Gonzales (2002) suggests that excessive spending by incumbent parties is likely to be observed in new democracies and in countries where the margin between the incumbent party and the main opposition party is narrow. Given the narrow margin between the incumbent party and the opposition in Ghana over the last three national elections, a hypothesis that emerges is that political spending is likely to be relatively large in election years in this country.

Political succession through elections can be considered as a *form of game* that can also be conceptualized as an investment project. In such a game there are winners and losers whose payoffs cover a time horizon of several years thus necessitating an analysis from an investment perspective. Voters choose a group of people or party to manage their affairs over a four-year period. This choice confers on the winning party or group the management of government policies costing about 100 billion Ghana cedis over the four-year period (based on an average budget of 25 billion Ghana cedis of national government spending per year using actual government spending for 2012 of the current government as a guide and adjusting for inflation). With government spending averaging between 25 to 35 per cent of the gross domestic product of the country, the elected government has considerable amount of power and resources to manage (or mismanage) the affairs of the country.

Democratic political transition can be also analysed from an economic viewpoint based on the welfare economics ideas first proposed by Vilfredo Pareto. Pareto`s optimality criterion states that a societal project or programme, such as democratic political transition, is efficient for society if it improves the welfare of one group without making other groups worse off. Pareto optimality is rarely obtained in real life as societal change, by its very nature, often makes some people worse off while others may gain from the change. Democratic elections create winners and losers. In Ghana's winner-take-all electoral system, winners take all the spoils of the electoral contest leaving losers with personal debt, the pain of loss, and other intangible costs.

The Potential Pareto Improvement Criterion is the theoretical basis of modern cost-benefit analysis. It also provides the theoretical tool to analyse societal changes that result in the kind of winners and losers that is obtained from national elections in a competitive multi-party political system. This criterion asserts that if the winners can hypothetically compensate the losers, then from a societal viewpoint, the programme is desirable. The compensation noted here is hypothetical (see also Kaldor 1939 and Hicks 1939). Note that the reverse situation may exist and this implies a deterioration or net negative societal outcome. We argue that democratic political change is a societal change where there are winners and losers and these are directly related to the winner-take-all political system where there are winners and losers.

Democratic transitions, such as those that occurred in Ghana in January 2001 and January 2009, create winners and losers. Given the dominance of Ghana's two major parties, the National Democratic Congress (NDC) and the New Patriotic Party (NPP), the winners and losers in a democratic political transition are those people and institutions directly connected to the political parties in terms of the level of activism and leadership position in the party. They are the most directly affected by democratic political transitions. Given the traditional social structure of the support system in Ghana, chief wage earners or breadwinners are the major financial backers of activities of a large number of people. The loss of employment by the chief wage earners during democratic transition therefore has a multiplier effect on the number of losers affected by the change. The opposite effect holds for principal wage earners whose positions may have been enhanced by the democratic transition. In the next section, we discuss the impacts of democratic transitions on the macroeconomy.

Macro-economic Impacts of Democratic Transitions

The macroeconomy while impossible to touch like bread or butter is a useful concept that captures the aggregation of small economic units of a society. It does not imply a linear aggregation of small economic units but a concept that articulates the composite nature of the aggregate of all economic units. The performance of the macroeconomy affects human development through several sources. These include the impacts generated through change in purchasing power (inflation), change in incomes of individuals (economic growth) and changes in the quantity and quantity of economic sectors or industries that employ people.

A major function of government is the stabilization of the macroeconomy by controlling inflation and increasing employment opportunities. In this chapter, the impacts of democratic transition on the macroeconomy are assessed through the changes in the following parameters: (1) inflation (2) economic growth based on changes in real gross domestic product (3) money supply and exchange rate, and (4) government expenditures, revenues and budget deficits.

Inflation

Inflation, defined as the general increase in the price level of the economy, erodes the purchasing power of individuals through increases in prices, and reducing the real amounts of goods and services that can be purchased by individuals with their existing incomes. If democratic transition results in rising inflation, then society on the whole suffers. However increased inflation has losers and winners. Losers from increased inflation, as a result of democratic transition, include people on fixed incomes such as retirees, civil servants and others who lack the capacity to adjust their incomes upwards in line with increasing inflation.

On the other hand, there are winners from increased inflation and these include owners of physical assets that generate services in high demand by consumers and producers of commodities with fast rising prices. Such owners can quickly adjust their prices.

A major impact of political transition in Ghana has been a rise in inflation. Inflation is generally known to increase around the year of political transition, whether it is a democratic or abrupt change of government through a military coup. The average annual inflation in Ghana from 1999 to 2010, based on the Classification of Individual Consumption by Purpose (COICOP) series, is presented in Figure 6.1. The COICOP-based index was adopted by the West African Monetary Union as a basis for harmonizing CPI measures among its members. It has a base year of 2002 and the Ghana Statistical has recalculated inflation based on the COICOP series from 1999 to 2010. These inflation figures were used for this study.

Since 1999, the year during which elections were held and the immediate year after the elections are marked by significant increases in inflation, for example, from 1999 to 2000 and then again in 2001. A moderate rise in inflation was also recorded from 2007 to 2008 and then in 2009. Inflation increased from 12.5 per cent in 1999 to 24.9 per cent in 2000 and then to 33.6 per cent in 2001 before falling to 14.9 per cent in 2002. Again, inflation increased from 10.7 per cent in 2007 to 16.5 per cent in 2008, then to 19.3 per cent in 2009 before falling to about 10.8 per cent in 2010. However, during the period that the incumbent government retained power, as in 2004 and 2005, inflation actually fell. *Thus the Nordhaus-Gonzalez's hypothesis appears to be upheld in Ghana at least for the phenomenon of inflation related to democratic political transition.*

Figure 6.1: Graphical Illustration of Annual Average Inflation Rate in Ghana, 1999 to 2010

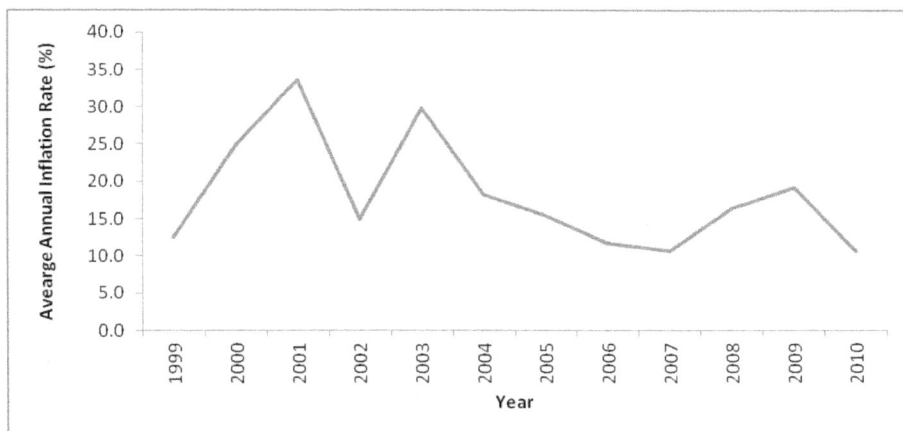

Economic Growth

The annual growth in the real GDP of Ghana from 1984 to 2010 is illustrated in Figure 6.2. The 1984 to 2010 period is the longest stretch of continuous growth in Ghana with positive annual growth in each year, with growth ranging from 3.2 per cent in 1984 to a high of 8.4 per cent. In 2000, an election year which saw the incumbent government lose power, annual economic growth was only 3.7 per cent. This was caused by external trade and financial shocks, low internal production and the relatively limited room for government overspending. The opposite growth rate occurred in 2008 when the incumbent government lost power. Economic growth reached about 8.4 per cent in 2008 achieved through very high government spending that was made possible by the financial space created through massive foreign debt cancellation in 2006 involving the forgiveness of two-thirds of Ghana's external debts. Economic growth declined in 2009 due to the reduced real government spending as a means of curtailing government deficits accumulated by the previous government from 2006 to 2008 and external economic downturn in Ghana's principal Western development partners. Finally, economic growth rebounded in 2010 based on 7.7 per cent change in real GDP. *Hence there is a mixed picture of positive and negative effect from the impact of democratic political transition on economic growth.*

Figure 6.2: Graphical Illustration of Annual Economic Growth Rates Based on Changes in GDP from 1984 to 2010

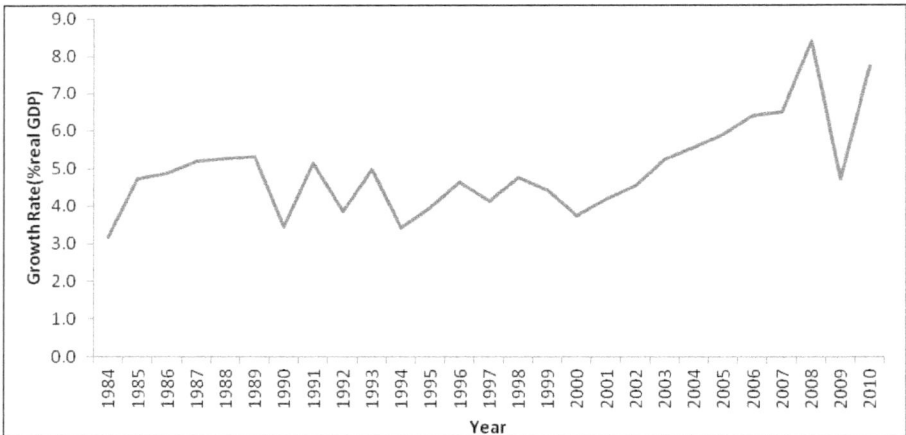

Money Supply and Exchange Rate

The growth of broad money supply in Ghana from 1997 to 2009 is presented in Figure 3. The growth of money supply was largely in tandem with increasing economic growth. However, the growth in money supply was substantially high from 2007 to 2009. Figures 4 and 5 depict the trends of exchange rate movements and depreciation over the period 1992 to 2009. It is clear from the two figures that during election years, the Ghana cedi depreciated significantly as was observed in 1996, 2000 and 2008. The depreciation was partly due to adverse external factors such as low commodity prices as occurred markedly in 2000. Nevertheless, government financial indiscipline during election years was an important factor in the depreciation of the cedi. This indiscipline resulted in inflationary pressures that contributed to the weakening of the local currency. Exchange rate depreciation may favour exporters as the local currency of the exported good increases. However, it also leads to an increase in domestic inflation. Not surprisingly, during election years, especially 2000 and 2008 that saw the defeat of the incumbent government, inflation increased as compared to the preceding non-election years. *In sum, democratic political transition led to the weakening of the local currency.*

Figure 6.3: Graphical Illustration of Money Supply Growth from 1997 to 2009

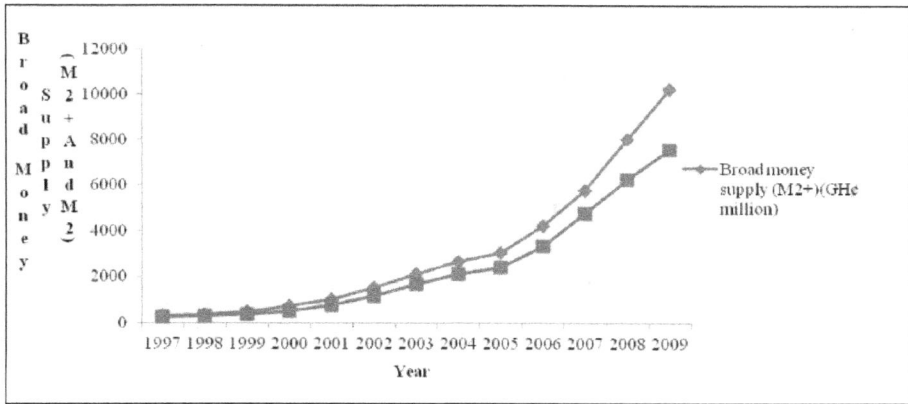

Figure 6.4: Graphical Illustration of the Annual Average Exchange Rate (GHS) in Ghana, 1992 to 2009 Measured as Ghana Cedis per One United States Dollar

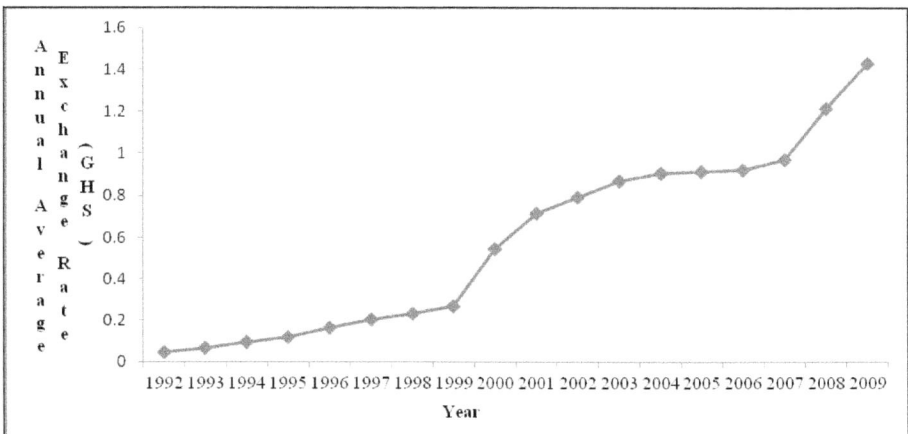

Figure 6.5: Graphical Illustration of the Annual Average Depreciation of the Exchange Rate (GHS) in Ghana, 1992 to 2009 with Respect to the United States Dollar

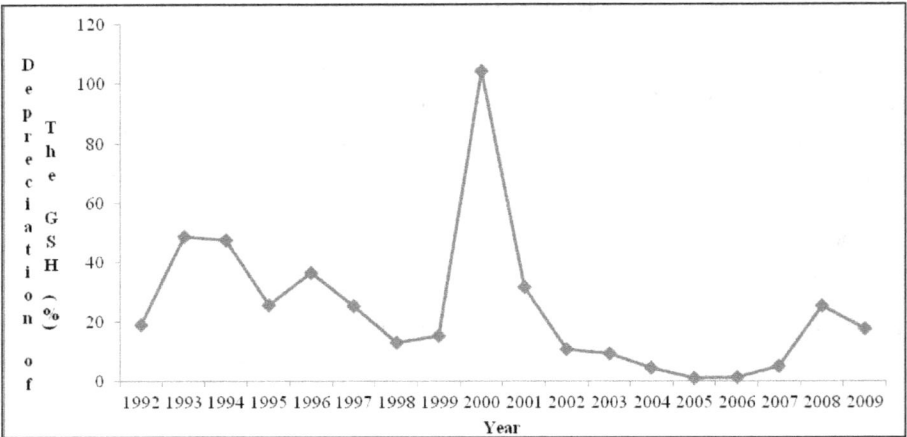

Government Revenues, Expenditures and Budget Deficits

A markedly clear effect of democratic political transition in Ghana has been the large government budget deficits accumulated during election years as a result of the incumbent government proclivity to overspend to win more votes. This observation can be gleaned from the government budget deficits calculated as a proportion of the GDP based on both old GDP and rebased GDP figures that are reported in Table 1. In 2000, the budget deficit was 8.5 per cent of old GDP partly due to the government's excessive campaign expenditures aimed at retaining power. The new government that assumed office in January 2001 restored financial sanity and kept the budget deficit under control, averaging 2.4 per cent of old GDP over the period 2001-2005. Budget deficits increased sharply from 2006 reaching a peak of 11.3 per cent of the old GDP in 2008, an election year. In 2010, total government expenditure was GHS 11,532.209 million (Ministry of Finance and Economic Planning 2011). In terms of the old GDP, the government budget deficit of GHS 2,999.866 million for 2010 was very close to the high of 2008; a sign that the government overspending in the election year 2012 could be very high.

Indeed, although 2004 was a year of national elections, the government's overall budget deficit was remarkably small and in terms of primary domestic balance, the government's budget was in surplus (refer to Table 1). The lack of excessive government spending in 2004 was due to the implementation of conditionalities and controls exercised on government spending as a result of the government's implementation of the Highly Indebted Poor Country (HIPC) initiative. This initiative was supported by international development agencies such as the International Monetary Fund and the World Bank. Ghana opted for the HIPC initiative in 2001. It completed the HIPC process of steps in 2006, paving the way for cancellation of two-thirds of Ghana's total external debts worth 4.2 billion United States (US) dollars in 2006. In fact, during the 2001- 2005 period, the primary budget balance was just positive by 0.34 per cent of the old GDP. This meant that the government was practically living within its means during the 2001-2005 period using internally generated revenues and some foreign grants to finance its domestic expenditures.

Further results of the analysis of the impact of democratic transition on government expenditures, revenues and deficits can be observed from Tables 1 and 2. Table 1 also provides some information about grants received by the government. Grants as a proportion of GDP were relatively smaller in the election years of 2000 and 2008 and these grants increased during the immediate years after the elections that saw a democratic transition. The increase in grants was largely due to the need of the new government to stabilize the economy after the excessive spending of the previous government during the national election year.

Table 2 provides information on total government expenditure as a proportion of the old GDP over the period 2000 to 2009. This proportion reached its maximum in the fourth and final year of the term of the government. This fourth and final year also coincided with national elections. Thus the years 2004 and 2008 saw peaks for this proportion. Further, this proportion declined during the first year after election. The prominence of recurrent expenditures in total government expenditure during years of national elections can also be observed in Table 2. This proportion peaked to about 30 per cent of old GDP in 2008, which was an election year. Furthermore, wages and salaries as a proportion of old GDP peaked during election years (refer to Table 6.2).[1]

Balance of Payments and Gross National Reserves

Table 6.3 provides information about the balance of payments and gross international reserves of Ghana over the period 2000 to 2009. This information reveals that during the years of national election years over this period, the overall balance of payments was negative. Further, gross international reserves declined during the year of national elections that coincided with democratic political transition (i.e. 2000 and 2008). Not surprisingly, months of cover of imports of goods and services for the country reached low levels in 2000 and 2008. These months of cover for imports of goods and services were 0.8 and 1.8 respectively compared to the ten-year average of 2.5 months. While declining terms of trade were a principal factor for the relatively poor positions of the country with respect to balance of payments and gross national reserves, poor management exemplified by excessive government expenditures was a major factor. The latter factor was linked to democratic political transition due to national elections during which incumbent governments overspent to try and win.

Table 6.1: Composition of Government Revenues and Grants, as % of GDP, 2000-2009

Indicator	2000	2001	2002	2003	2004	2005	2006	2007	2008	2009
Total revenue and grants	19.8	22.3	23.6	25.8	30.0	29.1	27.8	32.1	32.2	31.3
Total revenue	17.7	18.2	20.5	21.1	23.8	23.9	22.3	26.0	27.5	26.1
Tax revenue	13.7	15.6	17.9	19.6	21.8	20.8	20.3	23.6	24.6	21.4
Grants	2.1	4.1	3.2	4.8	6.2	5.3	5.6	6.1	4.7	5.1
Amount of grants in million Ghana cedis	57.0	156.1	156.4	317.6	495.3	515.5	653.6	856.8	828.0	1103.2
Amount of grants in million US dollars	104.5	217.7	197.2	366.0	547.2	564.6	707.7	882.9	682.0	772.4
Overall budget balance (using old GDP)	-8.5	-3.2	-1.6	-2.7	-2.9	-1.7	-7.8	-8.1	-11.3	-9.7
Overall budget balance (using rebased GDP)	-	-	-	-	-	-	-4.9	-4.9	-6.6	-5.7
Nominal GDP in million Ghana cedis based on the old method with data released on 30 June 2010	2715.3	3807.1	4886.2	6615.8	7988.7	9726.1	11672.0	14045.9	17617.6	21630.7
Nominal GDP in million Ghana Cedis based on the rebased figures released on 3 Nov. 2010	-	-	-	-	-	-	18705.1	23154.4	30178.6	36867.4

Sources: Compiled from data from the Ghana Government Budget Statements from 2001 to 2010 and updated by data released in 2011.

Table 6.2: Recurrent and Capital Government Expenditure, 2000-2009, % of old GDP

Item	2000	2001	2002	2003	2004	2005	2006	2007	2008	2009
Total expenditure	27.7	25.5	25.3	28.6	32.9	30.8	34.9	40.6	45.9	41.7
Recurrent expenditure			19.4	18.9	20.4	18.8	22.3	26.2	30.1	25.9
Non-interest			14.1	13.3	16.1	15.1	18.9	23.1	26.2	21.2
Wages & salaries		8.0	8.7	8.7	8.7	8.5	10.0	10.0	11.4	11.4
Administration services		1.9	3.0	2.7	3.0	3.2	3.7	4.0	3.7	2.9
Transfers		0.8	2.4	1.9	4.4	3.4	5.2	7.6	8.4	6.1
Domestic		6.1	4.2	4.3	3.2	2.8	2.6	2.3	2.8	3.6
External		4.9	1.1	1.3	1.2	0.9	0.8	0.8	1.1	1.2
Capital expenditure	9.2	4.9	5.9	8.4	10.1	10.0	10.0	11.6	14.2	10.7
Domestic financed		0.6	2.4	3.7	4.4	3.9	5.4	6.4	9.0	3.2
Foreign financed		4.3	3.5	4.7	5.7	6.1	4.6	5.2	5.3	7.5

Sources: Compiled from data from the Ghana Government Budget Statements for various years from 2001 to 2010 and updated by data released by the Ministry of Finance and Economic Planning in November 2010. N/A denotes that the data were not available.

Table 6.3: Balance of Payment and Gross International Reserves of Ghana, 2000-2009

Indicator	1999	2000	2001	2002	2003	2004	2005	2006	2007	2008	2009
Overall balance of payments (million US$)	-90.7	-117	8.6	39.8	558.3	-10.5	84.3	415.1	413.1	-940.7	1,158.8
Gross international reserves (end of year in million US$)	420.1	233.4	364.8	640.4	1,425.6	1,732.4	1,894.9	2,266.7	2,836.7	2,036.2	3,164.8
Months of cover for imports of goods and services	1.2	0.8	1.2	2.2	3.9	3.0	3.8	3.0	2.7	1.8	3.0

Sources: Compiled from data from the Bank of Ghana Annual Reports from 2001 to 2010.

Microeconomic Impacts of Democratic Transition

Democratic Transition and Performance of Industries or Sub-sectors of the Economy

Microeconomic analysis, based on the performance of individual industries, was captured by analysing the real growth rates of these industries using 1974 to 2009 data released by GSS on 30 June 2010 using the nomenclature of the old GDP system. Simple statistical analysis of the real outputs of industries would capture the spikes and trends of their real growth rates during periods of democratic transition. Fourteen industries or sub-sectors are reported by GSS. These are (1) crops and livestock, (2) cocoa, (3) forestry and logging, (4) fishing, (5) mining and quarrying, (6) manufacturing, (7) electricity and water, (8) construction, (9) transport, storage and communications, (10) wholesale and retail trade, restaurants and hotels, (11) finance and insurance, real estate and business services, (12) government services, (13) community, social and personal services, and finally (14) producers of private non-profit services.

The results of the analysis showed that all the industries increased their real total output over the 1993 to 2009 period. Of particular importance to this study is the result over the election years and the years immediately after those years. The real value of outputs of all the industries increased over the transition years (2000 to 2001) with the exception of the mining and quarrying industry. The sharp drop in the production of electricity and water from 2006 to 2007 was due to power rationing from August 2006 to September 2007 as a result of the low volume of water in the Akosombo dam, the principal source of energy of the country. In terms of the absolute size of the industries, we observed no major impacts of democratic transition on the size of the various industries. However, the manufacturing industry continued to shrink in relative size (proportionate to GDP) over the period.

Democratic Transition and the Ghana Stock Exchange

The Ghana Stock Exchange (GSE) is part of the finance, real estate and business services subsector of the economy described above. The GSE was established in 1990. The performance of the GSE is measured by the GSE All Share Index. The performance of the GSE in its first decade (1990 to 1999) was consistent. However from 2000 to the present, the performance of the GSE appeared to be influenced by developments during democratic transitions. GSE performance was relatively high in an election year and then declined in the year following an election (refer to Figure 6). For example, in 2009, considered to be a democratic transition year, the GSE All-Share index dropped by 46.6 per cent making the GSE the worst performing market in Africa for that year. In 2008, which was an election year, the GSE All Share Index increased by 58 per cent from its 2007 closing level making the local market the best performing stock market in Africa. In 2010, the GSE rebounded after the bearish run in 2009 and was adjudged the Africa's second best market in terms of return to investors this same year (Databank 2011).

In Box 1, the impact of democratic transition on the performance of the firms listed in the GSE is reported based on an econometric panel data study by Anaman and Agyei-Sasu (2012). They analysed the factors influencing the performance of GSE firms based on several sets of factors as follows: internal governance factors, non-governance factors and external environmental influences including democratic political transition. Performance is measured as the rate of return on equity (ROE) based on data from 22 firms over a twenty-year period from the inception of the GSE in 1990 to 2009. Governance factors evaluated were the governance structure of the firm whereby the chief operating officer (CEO) also acted as the chairman of the board of the company, the size of the board and the proportion of total board members made up of non-executive directors. The two non-governance factors were debt to equity ratio and firm size. Macroeconomic factors were inflation rate and economic growth based on annual changes in the real gross domestic product (GDP). Democratic political transition was incorporated using dummy variables for both the election year and the transition year after an election year, and an interaction term variable combining government budget deficit as a proportion of GDP and election year. The analysis indicated that firms having the chief executive officer as the chairman of the board had significantly less return than those where the chief executive officer was not the chairman. Further, the size of the board negatively affected ROE. Economic growth and inflation positively affected ROE. The effect of democratic political transition on ROE was mixed; return increased in an election year but declined in a transition year after an election. Government budget deficit in an election year had a negative impact on ROE.

Figure 6.6: Illustration of the Performance of the Ghana Stock Exchange from 1991 to 2009

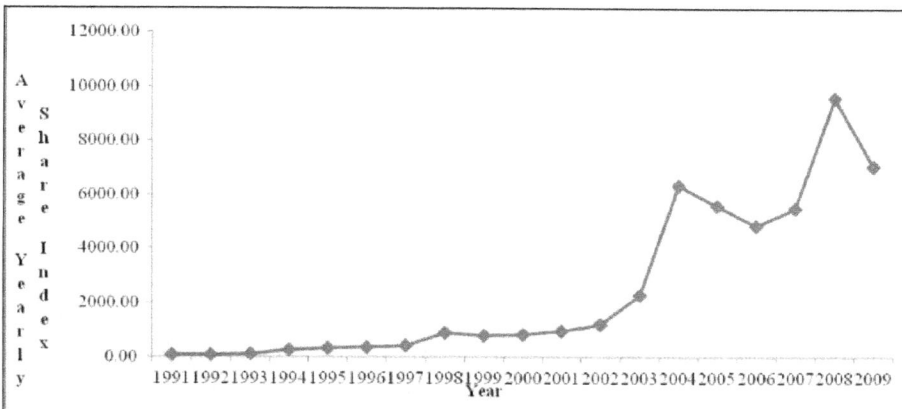

Box 6.1: The Effect of Democratic Transition on Stock Market Performance in Ghana

Econometric analysis was conducted using both cross-sectional and time-series data for 22 firms who were listed in the Ghana Stock Exchange (GSE) from 1990 to 2009 (Anaman and Agyei-Sasu 2012). The variables in the model were return on equity of the firm listed on the GSE (ROE), the number of the members of the board of the firm (BODSIZE), the proportion of non-executive directors in the firm (NED), debt-to-equity ratio (per cent) (DER), real size of the firm measured as the turnover in millions of Ghana cedis deflated by the GDP deflator with 2000 as the base year (SIZE), the rate of inflation in Ghana, measured as the change in consumer price index (INFLATION), the annual growth of the real GDP for Ghana (EGROWTH), the Fourth Republican democratic political transition year variable dealing with a year of national elections, measured as the dummy variable with 1 for 1992, 1996, 2000, 2004 and 2008 and 0 for all the other years between 1992 and 2010 (ELECYEAR), the Fourth Republican democratic political transition year variable dealing with the immediate year following the year of national elections, measured as the dummy variable with 1 for 1993, 1997, 2001, 2005 and 2009 and 0 for all the other years between 1992 and 2010 (TRANYEAR), and an interaction term consisting of the product of overall government budget deficit as the proportion of GDP and election year to measure the joint impact of democratic political transition during an election year when government budget deficits normally go up (DEFICITEYEAR). The estimated fixed effects panel model is presented below with the estimated parameter figures with their student statistics in parentheses.

$$ROE = 37.693^*CEOCHAR + 5.329^*BODSIZE + 0.015^*NED + 22.835^*DER +$$
$$\qquad\quad (12.526) \qquad\qquad (16.248) \qquad\qquad (0.593) \qquad\qquad (1.692)$$

$$0.000001^*SIZE + 2.369^*INFLATION + 1.938^*EGROWTH + 9.412^*ELECYEAR +$$
$$\qquad (1.103) \qquad\qquad (50.851) \qquad\qquad (2.878) \qquad\qquad (2.257)$$

$$9.084^*TRANYEAR + 223.672^*DEFICITEYEAR$$
$$(4.996) \qquad\qquad (6.136)$$

$^*R2 = 0.995$ \qquad Adjusted $R2 = 0.994$ \qquad Degrees of freedom = 206

Summary of Winners and Losers from Democratic Political Transition

As indicated earlier in this chapter, democratic political transition, like major historical events, and also public investment projects, results in winners and losers due to changes in people's economic conditions. Table 4 provides examples of winners and losers from democratic political transitions in Ghana that occurred in 2000/2001 and 2008/2009. These winners and losers are linked to effects of the transition that shape the fortunes of people. Inflation, as indicated earlier, is a clear feature of democratic political transition in Ghana, and this adversely affects people on fixed incomes such as pensioners and public servants. Given the polarized two-party system in Ghana, presidential appointments tend to favour the elites from the dominant social/cultural/ethnic groups tied to the ruling party. Similarly, awarding of government contracts tends to favour firms and businesses closely associated to the ruling party. Firms closely associated with the losing party tend to suffer from reduced levels of government contracts after national elections have changed the previously ruling party.

Table 6.4: Examples of Winners and Losers from Democratic Political Transition

Indicator	During Election Year		Post-election Transition Year	
	Winners	Losers	Winners	Losers
Inflation	Landlords	People on fixed incomes	Landlords	People on fixed incomes
Presidential appointments			Elites of major social or ethnic groups closely allied to the ruling party	Elites of major social or ethnic groups closely allied to the former ruling party
Budget deficit	Incumbent government			Incoming government
Awarding of contracts and projects	Firms closely associated with the ruling party	Firms closely associated with the main opposition party	Firms closely associated with the ruling party	Firms closely associated with the former ruling party
Exchange rate	Exporters	Importers	Exporters	Importers
Private sector	Stock market investors			Stock market investors

Conclusion

Overall, in terms of human development, it is observed that election years produce poorer macroeconomic management which is characterized by higher inflation, higher budget deficits, negative balance of payment figures and lower levels of gross international reserves. The poorer macroeconomic management translates into poorer economic conditions of the people and a lower quality of human development. The incoming government (after national elections) seeks international development assistance to stabilize the economy. Clearly, a major impact of political transition in Ghana has been the increase in inflation that impacts on the poorer sections of society more severely through loss of purchasing power for goods and services.

Government expenditure during election years is atypical, raising questions on the mode of operations of government in election years. Our analysis suggests that there is an emerging culture of high government deficit arising from government spending during election years that is driven primarily by the excessive desire to retain power. Budget deficits are expenditure beyond the revenues and grants raised by the country. Hence they represent substantial shortfalls in revenue mobilisation. The atypical case of 2004 was due to the strict conditionalities and controls on government spending imposed on the government after it opted for the HIPC initiative. It is imperative that legislative rules and laws are enacted in an attempt to eliminate the culture of excessive budget spending in election years.

Acknowledgments

The author thanks Dr. Jemima Agyare (formerly of the Institute for Democratic Governance, Accra), and Messrs Charles Yaw Okyere and Felix Agyei-Sasu for their assistance in completing the study. The support of the Institute for Democratic Governance, Accra, Ghana and the United Nations Development Programme Office, Accra, Ghana for the development of this paper is gratefully acknowledged.

Note

1. On November 2010, the Ghana Statistical Service formally announced the completion of the rebasing of Ghana's GDP. The rebasing was based on 2006 social accounting and use tables and concluded that Ghana's GDP was about 60 per cent larger than previously thought (refer to rebased figures in Table 1 for the period, 2006 to 2010). Hence the budget deficits as a proportion of the rebased GDP are significantly smaller.

References

Acemoglu, D. and J.A. Robinson, 2001, 'A Theory of Political Transitions', *The American Economic Review*, 91(4), pp. 938–963.

Anaman, K.A. and Agyei-Sasu, F., 2012, 'Impact of Democratic Political Transition on the Performance of Business Firms in Ghana', *Economic Papers: A Journal of Applied Economics and Policy*, 31, pp. 391-400.

Bollen K.A. and Jackman, R.W., 1985, 'Economic and Noneconomic Determinants of Political Democracy in the 1960s', *Research in Political Sociology*, 1, pp. 27-48.

Burkhart, R.E., and Lewis-Beck, M.S., 1994, 'Comparative Democracy: The Economic

Development Thesis', *American Political Science Review,* 88, pp. 903-910

Cutright, P. and Wiley, J.A., 1969, 'Modernization and Political Representation: 1927-1966', *Studies in Comparative International Development*, 5(1), pp. 23-44.

Databank, 2011, *Investment and Macroeconomic Developments in some African Countries,* Accra, Ghana: Databank Research Department.Gonsalez, M.D.L.A., 2002, 'Do Changes in Democracy Affect the Political Budget Cycle? Evidence from Mexico', *Review of Development Economics*, 6(2), pp. 204-224.

Helliwell, J., 1992, *Empirical Linkages between Democracy and Economic Growth*, National Bureau of Economic Research Working Paper No. 4066, Washington DC, USA.

Hicks, J.R., 1939, 'The Foundations of Welfare Economics', *Economic Journal*, 49(196), pp. 696-712.

Kaldor, N., 1939, 'Welfare Propositions and Inter-personal Comparisons of Utility', *Economic Journal*, 49(195), pp. 549-552.

Libich, J., Savage, J. and Stehlik, P., 2010, 'Fiscal Neglect in a Monetary Union', *Economic Papers*, 29(3), pp. 301-309.

Lipset, S.M., 1959, *Economic Development and Political Legitimacy*, London: Bobbs-Merril.

Ministry of Finance and Economic Planning, 2011, *2010 Fiscal Data Final*, 31 May, Accra, Ghana: Ministry of Finance and Economic Planning.

Nordhaus, W., 1975, 'The Political Business Cycle', *Review of Economic Studies*, 42, pp. 169-90.

Rodrik, D. and R. Wacziarg, 2005, 'Do Democratic Transitions Produce Bad Economic Outcomes?', *The American Economic Review* 95(2), pp. 50–55.

Sen, A., 1993, 'Markets and Freedom: Achievements and Limitations of the Market Mechanism in Promoting Individual Freedoms', *Oxford Economic Papers*, 45(4), 519-541.

Welzel, C. and Inglehart, R., 1999, *Analyzing Democratic Change and Stability: A Human Development Theory of Democracy*, Paper FS III 99-202, Berlin, Germany: Wissenschaftszentrum Berlin für Sozialforschung GmbH.

Winham, G.R., 1970, 'Political Development and Learner's Theory: Further Test of a Causal Model', *American Political Science Review*, 64(4), pp. 810-818.

7

Political Transitions, Electoral Mobilization, and State Institutions[1]

Kwame A. Ninsin

Introduction

In November-December of 1992 Ghanaians went to the polls to elect a new government to climax their struggle to live no longer under a military regime but under a democratically elected government. Since then the country has undergone a democratic transition every four years. In practical terms the transitions have entailed the transfer of political and administrative power from one group of political elite to another either within the same political party or of another political party. Following the 1996 and 2004 elections the political transition occurred within the incumbent political party – the National Democratic Congress (NDC) and the New Patriotic Party (NPP), respectively. However the 2000 and 2008 elections resulted in a change of government from the NDC to the NPP, and from the NPP to the NDC, respectively. This chapter dwells on the second instance of political transition. Despite the formal change of government the practicalities of political transitions to date have exposed informal and unwritten dimensions which threaten the stability of the nation- state. First the election that ushers in political transitions has created a nation of winners and losers. In particular for the winners an election has meant opportunities for them to emerge as a new ruling elite – a group of new political actors and their political allies that enjoy almost untrammeled access to political power and wealth. For the losers on the other hand an election means a fall from power and loss of access to wealth and privileges associated with public office. In effect, an election – especially transition elections[2] – is an opportunity for a faction of the political class to win state/political power in order to gain unqualified access to the wealth of the nation.

On the whole, political transitions have always become moments for some groups to jubilate and others to grieve. They open old cleavages and create new ones, and in so doing divide society along multiple fault lines, leading to conflict as well as intense and desperate rivalry in the political arena. Transitions have also engendered tension and uncertainty, and raised questions about individual as well as group survival, identity and national cohesion. The fear, insecurity and anguish that transitions have generated at the personal level impact adversely on state institutions and diminish the latter's capacity to discharge their governance responsibilities effectively. In short, political transitions in Ghana since 1992 have turned out to be conflictual; because the ultimate prize at stake is the control of state power and wealth, the protagonists engage in intense political competition to a point that threatens the capacity of state institutions, national stability and security.

In what follows I first examine the key features of Ghana's democratic transitions. This is followed by an analysis of how the intense political competition that has characterized political transitions since the return to democratic rule has impacted adversely on the capacity and stability of the state, and on national cohesion.

Transition Politics: Politics Without Rules

Normally electoral mobilization for the citizens' mandate to govern should follow the quadrennial election cycle stipulated in the 1992 Constitution. On the contrary Ghanaian politics has been characterized by permanent mobilization of the electorate, especially by leaders of the defeated political party, immediately the presidential election results have been declared. Permanent electoral mobilization is most pronounced during periods immediately following the end of transition elections. At the end of transition elections the political party of the defeated presidential candidate immediately embarks on a project of permanent criticism and agitation against the newly elected government with the aim of discrediting it and delegitimizing its mandate to govern. The intensification of electoral mobilization compels the new government to contest the adversarial politics of the defeated political party. Quite often this contestation drags on, with rising crescendo, as the nation moves closer to the next elections - as was the case in 2012. In this intensely contested political environment the new government is unable to immediately grapple with the imperatives of governing for the good of the nation.

Since 1992 the country has gone through two transition elections - in 2000 and 2008. Those two elections involved the transfer of political and administrative power between the political elites of the NDC and those of the NPP in 2000/2001 and 2008/2009. However, contrary to the present situation when Parliament recently enacted the *Presidential (Transition) Act 2012, Act 845*[3] the country had not legislated agreed rules and procedures to manage the formal transfer of power. The existing institutional vacuum enabled the competing elites to determine their own rules for managing the transition process claiming to ensure political stability and firm control of state power from the outgoing political elite. The democratic electoral system of winner-takes-all provides a powerful justification for the appropriation of state power and the associated material resources by the in-coming political elite against any presumed right by the outgoing political elite to contest that claim.

The actual transition process can only be described as transition without rules. Here is what happened. After the transition elections of 2000 and 2008 the transition teams of the outgoing government and the incoming government were set up on the spur of the moment. In the heat of the moment the representatives of the two rival political parties faced each other to try and jointly manage the process, first to lay down the modalities to guide the process and second to implement it. In reality they met to contest each other's claim to the state apparatus[4] and state assets. In the 2000/2001 transition the two teams first met on 1 January, 2001 which gave them barely one week to manage the very sensitive and intricate process of formally handing over state power to administer the country to the incoming government on 7 January 2001.[5] The situation in 2008/2009 was not different.

Bringing the representatives of the two rival political parties face to face and expecting them to consummate a process in which both of them had a huge stake was a recipe for open hostility and acrimonious exchanges. In the absence of settled rules and procedures for regulating the process each transition team determined its own rules to guide the process. This was compounded by the limited time available for the outgoing government to hand over the administration of the nation to the new government. The result was the acrimonious exchanges that characterized each transition process. In 2008 the incumbent NPP government had made some preliminary transition arrangements,[6] but those preparations were considered by the in-coming government to be partisan, lacking the essential attributes of neutrality, in particular, consensus. Those arrangements could therefore not be considered binding on the transition team of the President-elect. Especially as both the defeated presidential candidates in the 2000 and 2008 transition elections[7] disputed the victory of the other candidate, each transition team approached the process from a hostile position.

Because the transition elections had settled the question of which rival political elite was entitled to exercise state power, as per the constitution, the controversy between the two contending political elites took the form of intense dispute over the stock of state assets – including lands, houses and cars; who gets what, from what stock and under what conditions. There was also dispute over the state of the economy: the rate of inflation in the economy, the size of the national debt and its ratio to the GDP, etc. Indeed the transition process was nothing more than a dispute over the size of the wealth of the nation and who had pre-eminent right to control it.

The tension, insecurity, and anxiety generated by the transition politics affected both the political elite of the outgoing government and people in senior administrative and executive positions. During the two transition periods the incoming government issued directives requesting outgoing ministers of state and other political appointees and functionaries to vacate government/state-owned houses that had been assigned to them for official use, and also return specified official vehicles which were in their custody. The enforcement of such directives often dragged into the first few months of the tenure of the new government as some personnel of the outgoing government challenged or defied the directive. In several instances the new government found it expedient to deploy personnel of the state security agencies to enforce compliance.

There were other sources of recrimination and anxiety within the ranks of the feuding political elites, such as the retention, redeployment or retrenchment of public officers who were regarded as political appointees, including those engaged in the country's diplomatic missions abroad. The new government's policy affected the heads of a wide range of state institutions such as the civil service (e.g., Chief Directors and Directors), public corporations (engaged in production, and service delivery), educational institutions, district assemblies, governing councils of public boards and corporations, the Council of State and the Bank of Ghana. The governing councils and officers of the security and quasi security agencies are also reconstituted. Between May and July 2009 the President made about 272 new appointments to the governing boards/councils of not less than 60 state/public bodies. A number of such new appointments were made about 3 months after the President had issued a directive dissolving the previous governing boards/councils. Effectively, such changes in the top hierarchy of the public service would leave the affected institutions in a state of uncertainty and paralysis as they waited for the vacancies to be filled and for new policy direction.

At the individual level the transition politics manifested itself as a sense of loss, fear and insecurity among politicians and political appointees, public sector administrators and their relations. Some of the affected persons might have occupied key decision-making positions at various levels of state and quasi-state institutions; others may remain in their current official positions but would be weighed down by a sense of uncertainty and fear. Invariably personal responses to the tense transition situation impacted adversely on state institutions in various ways – either as institutional weakness or as institutional paralysis. Such impacts were transmitted as actions or inactions of the individual agents of state who occupied key positions in the state machinery – e.g., the judiciary, the civil service, public corporations, the security agencies and other state and quasi-state institutions – with serious national security implications.

The tension, uncertainty about one's position or the direction of public policy under the incoming government, the fear of redeployment, retrenchment or fear of prosecution, cumulatively affected the morale, disposition and commitment to work on the part of people operating in the institutions of state. Similarly, uncertainty about policy direction of the new government, including policies and attitude towards the private sector, especially with regard to macro-economic management policy, the state's fiscal matters, as well as the management of existing contracts, including payment of arrears owed to private sector companies and to its debtors affected more or less the capacity of private sector corporate entities to do business.

Electoral Mobilization

Transition politics, which manifests itself immediately as the struggle to control the wealth of the nation, inaugurates the next phase of the transition process which is electoral mobilization towards the coming elections. It is launched by the political party that has lost the immediate past elections with the resolve to reverse its fortunes in the next elections. The victorious political party responds immediately with similar tactics. In such a highly adversarial political environment, electoral mobilization by both the ruling and opposition political parties is scarcely driven by a set of policy alternatives. Rather each of the contending political parties mobilizes primordial identities such as tribe/ethnicity and region rather than ideas and policies. Where a region is dominated by a single tribal or ethnic group, the entire region becomes the focus of electoral mobilization. The mobilization of ethnic identities is crucial for the two main contending political parties because increasingly the tribe or ethnic group has become a salient factor in electoral politics (Jonah 1998:229-257; Gyimah-Boadi 2001:67-68; and Frempong 2006). The mobilization of ethnic identities enables these political parties to secure vital political capital for the coming electoral contest; it promises a short-cut to electoral victory.

Ethnic elites benefit from the electoral victory of their political party: they become beneficiaries of government contracts, access to huge bank credit, appointment to elite public offices, and other forms of patronage. On public appointments, Asante and Gyimah-Boadi (2004) have pointed out that an audit of presidential appointments to various offices since the dawn of the Fourth Republic is most likely to reveal a palpable trend towards ethnic appointments.

Because electoral mobilization tends to assume tribal/ethnic and regional dimensions, the winners and losers in transition politics also tend to segregate along tribal/ethno-regional lines. Where the winners-losers divide is coterminous more or less with people in the geo-political division of the country: for example,

Ewes in the Volta Region, Asantes in the Ashanti Region, and northern tribes who tend to associate en bloc with the northern Regions (their internal differences notwithstanding), the politicization of primordial cleavages is exacerbated, and political discourse tends to capitalize on such cleavages instead of becoming a discourse on alternative public policy. Transition elections therefore have a strong tendency to open up social cleavages where some of them may be dormant. Such cleavages could easily become the source of a variety of conflict and instability, thereby jeopardizing the cohesion and peace of the nation.

State Patrimony and Endless Electoral Mobilization

Why is the Ghanaian elite so keen on winning state power? As Dunn has pointed out, democratic elections provide an orderly and legitimate means for exercising state power.[8] After decades of military rule the Ghanaian political elite is justified in celebrating democratic elections. Apart from affording them a secure and orderly procedure for winning state power, elections also protect their claim to govern the country. Ghana's political elite cherish democratic elections for another reason, which is the control of the state and through it to gain access to the vast state resources available for distribution. Since the end of colonialism politicians have viewed the state as the means for securing access to the vast economic resources of the nation. Edie argues, 'For the elites the loss of influence over the state meant the loss of everything. Losing an office meant not only losing political influence but also access to economic resources. The state had the power to determine success or failure of economic actors.' (Edie 2003:65-66) Accordingly the political elite indulges in intense competition among themselves, sometimes to absurd limits, to win control over it. Hence since 1992 competition for parliamentary seats has become quite aggressive: in 1992 there were 463 candidates competing for 200 seats; in 1996 there were 778 candidates competed for 200 seats; in 2000 the number increased 1,074 candidates competed for 200 seats; in 2004 the nuber fell 951 candidates competed for 230 seats; in 2008 1,060 candidates competed for 230 seats; and in 2012 the nuber inceased again 1,332 competed for 275 seats. In 1992 the average number of candidates per constituency (a total of 200) was 3. Despite the fact that the number of constituencies had increased from 200 in 2000 to 230 in 2008 (an increase of 15%) and then to 275 in 2012 (an increase of 19%), the average number of candidates per constituency in 2012 had increased by 66.67 per cent in the 2008 and 2012 elections when the average number of candidates per constituency had risen to 5.

In effect therefore elections have become a method for conferring a veneer of democratic legitimacy on what the political elite regard as the proprietary right to power which is power to control the state, its bureaucratic apparatus as well as the wealth and other assets of the nation. This culture of power as a proprietary right is strengthened by the Constitution which confers almost unbounded power on the victorious political party to control public wealth and other assets. Anaman[9] puts the total wealth that the victorious political party elite controls at 'about 50 billion Ghana cedis over the four-year period (based on an average budget of 12.5 billion Ghana cedis of national government spending per year using actual government spending for 2010 of the current government as a guide). With government spending averaging between 25 to 30 per cent of the gross domestic product of the country, the elected government has considerable amount of power and resources to manage (or mismanage) the affairs of the country.' To win control of the state therefore means securing control of this huge national wealth (which has been increasing exponentially with the discovery of oil in commercial quantities) and using it for purposes that are often unaccounted for and perverse, and offends the citizens of the country.

The electoral mandate further confers on the victorious political party, represented by the president, the power to make infinite number of appointments, from cabinet ministers and top executives in state and quasi-state organizations (including board members of public boards and corporations) to lower level political and executive appointments such as district chief executives and executive heads of, for example the Ghana Youth Empowerment and Entrepreneur Development Agency (GYEEDA), National Health Insurance Scheme (NHIS), National Disaster Management Organization (NADMO) and National Identification Authority. These constitutionally mandated appointments alone make the president a very powerful head of an extensive and rich patrimony, and the rank and file of his party become privileged beneficiaries of financially rewarding patronage. The attraction of such patrimony binds the rank and file of a party together, infusing them with a passion for permanent electoral mobilization.

Transition Politics and State Institutions

The mass redeployment of public servants of talent and experience during transition periods adversely affects the capacity of the state bureaucracy and other public sector institutions. The unavoidably slow process in redeploying personnel and replacing them with new appointees compounds problems for both institutions and individuals who are caught in the redeployment politics. In particular, the processes for new appointments which are regulated by the Constitution virtually paralyzes public institutions and stalls the business of managing public affairs. For example, Articles 71, 72, 74 (1), 183 (4.a), 185 (3) and 189 (1.a) of the Constitution provide that the President shall make a number of key executive appointments in consultation with the Council of State. However, over the years change of government has also meant change in the membership of the Council of State whose re-constitution is often held up by other constitutional requirements. For example, when there is change of government, fresh elections should be organized to choose the 10 regional representatives on the Council of State. This constitutional requirement further makes it obligatory that the Metropolitan, Municipal and District Assemblies (MMDAs) would be re-constituted[10] through the appointment of new Chief Executives and new government appointees. Furthermore, the new MMDAs have to hold fresh elections to choose a presiding member and other principal officers. The election of new presiding members as well as the approval of new MMDCEs could be held up by internal, largely partisan squabbling, leading to long delays in reconstituting the MMDAs. The reconstitution of the Council of State could therefore be delayed, becoming a huge obstacle to the early appointment of top public officers in accordance with the Constitution. In 2001, for example, the Council of State was sworn in on 19 July and had to start work immediately.[11] Meanwhile, with the good intention of saving precious time and getting the central government machinery to start functioning, pending the inauguration of the reconstituted Council of State, the new President had decided to make a number of senior-level appointments. Before long, a member of the out-going government had filed a writ in court restraining the President from making appointments without consulting the Council of State, arguing justifiably that any such appointments contravened the Constitution (see Daily Graphic 2 January 2001).

Conclusion

I have argued that elections that usher in political transitions have divided the nation into winners and losers, where for the winners the election propels them to the position of a new ruling elite with almost unqualified access to political power and wealth, and the losers a fall from power and loss of access to wealth and privileges associated with public office. The notion that control of the state is the key to controlling and appropriating the wealth of the nation emboldens the protagonists to engage in intense political, often vindictive, competition to a point that threatens the capacity of state institutions, as well as the unity, stability and security of the nation. In the heat of this adversarial politics political competition tends to mobilize tribal/ethnic, and other primordial cleavages instead of unleashing a discourse on alternative public policy. Transition elections, and by extension politics in general, therefore have a strong tendency to open up social cleavages even where some of them may be dormant. This has become the bane of Ghana's politics in general.

The notion that control of state power is a means to monopolize public resources in the form of financial and other assets, appointments and other reward systems underscores three inter-related features of transition politics. First it underscores the nature of power as an inherently priceless value that political elites should fight for at all cost – even if it means fighting for it at the cost of one's life. Hence a leading contender of the presidency in the 2012 elections would admonish his followers to be prepared to fight even if it would cost them their lives. After all, 'All die be die.'[12] Second, it makes electoral mobilization a political imperative for any political party that would like to win state power at the next elections. Hence the endless nature of the transition process and why electoral mobilization does not end with the declaration of the just-ended presidential election results. Third, permanent electoral mobilization diminishes the capacity of the state to govern effectively. This in turn makes it easier for the elites of the two leading political parties to politicize such institutions in their struggle to 'capture' the state apparatus, and control the wealth of the nation.

Notes

1. This chapter was developed from several draft reports on Ghana's political transition that I prepared for the Institute for Democratic Governance (IDEG) as part of a project sponsored by the UNDP titled 'Democratic Transitions and Human Development in Ghana' in 2010-2011. I acknowledge the contribuition made into the clarification of the concept of 'permanent mobilization' by Dr Emmanuel O. Akwetey of the Institute for Democratic Governance, Accra.

2. Since the1992 general elections Ghana has changed government every 8 years, that is, after the second tenure of the ruling political party, which seems to suggest an evolving tradition that there will be a change of government every 8-year election cycle. The elections that climax this eight-year cycle are here referred to as 'transition elections'.

3. See the *Presidential (Transition) Act, 2012, Act 845*

4. The state apparatus must be distinguished from state power the control of which is usually decided at the polls.

5. Interview with a member of the NPP's 2000/2001 transition team. According to this source, it was most unlikely that the outgoing NDC government had thought it imperative to establish a transition team as a contingency measure. The most probable explanation for this is that the NDC did not expect to lose the elections. Hence, without reference to the representatives of other political parties or any established authority with responsibility for managing the transition, it had gone ahead to initiate preparations for the swearing-in of the President and the inaugural dinner, including the compilation of a list of guests who would be invited to the two events.

6. According to Mr Kwadwo Mpiani, Minister of State and Chief of Staff at the Office of the President, the government had prepared a transition handbook with the help of the Canadian Government, and all the Chief Directors had been directed to prepare detailed handing-over notes on their respective ministries in preparation for a smooth handing over of the administration to a new government. See Daily Graphic, December 2000.

7. In the 2008 presidential elections, for example, the NDC presidential candidate had obtained 4,521,032 votes against the NPP candidate's 4,480,446 following the run-off, winning with a very slim majority.

8. Dunn celebrates democracy as a preferred form of governance because it provides the framework for orderly and legitimate exercise of power. See his introduction in Dunn (1992) Democracy, The Unfinished Journey 508 BC to AD 1993 Oxford: Oxford University Press.

9. See Chapter 6 of this volume.

10. A new president normally removes the MMDCEs and terminates the tenure of the government appointees on the MMDAs.

11. According to our interview with a member of the 2000/2001 Transition Team of the President-Elect, the reconstituted Council of State had to get down to work immediately even when it did not have records from the previous Council of State; it did not have secretarial staff, handover notes or no adequate furniture for serious Council deliberations.

12. This political declaration was made at the political party's public rally on Tuesday 8 February 2011 in the Eastern Region of Ghana.

References

Asante, R. and E. Gyimah-Boadi, 2004, 'Ethnic Structure, Inequality and the Governance of the Public Sector in Ghana' in Yusuf Bangura (ed.) Ethnic Structure, Inequality and Governance of the Public Sector Geneva: UNRISD.

Dunn, J., 1992, Democracy, The Unfinished Journey 508 BC to AD 1993, Oxford: Oxford University Press.

Edie, C.J., 2003, Politics in Africa: A New Beginning? Belmont: Wadsworth.

Gyimah-Boadi, E., 2001, 'The December 2000 elections and prospects for democratic consolidation' in Joseph R A Ayee (ed.) Deepening Democracy in Ghana: Politics of the 2000 Elections, Vol. One, Accra: Freedom Publications.

Frempong, A.K.D., 2006, 'Ethnicity, Democracy and Ghana's Election 2004' in K. Boafo-Arthur (ed.), Voting for Democracy in Ghana Vol. 1.

Jonah, K., 1998, 'Agency and structure in Ghana's 1992 and 1996 presidential elections' in Joseph R A Ayee (ed.) The 1996 General Elections and Democratic Consolidation in Ghana, Legon: Department of Political Science, University of Ghana.

8

Democracy without Development: The Perils of Plutocracy in Ghana

Maxwell Owusu

By the close of the first decade and a half of the 21st century, a preponderant majority of the 54 independent African countries, including Ghana which won independence from British colonial rule on 6 March 1957 after a hard, long, and bloody struggle, will have marked or celebrated their 50th anniversaries of independence from European rule. The first wave of African decolonization that occurred in the 1950s affected only a handful of countries, namely Libya, Morocco, Tunisia (North Africa); Sudan (East Africa) and Ghana and Guinea (West Africa). The second and larger wave followed in the 1960s when thirty-one countries, more than half of them former French colonies, gained their independence. This provides a good opportunity for the historically-minded student of African democracy and political economy, in the sense of the principles governing the generation and distribution of surplus wealth among the different socio-economic classes and the state's role in the process, to step back and assess, on the basis of the available empirical evidence and relevant historical facts, the socio-economic and political development achievements, failures and challenges of Ghana to derive some lessons, parallels and wisdom, if not inspiration, for national policy for the next half-century.

The present study draws heavily on, expands and clarifies some of the observations made on the subject of the role of money and wealth in the politics of democratization and development in Ghana in earlier publications by the author: *Money and Politics: 'The Challenge of Democracy in Ghana* (Owusu 2009), 'Two Cheers for Ghanaian Democracy: Lessons from the Last Half Century for the Next Half Century: A Review Essay' (Owusu 2006) and *Uses and Abuses of Political Power: A Case Study of Continuity and Change in the Politics of Ghana* (Owusu 2006).

A large body of literature on Ghanaian elections, politics, democracy and development by foreign and Ghanaians scholars, notably E. Gyimah-Boadi, Kwame Ninsin and others, suggests that there exists in Ghana (and several other African countries) a viable and resilient political culture that combines indigenous African and British traditions: a pattern of political attitudes, values and beliefs and an underlying set of social attitudes and practices that is supportive, paradoxically, of both popular revolt and uprising against authoritarian and dictatorial rule, or simply bad governance, as well as a peaceful and stable democratic process and rapid socioeconomic development. In an earlier essay, I argue that the precolonial '…tradition of rebellion, rooted in evolving African customary law concepts of the subordination of the chief to 'constitutional law' and the 'right' and duty of the subject to disobey and even kill an autocratic or tyrannical ruler, has persisted and adapted to modern conditions (see Owusu 1986:69-99)

As a result, Ghanaians never despaired even in their darkest days of one-party government, *coups d'etat* and military rule, about the prospects for democracy and development in Ghana. Indeed, one obvious lesson to be learnt from the chequered experience of the past 50 years is that if full participation. that is, including and beyond regular elections, in the political system at all levels (centre and periphery) and access to the channels and opportunities for social and economic improvement and welfare are limited to a privileged, well-connected or fortunate few and denied to a large segment of the Ghanaian population, Ghana's democratic and development promise will continue to remain unfulfilled. And that this will pose serious challenges to the self-image of Ghana as a prosperous, peaceful, democratic society and the political lodestar of Africa.

African Democracy in the World Context: The Ghana Case

In the period between 1966 when the Nkrumah CPP one-party democracy was overthrown by a police/military *coup d'etat* and 1993 when multi-party constitutional democracy was restored in Ghana and several African countries, no less than 63 military *coups* had occurred on the African continent. Meanwhile there had been successful wars of national liberation in countries such as South Africa, Namibia, Zimbabwe and the former Portuguese colonies of Angola, Mozambique, Guinea-Bissau and São Tomé and Principe, and bloody civil wars in Nigeria and Liberia among others (Legum 1999:31-32). The widespread political instability and general economic decline and mass poverty obliged The Economist magazine to describe Africa, rather cynically, as 'the hopeless continent' (*The Economist* May 2000.) This is hardly surprising, given the contradictory policies, purposes, influences and legacies of European colonial rule in Africa. Simply put, colonial rule in Africa simultaneously encouraged and retarded Africa's political and socio-economic transformation depending on the dictates of the perceived national interest (military, geo-political, commercial, trade and social) current at the time.

According to Carrington, '...the [merchant] adventurers who conducted the partition [of Africa] whatever their motives, alike failed to interest capitalists in their enterprises' (1961:36). European capital went mostly to the white settler colonies such as Australia and South Africa where there were much safer investments. Ross Johnston also notes that 'the thinking of the British government and British business interests was that Western industrial might was sufficient to meet all the manufacturing needs of the African colonies – they could supply the raw materials which Europe would process'. Johnston again claims that 'Lugard set the pattern when he proclaimed that 'a Government would not be wise to hasten the advent of the factory in Africa. ...Mineral exploitation, however, was accompanied by some degree of industrialization' (Johnston 1981:148). Indeed, Frederick Lugard, one of the most famous British colonial administrators in Africa, candidly admitted in the *Dual Mandate in British Tropical Africa* (1929) that 'European brains, capital, and energy have not been and never will be expended in developing the resources of Africa from motives of pure philanthropy' (quoted in Owusu 1992:375).

In effect, colonial policies and practices thus routinely cut off Africa from new technology and new capital investments from abroad, which alone could have released her full development potential (see also Rodney 1972:162-310).

In post-colonial Africa, the culture of corrupt and autocratic political leadership, whether instigated or propped up by foreign powers and interests or by pure self-interest, has also contributed immensely to mounting international debt, political violence and repression and persistent poverty. Colonial education created a small African political class, an elite with oligarchic or authoritarian tendencies, which preferred to perpetuate its own ascendance and privileged status after independence rather than to share power and national wealth with the less privileged groups in African society. After decolonization, most African countries were basically poor, underdeveloped, predominantly extractive mineral and agrarian monocrop export economies, with small, but rapidly growing, mostly illiterate populations.

It is important also not to forget, as Ivor Jennings has correctly pointed out in his classic *Democracy in Africa* (1963), that 'the essential problem of African democracy is... the essential problem of democracy everywhere – and it is wise to remember that only a few countries in the world have really made a success of it. Democracy has succeeded in Northwestern Europe and in a few countries outside Europe because it has become *entwined* in the *traditions* of the people' (Jennings 1963:68-69).

Jennings further notes that the consolidation of democracy requires several favourable events. These include strong political organization with its roots in the villages, as well as efficient and honest leadership (Owusu 1992). Among the obvious risks, Jennings warns, are nepotism and corruption; racialism, communalism or tribalism; dictatorship, anarchy or economic breakdown. There is no sure way of guarding against the risks. Constitutional safeguards help, but they can be overridden.

Moreover Miliband (1992) claims that *capitalist* democracy 'is a contradiction in terms, for it encapsulates two opposed systems': on the one hand is capitalism a system of economic organization that demands the existence of a relatively small class of people who own and control the main means of industrial, commercial and financial activity, as well as a major part of the means of communication; these people thereby exercise a totally disproportionate amount of influence on politics and society both in their own countries and in lands far beyond their own borders. On the other hand, there is democracy, which is based on the denial of such preponderance and which requires a rough *equality of condition* that capitalism... repudiates by its very nature' (Miliband 1992:109) (see also Perham 1962, Carrington 1961:36, Johnston 1981:148 and Rodney 1972). The poverty of Africa has direct implication for sustainable democracy. The evolution and development of modern democracy in Western societies and in the non-western world colonized by Western powers since the 19th century clearly demonstrate a mixed record of achievement. For each of the unique constellations of political institutions and practices distinguishing democracies today from non-democracies, such as universal suffrage, freedom of political association and institutions that ensure the peaceful transfer of power from the losing party leader to the winning party leader after elections, seems to have a relatively independent history and pattern of development depending on the particular country. For example, in a majority of African countries, the universal adult franchise and its exercise was achieved long before other democratic elements had time to take root. In contrast, in many of the mature or older democracies of Britain, U.S. and Western Europe, universal suffrage was preceded by industrialization of the economy, improved standards of living and mass literacy, all of which are beneficial to, if not necessary prerequisites, for sustainable modern democracies. But even in the older, more prosperous democracies, it was not until, in some cases, after World War I or World War II that the vote was extended to every adult citizen, regardless of race, gender, class, property or level of education.

The Meaning of Elections in a Democracy

From the wider historical perspective of global democratization in the modern age, the record since independence of Ghana and other African countries (notably Botswana, Mauritius, Senegal and Benin) that have comparatively fewer resources or advantages, such as high levels of literacy and a prosperous economy which favour the consolidation of modern democracy, is commendable in many respects. Despite David Apter's sensible and timely caution about democratization in Uganda against 'the ease and confidence with which pronouncements about prospects for democracy are made by political scientists with reference to countries about which they have not the foggiest notion of complexities faced by the people on the ground' (Apter 1995:158), there are good grounds for optimism about the future of democracy and development, not only in Ghana, but in most of the rest of Africa in the first half of the 21st century.

Ghana's democratic achievement since the inauguration of the constitution of the Fourth Republic in 1992 is an iconic testament to the progressive consolidation and routinization of electoral democracy in an increasing number of African countries. There is hard evidence for this assessment. First, it is noteworthy that one of the severest critics of the lack of meaningful progress in postcolonial African economic and political development, *The Economist* magazine, which in an editorial a couple of years before had described Africa as a 'hopeless continent' had this to say following the controversial Nigerian presidential election of 2007 won by the late Umaru Yar' Adua: 'Nigeria's latest shameful and rigged election does not mean that all Africa is hopeless'. It adds: 'Nigeria is not typical of Africa' and that Nigeria's dismal performance as a would-be democracy does not cast a blight across the rest of Africa. For, 'Over the past decade or so, the rest of the continent has on the whole been taking modest, belated but encouraging steps towards greater prosperity, security and democracy.' It continues: '...Remember it was only in 1991 that, for the first time since independence, the leader of any African country (not counting the Indian Ocean State of Mauritius) was peacefully voted out of office – in Benin ... Since then many African countries [including Ghana] have followed suit. Multi-party elections, though often very messy, *have become far commoner*' (*The Economist* 28 April 2007: italics added).

Second, comparing the state of African politics and political leadership style from the late 1990s to the first decade of the 21st century, to that of the previous forty years, Kenyan Wangari Maathai, the 2004 Nobel Peace Prize winner, former parliamentarian and Deputy Minister for the Environment and Natural Resources, points out correctly in her recent publication, that

> Few African leaders today dare to be as autocratic as their predecessors. In nearly all sub-Saharan African countries, democratic space has increased and opposition movements are stronger than they were (although, of course, this varies by region and country). More leaders than ever before in post-independence Africa have their actions scrutinized or checked by an increasingly vocal and sophisticated civil society, and a freer and at times vibrant press. In addition, more heads of government have their time in office limited by set terms and elections (Maathai 2009:54).

It is noteworthy in this regard that the most recent results of the annual Ibrahim Index of African Governance indicate that African governance has continued to improve since 2000. According to this report 'multi-party systems are now more normal in Africa and most countries demand that their leaders step down after constitutionally mandated term limits.' The Index codes fairness of national elections and assesses opposition participation in elections at the executive and legislative levels, as well as press freedom, respect for civil rights and the absence of gender discrimination (as measured by women's economic, political and social rights). Governance in thirty-four of forty-eight sub-Saharan African governments have shown improvements. In 2006, the Ibrahim Index of African Governance ranked Ghana seventh in overall improvements after Mauritius (ranked first), Seychelles (ranked second), Cape Verde (ranked third), Botswana (ranked fourth), South Africa (ranked fifth), and Namibia (ranked sixth). Gabon was ranked eighth after Ghana, Sao Tome and Principe (ranked ninth) and Senegal was ranked tenth. Sudan, Chad, Democratic Republic of the Congo and Somalia were, not surprisingly, among the worst governance performers in Africa (Rotberg 2009:118-119).

Thirdly, and perhaps more significantly, Freedom House, using two broad categories of freedom namely, political rights and civil liberties, has developed composite scores which are averaged to determine the overall status of a country as either 'Free', 'Partly Free' or 'Not Free'. These terms may be used interchangeably with 'Democratic', 'Partly Democratic' or 'Not Democratic'. In addition to these terms, Freedom House describes as 'electoral democracy' states that have competitive multi-party polities, universal suffrage, regularly contested elections using a secret ballot and without huge voter fraud, and significant access of major political parties to the voters through the media and open political campaigning. For a country to qualify as an electoral democracy, the last presidential or parliamentary (legislative) election held in the country must be competitive (see 'Methodology', http://www.freedomhouse.org/template.cfm?page=1). Since 2003 Freedom House has rated Ghana as being 'Democratic' or 'Free' and as an 'electoral democracy' on the basis, among other factors, that John A. Kufuor, who succeeded Jerry John Rawlings, served two terms and in 2008 was succeeded peacefully by John Atta Mills. Freedom House concludes that democracy appears to have taken root in Ghana.

To underscore this remarkable sense of growing optimism about the future of democracy and development in Ghana and Africa generally, the front cover page of a recent issue of the *Economist* entitled *Africa Rising* portrays, symbolically, a young African school boy flying a kite in the shape of the continent of Africa in brilliant rainbow colours high up in the sky. The editorial notes that after decades of slow economic growth, Africa has a real chance to follow in the footsteps of Asia's fast growth rates. Pointing to the link between democracy and development the editorial explains, 'All this is happening partly because Africa is at last getting a taste of peace and decent government....' The editorial continues, '...since Benin set the mainland trend in 1991 [of peacefully ousting a government or president at the ballot box] it has happened more than 30 times – far more often than in the Arab World'.

However, *The Economist* was quick to stress that optimism about Africa 'needs to be taken in fairly small doses, for things are still exceedingly bleak in much of the continent'. The editorial goes on:

> Most Africans live on less than two dollars a day. Food production per person has slumped since independence in the 1960s. The average lifespan in some countries is under 50. Drought and famine persist, the climate is worsening, with deforestation and desertification still on the march. Yet against this depressingly familiar backdrop, Africa is making significant economic progress. Africa now has a fast growing middle class, according to the World Bank, around 60 million Africans have an income of $3,000 a year and 100 million will in 2015 (*The Economist* 3-9 December 2011:15).

But this is for a growing current African population of over 1 billion. Indeed, a recent report from the Africa Progress Panel led by the former UN Secretary-General Kofi Annan, a Ghanaian, found that African countries were growing faster than almost any other region with booming exports and more foreign investment. But it warned that there was a disturbing contrast between a growing yet still *relatively small middle class* and the large majority of Africans left behind. Annan's study found that almost half of Africans were still on incomes below the poverty benchmark of $1.25 a day. Ghana was the fastest-growing economy in the world in 2011 and Ethiopia expanded more quickly than China in the period from 2004-2009 according to the report, but it added that the current trickle-down pattern (without a real distribution of wealth in favour of the poor was leaving too many people in destitution. 'The deep, persistent and enduring inequalities in evidence across Africa have consequences' the report said. 'They weaken the bonds of trust and solidarity that hold societies together. Over the long run, they will undermine economic growth, productivity and the development of markets'. The Annan report added 'it cannot be said often enough, that overall progress remains too slow and too uneven; that too many Africans remain caught in downward spirals of poverty, insecurity and marginalization; that too few people benefit from the continent's growth trend and rising geo-strategic importance; that too much of Africa's enormous wealth remains in the hands of narrow elites and increasingly foreign investors without being turned into tangible benefits for its people' (*The Guardian Weekly* 18-24 May 2012:18 italics added). The Annan report clearly reveals the paradox and challenge of post-colonial African social transformation, namely economic growth without a broad-based development, that is without the benefits of growth translated into sustainable improvements in the material well-being of the common people, the pro-democracy voting masses.

The conduct of elections is critical to the determination of a country's status in Freedom House's scheme of things, but it is equally true that elections pose special problems, some historical, some cultural and social, and others economic and technical, that are not easy to overcome. As MacKenzie and Robinson (1960:1) have pointed out, in such circumstances elections *mean* not the same thing in different countries, especially where the colonial rule bequeathed ambiguous states and an amalgam of cultures in which elections were planted as the only ideological basis for constituting legitimate government. Moreover, certain conditions must be met for elections to be meaningful, including a body of dedicated officials who have high standards of honesty and routine competence. The existence of such an administration creates and steadies public confidence in electoral procedure, but unless it is supported by public confidence along with the active engagement of civil society in the political system this particular task is beyond it. In this regard, I believe also that the excellent performance of Ghana's electoral commission, since the inauguration of the Fourth Republic, under the leadership of Kwadwo Afari-Gyan (Chairman of Ghana's Electoral Commission) has no doubt contributed to both the international reputation of the electoral commission and to the public trust in the electoral process in Ghana, as well as to the designation of Ghana as an 'electoral democracy' by Freedom House. Afari-Gyan, a man of exceptional integrity, courage and administrative competence, is respected locally and in several post-conflict African countries, including Sierra Leone, Burundi and South Sudan transitioning to electoral democracy where he has advised, as a consultant, on how to organize and successfully hold free, fair, and transparent elections.

There are, of course, Herculean challenges facing every modern nation in her struggle for democracy and development. The widespread political instability and bloody internecine feud and rivalry between political factions and the general economic malaise in Tunisia, Libya and Egypt following the seemingly successful popular uprising, against long-sitting autocratic leaders, the so-called 'Arab Spring' beginning at the end of 2010 should make us cautious about predictions on the future of democracy and development. But the argument here is that Ghanaian society has taken a number of significant steps toward fulfilling popular demands for democracy and development; not without protest, not without countermovement and resistance, of course, but toward democracy and development nonetheless.

MacKenzie and Robinson (op. cit.) add further that for elections to be credible, there must emerge a new group of 'political persons' or politicians, who know how to work in and through the electoral system and the party system in a unified political system at the centre of which is an assembly based on free and fair elections. These new 'political persons', with varying interests and socio-economic backgrounds, will certainly pull against one another, seeking, as rivals, to extract their own advantage from it, yet once established such people have a common interest in stability, and may collectively be wise enough not to push rivalry to the point of mutual destruction (MacKenzie and Robinson (op. cit.:4-5). This sense of emotional and political maturity may take some time to take root.

Harold Laski has added a third factor that underpins the success of democracy in Europe. According to him the success of parliamentary democracy was

> .... dependent upon a conjuncture of economic circumstances [namely, capitalist development] the permanence of which could alone guarantee their effective functions. It required, first, the sense of security that came from the ability to go on making profit that enabled it, from its surplus wealth, to continue the distribution of amenities to the masses. It further required *agreement among parties in politics to all matters of fundamental social constitution in order that each might succeed the other as government of the day without a sense of outrage*. [Without the ability to meet these conditions, constitutional democracy] was powerless to settle differences in terms of reason (Laski 1962:157, italics added).

Money Matters: Poverty, Politics and Plutocracy

A plutocracy is a democracy in which institutions are formed whether or not by design such that only a person of some means or considerable wealth can aspire to office, or hold office, either because of the expenses necessary to compete for office or to maintain it. The second meaning of democracy as a plutocracy (for example, Ghana's) is that it is a democracy in which holding office is the occasion for acquiring wealth (through legal and corrupt means), higher status and power. The close connection between political liberalism and economic liberalism shown by Harold Laski and others is quite clear. In the older European democracies, industrialization, improvements in the welfare and material standards of living of the masses and mass literacy *preceded* full universal suffrage, or both developed in tandem. In the new states of Africa, the reverse is the case. In Ghana and elsewhere in tropical Africa, universal adult suffrage, which is at the core of political liberalism, was achieved before sustainable economic growth that makes possible higher incomes, better standards of living and the provision of social amenities for a majority of the ordinary people in villages, towns and cities. For example, in Ghana, as an internationally respected electoral democracy, the gap between political liberalism and socio-economic progress has produced a situation in which advances in political liberalism are not matched by equal advances in economic liberalism or the reduction of widespread poverty. Economic development lags woefully behind political development in Ghana, creating contradictions and crises of political legitimacy, characterized by popular cynicism about elected representatives and politicians in general. In the 2008 presidential and parliamentary elections that earned Ghana the covetous designation as electoral democracy by Freedom House (as well as in previous elections of the Fourth Republic), it was not uncommon to hear young people (poor, unemployed, often unskilled, semi-skilled or illiterate or semi-literate, mostly living on the street or in the mushrooming slums of the cities) express their utter frustration, a sense of betrayal, mistrust of government and political institutions in statements such as 'politicians are all the same, whether NPP,

NDC, CPP, PNC or under Kofi Wayo's party! Why waste our time to vote?' Few people have much faith in politicians as the people entrusted with the responsibility to bring improvements in the life of the poor masses. At best, the ordinary people regard government as a big lottery from which individuals, particularly if they are well-connected, may or may not benefit. The question is, who benefits? The answer to this question is not so simple. Obviously, it depends on who you are, what you are, and what your constituency is. In other words, who gets what, when, and how (la Lasswell 1972) is the attitude of practicing politicians and their constituents. That is, self-interest, rather than the national interest, as the principal thrust of politics and political behaviour in Ghana provides a major part of the answer to the question about the main beneficiaries of democratic politics in Ghana. This was the case in the 1950s and it is the case today.

Eating From the Same Bowl and the Politics of Plutocracy

Democratic politics in Ghana centred on elections consists of power and manipulation by selfish, self-seeking and self-indulgent ruling elites and counter-elites and their equally self-seeking supporters or followers. Culturally, this sort of relationship between leaders, potential leaders and the led, rulers and subjects is often couched or defined in a kinship or chieftaincy idiom which is deeply institutionalized, pervasive and, therefore, difficult to change. I have shown in an earlier publication (Owusu 1971:68-76) that individuals occupying positions of authority (such as teachers, landlords, employers, senior colleagues, religious leaders and political incumbents) are ritually treated deferentially and receive loyalty and respect in proportion to the extent to which they provide publicly and conspicuously solicitous care for their 'small boys' and 'juniors'. Coincident with their right to expect unwavering loyalty and service at their beck and call, if not their pleasure, the 'big men' or 'social superiors' are under a well understood obligation to offer generous assistance, tangible and intangible to their 'social inferiors': a relationship of superordination and subordination which is highly ritualized.

As I pointed out in that essay, the power or authority to command others is one important way of showing and maintaining one's superior status and respect. The other side of this picture is the desire of subordinates to please their superordinates, whether the latter are headmasters or headwaiters (Owusu 1971:73) This pattern of behaviour clearly contradicts and undermines a democratic civic culture which is based on individual initiative and rights, individual freedom, creativity and accountability, and equality of opportunity. More cynically, this political culture nurtures and sustains corruption and bad governance; it arrests development and perpetuates mass poverty.

The challenge facing the consolidation of representative democracy in Ghana and elsewhere in Africa is the universal predisposition of power holders and officials to use state power for their own ends rather than for the public good;

of ruling political parties to become vehicles and transmission belts of ethnic or regional blocs, special interests, patron-client networks, and of influence peddling chains of what Ghanaians aptly call 'connections'; their predisposition to use state-owned enterprises and public sector positions as a source of 'jobs for the boys' to meet the cravings of party activists and 'foot soldiers', and the delivery of public services as a source of self-enrichment for party bosses, the party faithful and their families and friends. The citizens have seen power corrupt their trusted leaders, though they may continue to vote for them out of habit, ethnic or personal ties or the hope of personal gains from those they vote for.

This style of electoral politics, the politics of plutocracy, detailed in Owusu (2006), has been well summarized by Dennis Austin, the father of modern Ghanaian political studies, in words which deserve extended quotation for their relevance to political practice in the post-1992 period which is characterized by 'instrumentalist' or 'extractive' conception and practice of politics rather than a 'public service, public interest' view of politics. Ghanaians, according to Austin, are:

> ... remarkably (and favourably) responsive to each change of regime. The crowds which gathered to listen delightedly to the CPP leaders at independence in 1957 actually danced in the streets to welcome Kotoka in 1966. They queued patiently in the sun to vote for Busia in 1969, but were ready again to turn to Acheampong in 1972. There was a hopeful acceptance of each turn of fate and popular expectation rode high at least until the second coup... [or another change of government]... of course there were many, at each turn of the wheel, who were disadvantaged since those who benefited, individually or communally, from a particular structure of power went out of business: but there was always the possibility that their chance would come again. Fortune's wheel could turn, when those who had been displaced might, if they survived, return to benefit not only themselves, but their kinsmen and dependents. What mattered therefore was to survive each castle revolution. The ordinary elector waited hopefully, while those who claim to act for him [or her] when their time came round, did what they could to capitalize on the resources which they could offer to the new rulers (Austin and Luckham 1975:6).

Dennis Austin then proceeds to comment on the 'instrumentalist' view of Ghanaian politics and its continuing relevance:

> Maxwell Owusu explores this notion of political stock exchange and its brokers. The Ghanaian world (it is argued) is essentially one of distributory politics. It embodies the values of the market – a political market place in which allegiance is determined by the good on offer. And if the distributory government runs out of benefits, the customers, if they can, will go elsewhere. Such an 'instrumentalist' view of politics – of governments as instruments of disbursements via an intermediary elite to the electorate at large – is not of course particular to Ghana. Clientage and brokerage are age old. It is simply that in many independent states, including Ghana, such trading relationships between the national government and the local centres of power may become the *prime matrix* of political life.

They reflect not only the poverty of trust in national institutions (whether parties or parliaments or trade union) but, the persistence of 'polyarchies,' – of semi-autonomous concentrations of power still largely territorial, in what was once a colonial artifact (ibid. 1975:7, emphasis added).

What makes the use of political power for private ends so common, as Hodder-Williams (1984) avers, can be explained in part by reference to a crucial element or strand in nearly all contemporary African political cultures called the 'extractive view of politics'. The inescapable assumptions or postulates underpinning or driving political actions are *instrumental* rather than *programmatic* (Hodder-Williams 1984:97-98). It hardly needs belabouring that in Ghana, and the rest of tropical Africa, ordinary people can readily point to individual politicians, party activists and party organizers, ministers, senior civil servants, parliamentarians, prominent traditional rulers and so on who could not have so enriched themselves without political power or connections to power holders (Owusu 1975:233-261).

Again, in their more recent article, Richard Sandbrook and Jay Oelbaum claim '[t]he few available studies of popular attitudes uniformly portray Ghanaians as expecting their politicians to be self-aggrandizing, and therefore hoping to receive some tangible benefits in exchange for their continued support. Political cynicism breeds, at the same time, a populist yearning which Rawlings initially satisfied' (Sandbrook and Oelbaum 1997:644). A survey of Ghanaian popular attitudes to democracy, the state and markets conducted in 1999 by Bratton, Lewis and Gyimah-Boadi confirms the plutocratic nature of Ghanaian politics. The survey reveals among other things, that Ghanaians overwhelmingly 'associate democracy – in practice with concrete delivery of basic political goods' and evinced a deep attachment to 'government provision of key goods and services', such as schools, clinics, roads, and agricultural credit. Furthermore, 'two out of three Ghanaians favoured the government as the main provider of employment' (Bratton, Lewis and Gyimah-Boadi 2001:231-250).

Persistent Problem of Ghanaian Democracy

Ghanaian popular attitudes toward democracy reflect the dangers of democracy *without* economic development, dangers foreseen by the British colonial administration and African nationalist leaders struggling for independence. Some of the obvious dangers were political corruption and incipient plutocracy. For instance, in 1950 James Griffiths, the British Secretary of State for the Colonies, in moving that the House of Commons take note of the Annual Report and Statement of Accounts of the Colonial Development Corporation (CDC) for 1949 said

...the essential purpose of our colonial policy is to guide the people of the Colonial Territories to responsible self-government within the commonwealth, and in partnership with them, to seek to establish with the Colonial Territories those *economic and social conditions upon which alone responsible democratic self-government can be built.* I am fully conscious of the need to ensure that *economic development* would go hand in hand with political progress and *I am equally convinced of the dangers of creating responsible states without adequate economic and social foundations.* ... Our policy combines economic development and political advancement, it is a policy which will eventually succeed' (quoted in Crabbe 1971:103-104).

The truth is that nearly all African countries achieved independence from colonial rule as economically poor and underdeveloped states thus lacking one of the critical and essential foundations for stable constitutional democracies. It is in this connection that Lord Hailey is quoted as saying, 'Africans would indeed have cause to reproach us if, when they ask for bread, we give them a vote' (reported in Owusu 2009:1-3).

According to Gower (1967), the British bequeathed to Ghana several legacies, two of which are particularly damaging to good governance and democracy, namely, economic exploitation and underdevelopment and an emotional and moral legacy, which he explained as follows: 'Colonialism, like enemy occupation, tends to instil contempt for the law and for the moral standards which it expresses. The government is an alien one; *to cheat* it is a patriotic duty. The law is that of the colonial oppressor; it has no moral sanction, and punishment for breaking it has no moral or social stigma' (Gower 1967:33-34). Colonialism thus encouraged the belief among subject peoples that conviction by a colonial government is an honour rather than a disgrace, thus encouraging crimes of political and administrative dishonesty and corruption. Not surprisingly, the Nkrumah government was plagued from the early 1950s by a steady rise in corruption that Nkrumah saw as a national defect and deficiency, the roots of which go deeper than that of the CPP. Suffice it to recall here that in his famous Dawn Broadcast at 5am on Saturday 8 April 1961, what Nkrumah himself referred to as 'homely chat', he called for high probity on the part of high party officials, ministers, ministerial secretaries, parliamentarians, civil servants, party members and the Ghanaian public in general, to rid the rank and file of the party and Ghanaian society as a whole of bribery and corruption, exploitation, patronage, nepotism, immorality and other evils which militated against the great socialist cause. Nkrumah called for the imposition of limits to property acquisition by ministers, party officials, ministerial secretaries and parliamentarians aiming for them to cease running businesses or involving themselves in other businesses or quit Parliament. He proposed a curb on ostentatious living by high party officials, chairmen of corporations and so on; ambassadors were to educate their children at home [that is, in Ghana] instead of sending them abroad; and there was to be no more 'red-tapism' in the civil service (see *The Party CPP Journal* (Accra) No 4, 1961:2) (see also Le Vine 1975). As Rattray has shown, through indirect rule, economic exploitation, inadequate education, poverty and underdevelopment, the colonial state contributed to the rise and institutionalization of corruption (Rattray 1934:22-36). It is significant that Nkrumah made a largely unsuccessful attempt to replace the elitist politics of plutocracy with the politics of mass democracy, socialism and the welfare state. For example, after assuming the position and title of Prime Minister, in March 1952 at a huge salary of £3,500 per annum with other ministers getting £3,000, and Members of the Legislative Assembly (MLAs) receiving a salary of £960 per annum (when the annual salary of a civil servant was about £120.00) it became clear to him that 'going to Assembly' was enticingly lucrative. This naturally led to fierce competition for office in a poor country with very low salaries, and in a culture that accords high value to money making. He warned the CPP leaders against accumulation of wealth and ostentatious living. In order that CPP MLAs would live humbly, instead of being allowed to be enticed by private economic interests, he set up three principles (in retrospect somewhat naively) consistent with his socialist vision for Ghanaian society, for his ministers and other political leaders to follow. First, ministers must not live in the plush bungalows that the British had always provided for members of the government. Secondly, only a minimum of social mixing with individual Britons would be permitted. Thirdly, members of his Cabinet must pay back one third of their salaries into a party fund or better still, surrender their salaries to the party and instead draw an agreed remuneration from the party in order 'to avoid class-conflict', but to no avail (Gunther 1955:805).

A Rising Plutocracy and the New Oil Economy

There is much evidence to suggest that as democracy in Ghana matures, it is becoming increasingly plutocratic in two senses of the word. It is progressively becoming a democracy dominated by wealth. This was clearly the case in the 2008 presidential and parliamentary elections in Ghana, for which it is believed, nearly GH¢50 billion (fifty billion new Ghana cedis) was spent by Nana Akufo-Addo, the NPP presidential candidate who lost the election (see *Ghana Palaver* 12 January 2009:31). Significantly, GH¢50 billion spent by a political party in a presidential election is far greater than the total average annual budgetary revenue of about GH¢43 billion collected by the government of Ghana. Concentration of presidential power as is the case in Ghana may lead to the acquisition of vast wealth and property by important office holders. Serious abuses of power in a democracy can produce elected autocrats and virtual kleptocracies.

The Nature and Persistence of Corruption

Carl Friedrich offers a minimum definition of corruption as where an 'official ... uses his office for private gain at public expense;' he explains further that corruption exists 'whenever a power holder who is charged with doing certain things, that is, a responsible functionary or office holder, is by monetary or other rewards, such as the expectation of a job in the future, induced to take actions which favours whoever provides the reward and therefore damage the group organization to which the functionary belongs more specifically the government' (Friedrich 2002:3). The publication in Accra of the results of the Ghana Corruption Survey conducted in Southern Ghana by the Ghana Integrity Initiative (GII) in March 2005 gives practical meaning to the incidence of corruption in Ghana. The report indicates that over 90 per cent of the representative sample of 900 interviewed agreed that corruption is not only prevalent, but a serious problem in Ghana and is on the increase. The GII survey report indicates that among the leading institutions or organizations perceived as highly corrupt by Ghanaians are as follows: Police Service; Ministry of Education; Customs, Excise and Preventive Services (CEPS); the Judiciary Service; Civil/Public Service; Ministry of Health; Members of Parliament; Ministers of State; Internal Revenue Service (IRS) and the Ghana Immigration Service. The survey results also indicate that the most common type of corruption experienced by victims or givers of bribe is the demand by public officials for money before rendering a service for which they are paid or taking money without issuing receipts i.e. in other words using their public office for private or personal financial gain (see *The Daily Dispatch* (Accra) Vol. 14, No. 13, Wednesday Edition, 20 July 2005:1,5,8). At a workshop in Accra on anti-corruption sponsored by Crown Agents (British) for West Africa in July 2005 the Chief Justice of Ghana, George Kingsley Acquah, further defined corrupt practices as including: '1) bribery; 2) hiring relatives (nepotism); 3) giving contracts to party supporters (cronyism); and 4) abusing privileged information to buy or sell stock (insider trading)'. These negative practices, according to him, thrived in markets where legal structures are weak or not well defined, where the rule of law is not strictly enforced, and where laws and the judiciary allowed government agents too much unsupervised and discretionary power. Certainly the Chief Justice had in mind the situation in Ghana and most African countries that are undergoing economic liberalization and democratization.

A good example of laws that are not enforced and contribute to corruption is Article 286 of The 1992 *Constitution of Ghana and the Public Office Holders (Declaration of Assets and Disqualification)* Act 1998 (Act 550). Both Article 286 of the Constitution and Section 4 of Act 550 require that 'A person who holds a public office submits to the Auditor General a written declaration of all property or assets owned by or liabilities owed by him whether, directly or indirectly, before taking office, at the end of every four years; and at the end of his term of office'. Article 286 (2) goes further to state that failure to declare or knowingly making false declaration shall be a contravention of the Constitution and shall be dealt with in accordance with Article 287 of it. To date there is no record of the enforcement of these two legal instruments. Recent Auditor-General's Reports on the accounts of the ministries, departments and agencies (MDAs) of government are replete with sordid corruption pervading the entire public administration of the country. The Public Accounts Committee (PAC), the accountability arm of the Parliament of Ghana, which has the constitutional mandate to ensure that public funds are applied as approved in the budget, has also been ineffective in ensuring that public officers found by the Auditor-General to have misappropriated funds are punished. The PAC is rendered ineffective by its own internal weakness and by the failure of extra-parliamentary bodies such as the Audit Implementation Committees of MDA's and Financial Administration Tribunals to ensure that officers found culpable by the Auditor-General are prosecuted. As the Chief Justice pointed out, institutions such as the Parliament of Ghana, which is a critical accountability institution for ensuring the prudent use of public funds, cannot control the manner in which such funds are used resulting in pervasive corruption.

In a remarkable telephone interview with the *Daily Graphic* (Accra), Ghana's leading national daily newspaper, Papa Kwesi, the flag bearer of the Progressive People's Party (PPP) in the 2012 general elections expressed disappointment over the dismissal by general secretaries of four political parties, namely National Democratic Congress (NDC), the New Patriotic Party (NPP), the Convention People's Party (CPP) and People's National Convention (PNC), of a report that described political parties as one of the perceived corrupt institutions in Ghana. Kwesi Nduom, who is also a wealthy businessman, affirmed in the interview that the perceived corruption among political parties is real. He pointed out that most of the political parties were unable to disclose the sources of campaign funds and could not even render accounts internally. He recalled that in the 2012 general elections the PPP challenged presidential candidates to declare the sources of the campaign funds, make their income tax returns public and declare their assets. Interestingly, he noted, 'the other parties ran away from the challenge. Only God knows where they get the funds to run their campaign. This is a recipe for corrupt acts in government'. The 2013 Global Corruption Barometer placed political parties second on the list of perceived corrupt institutions in Ghana. Nduom added that 'Nkrumah's dawn broadcasts were an admission that there were corrupt leaders in the CPP. All *coups* in Ghana have mentioned corruption as one of the reasons for the actions…Ghana cannot afford to have its political leaders burying their heads in the sand and pretending not to see, smell and hear corruption.' He continued, 'All of us must admit that corruption is killing our nation and making its people poor, for which, reason we must join hands to fight it.' (see *Daily Graphic*, Wednesday, 21 August 2013:3).

The problem of corruption is pervasive, running through successive governments, and seems to be getting worse especially with the recent discovery of oil and gas in commercial quantities. Following the victory of the NPP in the 2000 elections the new government heaped serious accusations and allegations of corruption against the leading functionaries of the defeated NDC government. Some of the corruption cases involving Francis Solormey resulted in long prison sentences for the accused. Since 2009 when the NDC was returned to power in a closely fought 2008 presidential election, the tide of accusations of corruption has turned against the leaders of the NPP, including ex-President Kufuor. For example, in a recent interview with William Wallis of the *Financial Times* (London) which touched upon ex-president J.A. Kufuor's alleged involvement and financial interest in a Ghanaian company EO and its link to Texan (US) company Kosmos that first discovered the Jubilee field oil block in 2007, ex-president Kufuor was unapologetic about his role in the development of the Jubilee field on terms which were said to be disadvantageous to Ghana's national interest. Following the defeat of his party in the 2008 presidential election, the new Ghanaian authorities initiated investigations into whether EO used access to senior government officials and the ex-president to gain the oil block back in 2004 when Kufuor was president, and win a more favourable contract both for themselves and Kosmos (Wallis 2010:7, Gyasi 2011:48). The NDC government has not been immune to similar accusations. Recall for example the recent rage of judgment debt, the most scandalous among which is the amount of GH¢51.28 million Ghana cedis paid to Alfred Agbesi Woyome. The judgement debt controversy that has gripped Ghana since November 2011 is, as expected, heavily politicized. Opponents of the NDC government have been quick to conclude that the judgement debt payment honoured by the Atta Mills' administration but which originated from the state's breach in suspicious circumstances of a contract going back to the preceding NPP government, and made to Woyome was a clever and complicated ploy i.e. robbing Peter to pay Paul, by government officials, to siphon money from state coffers to finance the NDC party in the 7 December 2012 presidential and parliamentary elections. The said contract in litigation was awarded for the construction and rehabilitation of stadia in Ghana in preparation for the Africa Cup of Nations (CAN) 2008, hosted by Ghana. Alfred Woyome is a businessman, considered by some as the bankroller of the NDC party (Achama, 'Woyome Faces Amidu' in *Daily Guide* (Accra) Thursday 7 November 2013:3-4; Bokor 'As Woyome Fights the Public Accounts Committee [Part 1] in *Daily Post*, Wednesday 28 August 2012:10.)

The ruling NDC party sees this as nothing but a cynical and hostile anti-NDC propaganda by the opposition NPP. Be that as it may, Woyome is currently (since July 2013) standing trial at the financial Division of the Fast Track High Court (Accra) on two counts of wilfully causing financial loss to the state and defrauding the state by false pretence. The state Attorney General is in court seeking an order for the refund of the judgement debt of GH¢51,283,480.59 paid to Woyome. According to the Attorney General, Woyome had no contract with the state and consequently lacked a cause of action and the capacity to make a claim for payment in any court of competent jurisdiction (Effah, 'Woyome's Case Back' in *The Ghanaian Times*, Friday 19 July 2013:1 and 3; Bonney 'Woyome Loses Appeal in GHC 51.2 Million Fraud Case' in *Daily Graphic*, Friday 10 May 2013:1 and 3).

William Wallis noted in his interview with ex-president Kufuor that the cycle of accusations is an emerging feature of Ghana's politics of elite-rivalry: the competitive strategies of a rising plutocracy in the context of a diffuse culture of corruption and strong 'instrumentalist' view of politics, a syndrome that is difficult to change. It should be noted here that the rivalry of the fortunate or privileged few, the elite and sub-elite, made up mostly of the more and better educated, for power, wealth and status is not new in West Africa. It has deep roots in pre-colonial and colonial history. Writing about the middle-class elite in West Africa in the 1960s after independence, Colin Legum observed that 'nowhere in the world are [the middle class elite] invested with more power and status than in Africa... It is ... a startling paradox that the continent with the highest illiteracy rate (85-90 per cent) should find its destiny entrusted to its smallest power group.' Legum continued

> ...Often the old and the new elites engaged in a power struggle for possession of the nationalist movement... The older elite – while politically conscious – were inclined to put a high value on their status for the *prestige and wealth* it brought their families, and were inhibited from action likely to jeopardize their bourgeois position. The newer elite, usually *no less concerned with wealth and prestige* affected to despise the older bourgeoisie and were willing to use their own status as an instrument to win power. Instead of basing their challenge for power on prestige and wealth... they sought to rest their power *on the people*.' (Legum 1965:134, italics added; Austin and Luckham 1974:122-123; and Owusu 2006).

Indeed, plutocracy is the root cause of political corruption in Ghana. Democratic elections are capital-intensive operations. As one Ghanaian observer puts it, an election in Ghana is lucrative business.

> It is an undeniable fact that ...there are political investors and business people engaged in political activities who do not have the interests of the people at heart, but basically what they stand to gain surpasses all... Now there is the emergence of some business tycoons in the Ghanaian political [world]...normally behind the scenes sponsoring political parties and their candidates to win elections. They give them money for their campaigns, print T-shirts for them and [lend out] a fleet of cars for their political activities...so after investing heavily in theses campaigns, they hope and [believe] that when their candidates do win the elections, the business tycoons would be awarded good contracts, given top board memberships and to have easy and daily access to the presidency. It is imperative to note that most of these people do not care about political ideologies; they put their money where they think they will get quick returns.' (Alagma 'Sponsorship of Political Parties: The State Must Take Responsibility' in *The Daily Dispatch*, 28 August 2012:5; Owusu 1975:233).

Accordingly, the real curse, if one exists, of Ghanaian politics and development, contrary to what several observers may believe, is not the recent oil find but rather the curse of unchecked human greed, self-interest and bad leadership in the management of the wealth of nations. As I have argued elsewhere, 'democracy of the franchise could hardly in itself, ensure peaceful and stable government. Good leadership is not necessarily assured by the free ballot; nor does civilian rule invariably produce social and economic democracy' (Owusu 1971:68).

Conclusion – Ghana and What President Obama Said

The official visit of U.S. President Barack Obama on 10-11 July 2009 to Ghana was hugely historic especially for Ghana and Ghanaian citizens. As the first sub-Saharan African country to visit after taking office in January 2009, Ghana was greatly honoured, a visit that Ghanaians are, understandably, deeply proud of and will never forget. There are important lessons to be learnt by Ghanaians and all Africans from the address he gave on Saturday 11 July 2009 in Accra at the Accra International Conference Centre that speaks directly and eloquently to the subject of my paper. The first lesson is closely linked to the theme of this chapter; namely, the complex relationship between democracy and development, especially economic progress and the role of the state and civil society and its leaders in the process of social transformation. The second lesson is a thoughtful assessment of the harsh realities of Ghanaian (African) experience of poverty, misery and misgovernment, and his advice that could simultaneously advance and sustain real democracy as well as promote economic development and prosperity, lifting the masses out of poverty and promising a peaceful and better future for all. President Obama's speech reminds Ghanaians of the dangers of equating democracy with elections. He points out:

> Repression can take many forms, and too many nations, even those that *have elections, are plagued by problems that condemn their people to poverty. No country is going to create wealth if its leaders exploit the economy to enrich themselves... or... if police can be bought off by drug traffickers. No business wants to invest in a place where the government skims 20 per cent off the top...or the head of the port authority is corrupt. No person wants to live in a society where the rule of law gives way to the rule of brutality and bribery. That is not democracy; that is tyranny, even if occasionally you sprinkle an election in there.* And now is the time for that style of governance to end. In the 21st century, capable, reliable and transparent institutions are the key to success - strong parliament; honest police force; independent judges...; an independent press; a vibrant private sector (and) civil society. Those are the things that give life to democracy, because that is what matter in people's everyday lives' (Sackey 2009:6, italics added).

He further advises that '*Development depends on good governance. That is the ingredient which has been missing in far too many places, for far too long. That's the change that can unlock Africa's potential. And that is the responsibility that can only be met by Africans.*' (2009:5, italics added).

We have seen that popular allegiance to the (colonial)/post-colonial state and its institutions and demands that Ghanaians (Africans) inherited at independence remain extremely weak producing a situation in which public property or interest (material and non-material) is routinely and wantonly abused or mismanaged by state office holders for self enrichment and status enhancement and for various personal ends. We have seen from post-colonial political experience that periodic elections (at both national and district levels) do not provide effective sanctions for exploitative and corrupt leadership in our fledgling electoral democracy. After more than fifty years of independence Ghanaians should reclaim the post-colonial state to ensure that the citizens' interest, security, prosperity, sustainable growth and development is passionately advanced by those who are given the mandate to govern. Especially the political class should replace the politics of self-service in pursuit of self-interest that is currently predominant with the politics of public service and the pursuit of the public good.

References

Apter, D.E., 1995, 'Democracy for Uganda: A Case for Comparison' in *Daedalus* Vol. 124:3 (Summer), p. 158 (155-190).

Austin, D. and R. Luckham, 1974, 'Education and Status [Ghana]' in *West Africa*, London, 4 February, pp. 122-123.

Austin, D. and R. Luckham, 1975, 'Introduction' in D. Austin and R. Luckham (eds.), *Politicians and Soldiers in Ghana 1966-1972*, London: Frank Cass, p. 6.

Bratton, M., P. Lewis and E. Gyimah-Boadi, 2001, 'Constituencies for Reform in Ghana' in *The Journal of Modern African Studies* Vol. 39, No. 2 June, pp. 231-250.

Carrington, C.E., 1961, *The Liquidation of the British Empire*, London: George G. Harrap and Co, p. 36.

Crabbe, A., 1971, *John Mensah Sarbah 1864-1910*, Accra: Ghana Universities Press, pp. 103-104.

Friedrich, Carl J, 2002, 'Political Corruption' in Arnold J. Heidenheimer and Michael Johnston, (eds), Political Corruption, Concepts and Contexts, Third Edition. New Brunswick (US) and London (UK): Transaction Publishers, p.3.

Gower, L.C.B., 1967, *Independent Africa. The Challenge to the Legal Profession,* Cambridge: Harvard University Press, pp. 33-34.

Gunther, J., 1955, *Inside Africa*, New York: Harper and Brothers, p. 805.

Gyasi Jr., S., 2011, 'Making Oil a Blessing in Ghana', *New African,* No. 503, February, p. 48.

Hodder-Williams, R., 1984, *An Introduction to the Politics of Tropical Africa*, London: George Allen and Unwin, pp. 97-98.

Jennings W. Ivor 1963, *Democracy in Africa,* Cambridge At the University Press.

Johnston, W.R., 1981, *Great Britain, Great Empire. An Evaluation of the British Imperial Experience,* St. Lucia: University of Queensland Press, p. 148.

Laski, H.J., 1962, *The Rise of European Liberalism An Essay in Interpretation,* London: Unwin Books.

Lasswell, H., 1972, *Who Gets What, When, How,* New York: The World Publishing Co.

Legum, C., 1965, 'Africa's Intellectuals: The Thin Black Line' in *Overseas Quarterly,* Vol. 4, No. 5, March, p. 134.

Legum, C., 1999, *Africa Since Independence* Bloomington: Indiana University Press, pp. 31-32.

Maathai, W., 2009, *The Challenge For Africa,* New York: Anchor Books, p. 54.

MacKenzie, W.J.M. and K. Robinson (eds.), 1960, *Five Elections in Africa: A Group of Electoral Studies,* Oxford: Clarendon Press.

Miliband, R., 1992, 'Fukuyama and the Socialist Alternative' in New Left Review (London) Vol. 193, May-June, p. 109.

Owusu, M., 1971, 'Culture and Democracy in West Africa: Some Persistent Problems' in *Africa Today* Vol. 18, No. 1, January, pp. 68-76.

Owusu, M., 1975, 'Politics in Swedru' in Dennis Austin and Robin Luckham (eds.), *Politicians and Soldiers in Ghana 1966-1972,* London: Frank Cass, pp. 233-261.

Owusu, M., 1986, 'Custom and Coups: A Juridical Interpretation of Civil Order and Disorder in Ghana' in *The Journal of Modern African Studies* Vol. 24, No. 1. 76 pp. 69-99.

Owusu, M. 1992 "Democracy and Africa: A View From the Village" in *The Journal of Modern African Studies ,* Vol. 30, No 3, pp.369-396

Owusu, M., 2006, *Uses and Abuses of Political Power: A Case Study of Continuity and Change in the Politics of Ghana, Second Updated Edition,* Accra: Ghana Universities Press.

Owusu, M., 2009, Money and Politics, 2009*: The Challenge of Democracy in Ghana* Cantonments, Accra: Institute For Democratic Governance, pp. 1-3.

Perham, M., 1962, *The Colonial Reckoning. The End of Imperial Rule in Africa in the Light of British Experience,* New York: Alfred A. Knopf.

Rattray, R.S., 1934, 'Present Tendencies of African Colonial Government' in *Journal of African Society,* Vol. 33, January, pp. 22-36.

Rodney, W., 1972, *How Europe Underdeveloped Africa,* Dar-es-Salaam: Tanzania Publishing House, pp. 162-310.

Rotberg, R.I, 2009, 'Governance and Leadership in Africa: Measures, Methods and Results' in *Journal of International Affairs,* Vol. 62, No. 2, Spring/Summer, pp. 113-126.

Sackey, E.K., 2009, *Yes You Can,* Accra: Achievers' Publications: pp. 1-16.

Sandbrook, R. and J. Oelbaum, 1997, 'Reforming Dysfunctional Institutions through Democratization? Reflections on Ghana' in *The Journal of Modern African Studies* Vol. 35, No. 4, p. 644 No. 102.

Wallis, W., 2010, 'Curse of Oil Follows Ghana's Hyperactive Ex-president: *Financial Times,* 26 October, p. 7.

Websites

1. http://www.america.gov/st/texttrans/english/2009/July/20090711110050abretn uh0.1079783.html
2. http://www.freedomhouse.org/template.cfm?page=415&year=2008
3. http://www.freedomhouse.org/template.cfm?page=1.

Newspapers and Magazines

Financial Times (London), 16-17 February 2008: p. 3.
Ghana Palaver, 12 January 2009: p. 31.
The Crystal Clear Lens, Wednesday 24 December 2008: p. 3.
*The Daily Dispatch (*Accra), Vol. 14, No. 13, Wednesday Edition, 20 July 2005: pp. 1, 5, 8.
The Daily Dispatch, 28 August 2012: p. 5.
The Daily Graphic, 10 May 2013: pp. 1 and 3.
The Daily Graphic, 21 August 2013: p. 3.
Daily Guide, 7 November 2013: pp. 3-4.
The Daily Post, 28 August 2012: p. 10.
The Economist, 28 April 2007: p. 14.
The Economist, May 2000.
The Economist, 3-9 December 2011: p. 15.
The Guardian Weekly, 20 February 2009: p. 25. Weekly Review 126
The Guardian Weekly, 18-24 May 2012: p. 18.
The Ghanaian Times, 19 July 2013.
The Party CPP Journal, No 4, 1961: p.2.
The True Democrat, 2 January 2008: p. 6.
Forbes, 15 March 2010, p. 76.
Financial Times, 26 October 2010, p. 7.

9

Ghana's 2008 Elections, the Constitution and the Unexpected: Lessons for the Future

Kofi Quashigah

Introduction

The 2008 elections took Ghana to the precipice and back. Ghana was held hostage over the results. The two main political parties, the New Patriotic Party (NPP) and the National Democratic Party (NDC), deliberately manipulated the electoral process and the legislative system to hopefully achieve desired ends. As argued by the Danquah Institute, 'in part this was the result of a deliberate strategy pursued by some parties over several months prior to the elections to cast doubt about the reliability of the results. In part it is based on credible charges against both parties of vote tampering and manipulation of results' (Danquah Institute 2010). In general so much money is spent on Ghana's electioneering campaign and related activities that the stakes become extremely high and loss becomes devastating. Consequently everything possible is done to win an election, even without regard to its repercussions for the whole democratic process or for the integrity and stability of the nation as a whole.

The 2008 elections were very keenly contested and stretched the electoral commission, the candidates and the electorate to the limit. The tension was felt even at the stage of second registration of voters; the electoral commission was overstretched and it became very clear that many potential voters were disenfranchised because they could not be registered before the close of the registration exercise. This was compounded by allegations of a bloated voters' register. The election itself was characterised by accusations and counter-accusations of intimidation of polling station agents, allegations of double voting and inflation of voting figures.

The timing of the election itself, the need for the organisation of the presidential re-run and the time required for a handover of government with its attendant complications of co-ordination of the handover process all created additional hiccups that damaged the 2008 electoral process.

On the other hand, the 2008 elections exposed a number of legal weaknesses inherent in both our constitutional provisions on elections and the ordinary legislation. The issues of concern are:

- Timing of elections
- The handover/transition process
- Lack of smooth voter registration process
- Disputes over counted votes
- Possibility of vacuum in the presidency due to delayed resolution of election disputes.

This chapter examines the possible legal response to these concerns. Could the legal position as it now exists have contributed to the situation, and how would a reform of the law address the matter? We intend to highlight weaknesses in the Constitution and the law, and suggest solutions.

Implication of Aspects of the 1992 Constitution Provisions on Elections

The 1992 Constitution of Ghana commits the country to democratic governance springing from the sovereign will of the people that is nurtured by the principle of universal adult suffrage.[1] Pluralism is the bedrock of the electoral system guaranteed by the Constitution. Article 3 (1) prohibits parliament from enacting a law to establish a one-party state and Article 3 (2) makes it unlawful for any person or group of persons to suppress or seek to suppress the lawful political activity of any other person or class of persons. It is to further guarantee the plural electoral process that the Constitution devotes a whole chapter (Chapter Seven) to the representation of the people. This chapter determines who qualifies to vote, the composition and functions of the Electoral Commission, and the process of election. Further, Article 63 imposes constitutional limits on the period during which presidential elections could be held (discussed further below). This constitutional mandate creates an inherent constraint on the electoral process with respect to the timing of elections and the time for a smooth handover to the incoming administration.

The Timing of Elections

The period between the declaration of the election results and the handing over of administrative authority to an incoming one has often posed a problem because of the short period in between the two events. By Article 63 (2) of the Constitution, a presidential election, where there is a President in office, shall not be held earlier than four months or later than one month before his term of office expires. Constitutionally therefore, since in 1993 the President was ushered into office on 7 January just as was the case in 2001 and 2009, the Presidential elections could not have been conducted before 7 September or after 7 December of those years. We have decided consistently to conduct Presidential elections in the month of December thus leaving barely four weeks between an election day and the handover date of 7 January. The matter is further complicated by the provision in Article 63 (3) which provides that to be elected as President the contestant must obtain more than fifty per cent of the total number of valid votes cast at an election. In the event of failure to secure that number, there shall be a run-off, within twenty-one days after the previous election (Article 63 (4)), between the two candidates who obtained the highest number of votes at the previous election (Article 63 (5)). This was the scenario in the 2000 and 2008 Presidential elections. The Electoral Commission and indeed the whole country were caught up in an electoral tension in the rush to keep within the constitutionally prescribed periods. The consequence is that there is barely any sufficient time left for a handover of political and administrative authority.

The inability of ex-President Rawlings to complete the nomination and confirmation of his ministers at the commencement of his second term of office resulted in the Supreme Court decision in the case of *J.H. Mensah v. Attorney-General* (1996-97 SCGLR 320). The facts of the case were that upon his re-election as President and assumption of the second term of office on 7 January 1997, the President announced the retention of a number of his previous ministers and also that since they had already been approved by the previous Parliament there was no need for them to go through a new process of Parliamentary approval. The Supreme Court held that prior approval is a constitutional mandate that must be respected. In his contribution to the judgment in the case of *J.H. Mensah v. Attorney-General*, Justice Hayfron-Benjamin opined that:

> …such is the nature of our 1992 Constitution that every President and every Parliament are assigned definitive terms of office and no more. There is no provision in the Constitution for an interregnum or 'caretaker government.' Consequently in order to prevent a failure of government, reasonable time must be allowed after the inauguration of the President and Parliament to enable the new institutions to be set in place and ensure smooth administration to avoid absurdity and unconstitutional action. Thus speaking for myself, I would incline to the view that not until the expiry of a reasonable time after a general and presidential election, ministers and deputy ministers may hold over their respective offices (ibid. per Hayfron-Benjamin JSC p. 35).

The fact that even a self-succeeding President was not able to quickly put together the Ministers for the new administration should have provided an insight into the inconvenience of the dates we have gradually settled with as our election dates.

Article 63 per se is not a problem if the elections are organised in September, for instance. There would be enough time to organize a run-off within twenty-one days if necessary and still leave enough time to conduct a smooth transfer of administrative authority of state. The problem is therefore not a legal one but self-inflicted.

The above proposition is possible but the difficulty with it is that there is the generally accepted position that it is preferable to have both the parliamentary and presidential elections conducted on the same day. It is the view that such an approach will save costs and also eliminate the influence of the outcome of one election on the other. Although constitutionally the presidential elections could be held four months to the date of expiration of the term of office of the incumbent president, the Constitution requires parliamentary elections to be organised within a period of thirty days before the end of the term of the incumbent Parliament as is prescribed by Article 112 (4).

The Constitution Review Commission's recommendation on this problem is intended to provide a solution. The Constitution Review Commission recommends and the White Paper accepts that Articles 112 (4) on the timing of parliamentary elections and Article 63 (2)(a) on the timing of presidential elections be amended to ensure that both elections are held within 60 days of the installation of a new government.

Voter Registration – Right to Be Registered

It is a constitutional right of every citizen to vote. That entitles every qualified Ghanaian citizen to be registered as a voter for the purpose of public elections (Article 42). The Electoral Commission therefore has the constitutional duty to facilitate registration by all qualified citizens who want to be registered. This is what the Electoral Commission sought to do when it re-opened the voter register to make it possible for those who though qualified were not captured in the register of voters, particularly those who turned eighteen after the last registration exercise. The re-opening of the voter register exposed the inability of the electoral commission to handle the backlog of unregistered potential voters. At the end of the stipulated period a large number of qualified voters remained unregistered and therefore effectively barred from participating in the electoral process. This of course is unconstitutional and goes contrary to the decision in the case of *Tehn-Addy v. Electoral Commission* (1996-97 SCGLR 589). In the said case the plaintiff was a 57-year old Ghanaian citizen who sought to invoke the jurisdiction of the Supreme Court to compel the Electoral Commission to register him as a voter. According to the plaintiff he was out of the country when the Electoral Commission embarked on a compilation of a register of voters in October 1995. Upon his return to the country in November 1995, he wrote to the Electoral Commission applying for registration and a voter's card. In May 1996, the Electoral Commission announced a re-opening of the register of voters from 1-9 June 1996. The announcement indicated that only citizens who had attained the age of eighteen since the beginning of the current registration exercise and those who were above eighteen years but could give tangible reasons for their inability to register in October 1995 would be allowed to register. The plaintiff claimed that when he presented himself for registration as announced, the Electoral Commission failed or refused to show up at the designated place to register him. In response, the Electoral Commission explained that it was compelled to abort the planned re-registration exercise because of an injunction from the High Court issued as a consequence of an action pending before the High Court initiated by two political parties.

The Supreme Court upheld the right to vote as a constitutional right following from Article 42 and that 'As a constitutional right therefore, no qualified citizen can be denied of it, since the Constitution is the supreme law of the land' (per Acquah JSC p. 594). The Supreme Court took particular note of the far-reaching consequences that attach to non-registration, particularly as provided by Article 94 (1)(a) which disqualifies any person not registered as a voter from qualifying as a member of parliament. Furthermore, disqualification as a member of parliament precludes one from holding office as a minister of state (Article 78 (1)), a member of the Electoral Commission (Article 44 (1)), as President or Vice-President (Article 62 (c)), as member of the Public Services Commission (Article 194 (3)(a), or as a member of the National Commission for Civic Education (Article 232 (3)).

The right to be registered as a voter is therefore not just a subsidiary to the right to vote. It is a substantive right in itself and the Electoral Commission breaches the Constitution anytime citizens are frustrated in their efforts to vote due to the often exhibited lack of capacity of the Electoral Commission to register all qualified voters within the brief registration period usually scheduled. The frustration of prospective citizens to vote also gives room for allegations that the Electoral Commission intends to favour the political party that is assumed to be lacking support in the particular area affected by the registration problem.[2] These accusations derogate from the integrity of the Electoral Commission and prepare the ground for orchestrated electoral disputes.

Biometric Registration

The 2008 Ghana elections called for a re-consideration of the manual registration and voting systems and gave support to the call for biometric voter registration and electronic voting systems to become the acceptable processes. The events in Kenya[3] and Cote d'Ivoire[4] related to disputes over the authenticity of the votes cast make the search for more credible vote ascertainment system even more urgent. Whatever the amount of money and time is spent to guarantee a credible electoral system can be justified because it is when our democratic enterprise is guaranteed that even the economy can grow to produce the wealth needed for the betterment and welfare of the people.

Going by the recurring inability of the Electoral Commission to efficiently register all qualified voters within the declared registration period it is questionable whether we should continue the strict adherence of the Electoral Commission to paragraphs 7 (1) and 10 (1) of the Registration of Voters' Public Elections (Registration Regulations) 1995, CI.12. This Constitutional Instrument requires that the Electoral Commission shall specify by notice in the Gazette the period during which the registration of voters shall take place and that the person entitled to be registered as a voter should apply for registration during the period specified. That the registration exercise should be completed within a reasonable period prior to the election time is without doubt very important. But if the right to be registered as a voter is that important as a constitutional right, and if our experience over the years has clearly shown that the periodic registration process has rather led to the disenfranchisement of large numbers of Ghanaians, then there is so much to be said for the review of paragraphs 7 (1) and 10 (1) of the CI.12 to make the registration process a continuous exercise. The continuous registration process is not impossible; the National Health Insurance Scheme (NHIS) registration is almost continuous and nothing should make it impossible to adopt a continuous registration process for the voter registration exercise. Indeed paragraph 26 (1) of CI.12 requires the Electoral Commission to revise the register annually.

A smooth voter registration exercise will be the prelude to a smooth electoral process because it is the misgivings and tensions that are started in the registration process that eventually seep into and pollute the whole electoral process. The confusion and recriminations that follow upon the heels of elections are not the best for the strengthening of our democratic enterprise.

E-voting

The tendency of the two major political parties, the National Democratic Congress (NDC) and the New Patriotic Party (NPP), to dispute election results is becoming established. The consequences of the refusal of a losing party to accept the results have been played out with dire consequences in Kenya and Cote d'Ivoire as well as a number of other African countries. Allegations of double voting and inflation of voting figures are regular renditions that follow our elections (Oquaye 2004 and NPP 1993). The potential of these events to degenerate into conflict and even physical violence is high. The allegations relating to the presidential elections run- off between President Atta-Mills and Nana Akufo-Addo, the presidential candidate for the New Patriotic Party, were such as could have plunged the country into turmoil. It has become very obvious that so long as we continue with the manual ballot system, the problem of allegations of double voting and inflation of figures will continue to damage our electoral process.

Regulation 18 of the Public Elections Regulation, 1996 CI.15 prescribes the equipment necessary for the polling exercise to include ballot boxes and ballot papers. Other materials for voting shall include instruments for perforating or stamping the ballot papers with the official mark; instruments for making the means of identification of the voter; a copy of the divisional register, the transferred voters list; the proxy voters list; the election officers list and the absentee voter list relevant to a polling station. This provision presupposes the utilisation of a manual voting system. The problems inherent in a manual system, coupled with the distrust and political tension that it generates, necessitate a review of the electoral process. The opportunity now exists for a shift to an electronic voting system. The National Identification biometric registration process provides an example for a move to an electronic voter registration and voting system.

Examples of the successful use of e-voting in India are available. Some have doubted the security of the e-voting system but if e-banking and other e-processes related to financial transactions have been deemed feasible then e-voting should be possible. In a situation where the major political parties have made it their stock- in-trade to dispute all election results, the electoral process cannot for long be based on a manual system.

Transition from One Administration to Another

The transfer of the administrative power of state from a defeated political party in government to a victorious party has been confused and acrimonious, particularly in 2000/2001 and 2008/2009 when the country experienced transitions of the type mentioned above. As stated above, this has been exacerbated by the incessant delay in the conduct of the Presidential elections. In 2001, there were six days for the transfer process while in 2009 the process had to be completed in only four days (Presidential (Transition) Bill 2010).

The absence of a clearly specified structure for the transfer of administrative authority is quite obvious, and the confusion that the whole exercise carries is pestilential. In well tested circumstances, where the working of the democratic system is entrenched and respected, the transition process should pose no problems. In the USA, for example, the transition process is regulated by the Presidential Transition Act 1963 which states its purpose in Section 2 as:

> 'to promote the orderly transfer of the executive power in connection with the expiration of the term of office of a President and the inauguration of a new President.'

It further recites in that same Section 2 that:

> the national interest requires that such transitions in the office of President be ac-complished so as to assure continuity in the faithful execution of the laws and in the conduct of the affairs of the Federal Government …

A smooth transition from one administration to the other is a legitimate expectation of the generality of the citizenry from the political players who are mere trustees.

In Ghana the fact of limited time coupled with other human factors render the whole exercise chaotic and vitriolic. It is to change this unpleasant trend that the *Presidential (Transition) Act, 2012 Act 845* has been formulated. The Bill recounts in its Memorandum a catalogue of problems that bedevilled previous transitions as including:

a) the shortness of the periods between the declaration of the results and the commencement of the transfer process in the two cases did not allow the losing party sufficient time to properly re-orientate itself for the transfer;

b) there seems to have been a lack of will on the part of both the incoming and outgoing officials on the teams to continue to work together beyond the handover date of 7 January in both 2001 and 2009;

c) the euphoria of victory and the disappointment of losing brought about some form of discord in the work of the teams and conflicting postures introduced irritation on both sides;

d) the ill-will developed during the acrimonious political campaign period unfortunately prevailed in the work of the teams and denied them much needed co-operation and good-will;

e) the absence of established procedures resulted in the use of discretion that was sometimes abused by the teams;

f) an intermediary or third party was not in place to help resolve differences that surfaced and the resultant stalemate;

g) deep-seated hostility between the two parties seemed to have influenced the process instead of factors that favoured the national interest (Presidential (Transition) Bill 2009).

This chronicle of frustrations and disaffection with our transition processes actually represents a lack of the political will to properly manage the democratic process. Nevertheless, it is believed that the putting in place of the proper legal structure may refine the process to a large extent. Hence, the *Presidential (Transition) Act 2010, Act 845* which was initiated by four political parties with representation in Parliament, that is, NDC, NPP, PNC and CPP (Presidential (Transition) Bill 2010).

The Presidential (Transition) Act provides for a Transition Team that shall be constituted within twenty-four hours after the declaration of the results of the presidential election. Where an incumbent President is re-elected for a second term the President shall designate the members of the Transition Team *(Presidential (Transition) Act 2012, Act 845*, Section 1(3)). Where however a person other than the incumbent is elected Section 1(1) of the Act mandates the incumbent President to appoint a team from certain specified office holders mentioned in Section 1(1) (a) while the President-elect is also at liberty to appoint an equal number of persons as the incumbent might have appointed (ibid. Section 1(1.b)). The Act further requires that the Head of the Civil Service, the Head of the Local

Government Service, the Secretary to the Cabinet and the National Security Co-ordinator shall be members of the team (ibid.) while the incumbent President and the President-elect will serve as co-chairpersons but with the proviso that each could delegate that function (ibid. Section 1(2)).

Taking into account the nature of previous transitions and the vitriolic approach of chasing out outgoing officials from official residences and the seizure of cars, the Act provides for how such matters should be handled. Hopefully this Act will introduce some civility and decorum into our transition exercises.

Possibility of a Vacuum in the Office of President

Another potential for a constitutional hiatus is the spectre of a vacuum in the office of the President on the eve of 7 January, when power must be handed over to a new President, as a result of unresolved challenges to the election of the President by the Supreme Court. According to the Constitution a person elected as President holds office for a term of four years beginning from the date on which he is sworn in as President (Article 66 (1)). It has become the practice to swear in the President-elect on 7 January following an election. The implication therefore is that the term of office automatically expires precisely four years thereafter at midnight on 6 January.

From the country's brief experience under the 1992 Constitution, and taking from the behaviour and disposition of our major political parties and their leaders, it is not inconceivable for things to be orchestrated to create a political crisis through the manipulation of the electoral process particularly from the judicial process with the consequence of a vacuum at the set date of 7 January.

Various scenarios can play out to frustrate a President-elect from assuming office on 7 January, as has become the tradition. The first is by the incidence of death of the President-elect just before 7 January. The second is by a legal challenge to restrain the Electoral Commission from declaring the results of the presidential election; and the third is a legal challenge of the validity of the election of the President. A fourth, though not a legal challenge, is an outright rejection of the declared results by the losing candidate(s) and the refusal to accept the winning candidate as elected. This fourth circumstance may create political tension in the country but cannot frustrate the constitutional process by which the President-elect assumes office on 7 January in accordance with Article 66. The possible steps to be taken in the scenario of the President-elect dying before his investiture on 7 January have not been provided for in the Constitution. Nevertheless, it is not beyond conjecture to project by analogy that just as how by Article 60 (4) of the Constitution ('a candidate shall be deemed to be duly elected as Vice-President if the candidate who designated him as candidate for election to the office of Vice-President has been duly elected...') it follows that the death of the President-elect will not derogate from the fact that the Vice-President has also become 'Vice-President-elect'.

In that circumstance, and again by analogy, going by Article 60 (6) which provides that 'whenever the President dies, resigns or is removed from office, the Vice-President shall assume office as the President with effect from the date of the death, resignation or removal of the President', it should be possible to argue that the Vice-President-elect shall step into the shoes of the President-elect and be sworn in as President. Thereafter, a new Vice-President shall be selected according to the process provided for in Article 60 (10) of the Constitution. The legal position as described is similar to that of the USA which has been described as follows: that 'if the President-elect dies before noon of 20 January, the Twentieth Amendment states the Vice-President becomes President.'[5] History recounts a near occurrence of this on 15 February 1933 when President-elect Franklin D. Roosevelt was fired at by one Gieseppe Zangara who missed him.

The other two possible situations were what the NDC and the NPP respectively had contrived to orchestrate in 2000 and 2008. In 2001 when the NDC party bigwigs sensed their obvious defeat after a large portion of the results had been declared decided to reject the totality of the results. The situation was saved by the then Presidential candidate, Prof. Atta-Mills, who came out to openly congratulate the winning candidate, Mr. John Agyekum Kuffuor, and thereby frustrated the designs of the NDC leadership. In 2008 when the NPP sensed defeat in the run-off of the Presidential elections, the Party proceeded to court seeking an injunction to restrain the Electoral Commission from releasing the final results. The court process was however aborted when the NPP withdrew the matter from court.

In the first case, the Electoral Commission could nonetheless have declared the results and the winner could still have been sworn into office on 7 January even without the blessing of the NDC. On the other hand if the 2008 scenario had continued, resulting in a possible judicial restraint on the Electoral Commissioner to release the final results and therefore incapacitated from declaring one of the candidates elected before the due date of 7 January, there would have been a constitutional uncertainty. There would have been no president-elect on that date to be invested with the authority of office. In consequence there would have been no president in office if Article 66 (1) is strictly interpreted. This was a prospect that troubled many during the events sequel to the presidential elections run-off in 2008.

There was the conjecture that, should that happen, the Speaker of Parliament should be able to step in to act as President according to Article 60 (11) which provides that:

> where the President and the Vice-President are both unable to perform the functions of the President, the Speaker of Parliament shall perform those functions until the President or the Vice-President is able to perform those functions or a new President assumes office as the case may be.

This is a possible solution taking into account the fact that it has become the tradition for the new Parliament to become constituted before the President-elect is sworn into office. The importance of the Speaker and Parliament in the transition process has been captured in the *Presidential (Transition) Act* with the suggested provision that within forty eight hours after the declaration of the results of the parliamentary election and the general election, the Clerk of Parliament shall summon a meeting of the elected members of Parliament to elect the Speaker (Presidential (Transition) Act, Section 11). The Speaker and Parliament would then have been properly constituted and ready for the swearing-in of the President that should take place on 7 January following the presidential election (ibid. Section 12). Should the new Parliament itself not be in place before the lacuna in the political structure occurs then the doctrine of necessity should be deployed to save the political situation.

The Doctrine of Necessity

The doctrine of necessity which is implied in law operates to legitimize that which is otherwise illegal or unconstitutional. The justification for any such otherwise unconstitutional act would be for the purpose of the protection of the constitution itself. Examples of circumstances in which actions that were otherwise unconstitutional but held to be permitted abound; for example, in the 1779 case of *R. v. Stratton and others* (21 St. Tr 1046) the accused were charged with arresting and imprisoning and deposing Lord Pigot, Commander-in-Chief of the Forces in Fort St. George and President and Governor of the settlement of Madras in the East Indies. In response to these charges the defendants claimed to have acted under necessity in order to preserve the constitution. Lord Mansfield in his direction to the jury exhorted them that:

> But the only question for you to consider is that whether there was that necessity for the preservation of society and the inhabitants of the place as authorizes private men… to take possession of the government, to be sure it was necessary to do it immediately. If you can find that there was that imminent necessity for the preservation of the whole, you will acquit the defendants.

For the doctrine of necessity to be applicable, there must be no other remedy available to avoid the impending consequences of the situation; the necessity, according to de Smith, must be proportionate to the evil to be averted (de Smith 1973). In this respect, Lord Mansfield was reported as follows:

> … to amount to a justification, there must appear imminent danger to the government and individuals; the mischief must be extreme, and such as would not admit a possibility of waiting for a legal remedy. That the safety of the government must well warrant the experiment… The necessity will not justify going further than necessity obliges: for though compulsion takes away the criminality of the acts, which would otherwise be treason, yet it will not justify a man in acting further than such necessity obliges him or continuing to act after the compulsion is removed.[6]

If therefore for any reason it should become impossible for the electoral process to yield a president-elect by 7 January, and if it should also be impossible for the Speaker of Parliament to step in to fill the vacuum thereby created, it should be possible for the Chief Justice to take interim control of the executive arm of government until a substantive president is subsequently sworn into office.

Indeed the doctrine of necessity would permit any other person with the ability to initiate remedial action to step in to face the threat that confronts the constitution and save the nation from slipping into total political chaos. In the old Nigerian case of *Lakanmi v. Attorney-General, Western State* (1971 1 UILR 201) the Supreme Court of Nigeria interpreted the assumption of office of the military following the disturbances of 1966 as understandably based on the doctrine of necessity.[7] Similarly in the Granada case of *Mitchell v. DPP* (1986 LRC (Const) 35) a completely new body of persons that replaced a previous government was held legally capable of administering the country on the doctrine of necessity. Thus a commitment to constitutional rule can always be achieved even in the face of unforeseen circumstances that may threaten to create a lacuna in the political system.

The idea of the outgoing President continuing in office until a new president is found is a possibility under the circumstances of necessity although it might not be politically prudent in an atmosphere of contestation for political power possibly between the incumbent President and his challenger from another political party. To reduce the chance of this happening, the Electoral Commission could as a matter of policy organise the Presidential and the Parliamentary elections, if it so wishes by or just after 7 September, that is exactly or a little into the period of four months. This should provide enough time for any incidental hiccups to be addressed before the handover date of 7 January.

Importance of a Vibrant and Independent Judiciary

So long as there are elections we should anticipate electoral disputes in one form or the other. It is for that reason that we have the superior courts that have been clothed with specific jurisdiction to deal with election disputes; the High Court has original and appellate jurisdiction in respect of electoral offences, while at the same time having original jurisdiction to deal with election disputes in parliamentary elections (1992 Constitution, Article 99 (1)); the Court of Appeal possesses final appellate jurisdiction in parliamentary election disputes[8] with the Supreme Court assigned original jurisdiction in all election disputes regarding presidential elections (1992 Constitution, Article 64 (1)).

When the disputing parties fail to agree the courts become the last bastion for peace; it is when there is loss of confidence in the judiciary that violence becomes the ultimate result of election disputes. Cote d' Ivoire and Kenya are examples of the consequences of failure of confidence in the judiciary. The Courts in Ghana have so far held sway in settling judicial disputes. The Supreme Court decision in the petition of the New Patriotic Party against the 2012 election of President John Mahama is the ultimate example of the degree of public confidence in the Ghanaian judiciary. This underscores the belief that a strong judiciary could make the difference even in cases where electoral disputes threaten the stability of the nation.

Conclusion

The success of a democratic system is more a reflection of principally the determination of political attitude rather than a matter of law or the constitution per se. Nevertheless the constitutional provisions could complement political attitude in ensuring a smoother operation of the electoral and transition processes. The experience in Ghana confirms the belief in the need for a complement between the political attitude and the constitutional and statutory aspects. The electoral process in Ghana could benefit from some conscious re-engineering of the timetable for elections as well as a statutorily regulated transitional process as has been the case in the American system.

Notes

1. See the preamble to the 1992 Constitution.
2. The incidence of missing names and mislocation of names from the register was reported even during the 1992 Elections. (See Larvie & Afriyie-Badu, 1996).
3. Electoral violence based on tribal sentiments led to the death of hundreds of ordinary citizens.
4. Disputed election results threw the country into chaos necessitating the forceful remov- al of the incumbent from office to pave way for the assumed winner of the elections.
5. Based on the Twentieth Amendment of the US Constitution.
6. For another example of the application of the Doctrine of Necessity see the case Mitch- ell v. DPP which case relates to the events in Grenada in which Mr. Bishop was removed as Head of State.
7. The military itself thought otherwise and preferred to label it a military coup d'état that abrogated the previous legal system.
8. *In re Parliamentary Election for Wulensi Constituency; Zakaria v. Nyimakan* [2003-2004] 1 SCGLR 1.

References

Afari Gyan, K., 1995, *The Making of the Fourth Republican Constitution of Ghana*, Accra: Friedrich Ebert Stiftung.

Danquah Institute, 2010, *Securing Africa's Democracy with e-voting – Ghana's civil society's relentless push for election automation technology*, in Danquah Institute Special Newsletter, p. 13.

Judicial Service of Ghana, 2012, *Manual on Election Adjudication in Ghana*, 2nd edition, Accra.

Larvie, J. and K. Afriyie-Badu, 1996, *Elections in Ghana, 1996*, Part 1, Accra: Electoral Commission of Ghana and Friedrich Ebert Stiftung. New Patriotic Party, 1993, *The Stolen Verdict*, Accra.

Ninsin, K.A. and F.K. Drah (eds.), 1993, *Political Parties and Democracy in Ghana's Fourth Republic*, Accra: Woeli Publications.

Oquaye, M., 2004, *Politics in Ghana, 1982-1992: Rawlings, Revolution and Populist Democracy*, Accra: Tornado Press.

Smith de, S. A., 1973, *Constitutional and Administrative Law*, 4th ed., p. 78.

Cases

In re Parliamentary Election for Wulensi Constituency; Zakaria v. Nyimakan [2003-2004] 1 SCGLR 1.

J.H. Mensah v. Attorney-General [1996-97] SCGLR 320

Lakanmi v. Attorney-General, Western State (1971) 1 UILR 201

Mitchell v. DPP [1986] LRC (Const) 35

Tehn-Addy v. Electoral Commission [1996-97] SCGLR 589

Constitutions and Legislation

1992 Republican Constitution of Ghana
US Constitution
Presidential (Transition) Bill, 2009
Presidential (Transition) Bill 2010
Presidential (Transition) Act 2012, Act 845

Index

B

ballots, 20, 49, 53–55, 57, 67, 116, 190
Baltimore, 12, 61–62
basis, 4, 8, 21, 38, 44, 73–76, 83–84, 92, 98, 100, 115–16, 135, 139, 163, 168
Bawumia, 64, 66, 72, 75–76, 78, 80
Bebli, 25, 27, 32
behaviour, political, 64, 116, 172
beliefs, 11, 85, 164, 175, 197
benefits, 11, 26, 83, 98–99, 118, 120–21, 127–28, 169, 172–74, 197
Better Ghana, 96–97, 113
Better Ghana Agenda, 97, 102
Bill, 17, 191–92, 198
billion, 104, 121, 123, 169, 176
billion Ghana cedis, 137, 159
BNI (Bureau of National Investigation), 132–33
Boafo-Arthur, 42, 45–47, 61–62, 73, 80, 99, 110–11, 131–34, 162
board, 65, 122, 147–48
Bob-Milliar, 15, 17, 19, 21, 23–25, 27, 29, 31–33
Bratton, 4, 12, 36–37, 61, 75, 80, 174, 182
British Political Parties, 112
budget deficits, 135, 138, 142, 149–50
Bureau of National Investigation (BNI), 132–33

C

Cabinet, 86–88, 92, 176, 193
Cambridge, 80, 111–13, 182
campaigns, electioneering, 120, 123
candidate nominations, 16, 29, 50
candidates, 6–8, 14–22, 24–27, 29, 48–53, 55, 65–72, 76, 79, 83, 101–3, 118–19, 158, 180, 193–94
average number of, 119, 158
defeated presidential, 154–55
field, 3
generational, 75–76
highest number of, 19
independent, 17–18, 20, 26, 89, 102
nominating, 13, 30

particular, 6, 26, 131
prospective, 20–21, 27
selecting, 22, 30
winning, 54, 193–94
Candidates Competing in Constituencies, 119
candidate selection, 13–17, 20, 23, 30, 33–34
presidential, 30
Candidate Selection in Britain, 34
Candidate Selection in Comparative Perspective, 33
Candidate selection in Ireland, 33
Candidate Selection Method, 34
candidate selection procedures, 15
candidate selection process, 14, 16, 22
capital, political, 67, 157
Caplan, 83–84, 109, 111
Carothers, 38–39, 58–59, 61
Carter Center, 42, 46–47, 58
CDC (Colonial Development Corporation), 174
CDD (Center for Democratic Development), 7, 30, 32, 36, 64, 131
CDD Election Monitoring Mission Document, 52–54
CDD-Ghana, 31, 33, 43, 52, 58, 61–62, 64, 110–11
CDD-Ghana/CODEO, 48–49, 60
CEC (Constituency Executive Committees), 20–22, 31
CEDEP (Center for the Development of People), 60
cent, 54, 57, 116, 140, 148
Center for Democratic Development. See CDD
Center for the Development of People (CEDEP), 60
Centre for Democratic Development Ghana, 131
century, 163, 166–67, 181
chairman, 27, 67, 75, 79, 94, 134, 147
change, 9, 11, 75, 77, 94, 99, 101, 113, 116, 137–38, 140, 148, 172–73, 180–81, 183
societal, 137
CHC Report, 122, 131

W

Y

www.ingramcontent.com/pod-product-compliance
Lightning Source LLC
Chambersburg PA
CBHW060036030426
42334CB00019B/2355